Reading MacIntyre's *After Virtue*

Reading Alasdair MacIntyre's *After Virtue*

Christopher Stephen Lutz

continuum

Continuum International Publishing Group

The Tower Building	80 Maiden Lane
11 York Road	Suite 704
London	New York
SE1 7NX	NY 10038

www.continuumbooks.com

ISBN: 978-1-4411-2616-0 (hardcover)
978-1-4411-4507-9 (paperback)

Library of Congress Cataloging-in-Publication Data
A catalog record for this title is available from the Library of Congress.

Typeset by Newgen Imaging Systems Pvt Ltd, Chennai, India

For my mother,
Suzanne Marie Stewart Lutz
(1924–2008)

CONTENTS

ACKNOWLEDGMENTS

The first person to thank in the acknowledgments of a book like this is Alasdair MacIntyre, for doing the work that allowed him to write a book of enduring value. In the original preface to *After Virtue*, he thanked his wife, Lynn Sumida Joy, and his longtime friends and colleagues Heinz Lubasz and the late Marx Wartofsky (1928–1997), along with those who helped him in the preparation and revision of the text and it seems appropriate to remember their contributions to *After Virtue* here as well.

After Virtue is truly a multidisciplinary work. It surveys the history of philosophy and delivers a powerful critique of modern ethics and Marxist political theory drawn from the philosophy of science, action theory, and the philosophy of Karl Marx. Then it proposes an ethics of virtue based on contemporary action theory, Elizabeth Anscombe, Aristotle, and the novels of Jane Austen. Commenting on this kind of a book is a daunting challenge, so I was most fortunate that I did not have to face this challenge alone.

In 2007, Kelvin Knight organized a conference in London to celebrate the philosophical achievements of Alasdair MacIntyre and to question the British Left's dismissal of his later work. This was the first international conference to gather a wide spectrum of scholars interested in explicating and extending the work of Alasdair MacIntyre. As we listened to each other that week, Thomist Christians and Marxist atheists, social scientists, philosophers, and political theorists, we were able to gain a richer understanding of a body of work that some of us had already spent a decade or more trying to master. The International Society for MacIntyrean Enquiry (ISME) was born at that London Conference, and I owe a debt of thanks to the members of ISME, particularly to Paul Blackledge, Neil Davidson, Kelvin Knight, and Ron Beadle, and Jeff Nicholas for answering my questions, commenting on my drafts, and helping me to see the things in MacIntyre's philosophy that my previous studies had left obscured.

I owe a special debt to Jeff Nicholas, who helped to organize and host the second annual meeting of the ISME, at Saint Meinrad Seminary and School of Theology in 2008. Jeff has also served as the executive secretary and webmaster of ISME since its foundation, providing invaluable administrative assistance to every one of ISME's annual conferences, and leading our work toward legal incorporation. Without Jeff's work—without ISME—this book would almost certainly present a narrower interpretation of *After Virtue*.

I owe another debt to Saint Meinrad Seminary and School of Theology, which supported my travel to the London Conference, and supported ISME's Saint Meinrad Conference with generous grants from the Adrian Fuerst Faculty Research and Development Fund, and provided outstanding hospitality to the members of ISME during the second annual conference. The Saint Meinrad Conference enabled ISME to become an institution that has continued to support research on MacIntyre's work through Dublin in 2009, Vilnius in 2010, Providence in 2011, and Nottingham in 2012.

Undergraduate students at Morgan State University in Baltimore, Maryland, and graduate seminary students at Saint Meinrad who have read *After Virtue* and other works of Alasdair MacIntyre in my philosophy courses over the past decade have also contributed to this volume, through their questions, insights, challenges, and complaints, and I thank them for the things they have taught me as we have worked together on MacIntyre's texts.

Jeff Gainey, who first proposed this book as a brief summary and interpretation of *After Virtue*, also deserves to be acknowledged here. Without his encouragement, I would not have started this project, and without starting, I would not have learned the things that I discovered I needed to learn in order to complete the task.

Thanks are in order too, to Haaris Naqvi of Continuum Books, and to Srikanth Srinivas and the production team at Newgen Imaging Systems for their help in polishing the final version of the manuscript and bringing it to the marketplace with remarkable efficiency.

Most importantly, I thank my wife and children, for their love, encouragement, and support over the course of this project.

Finally, I thank the following publishers for permission to reprint materials used in this book:

Alasdair MacIntyre, *After Virtue: A Study in Moral Theory*, 3rd edn (2007) ©1981, 1984, and 2007 by Alasdair MacIntyre. Reprinted with permission. Published by the University of Notre Dame Press, Notre Dame, IN 46556.

Alasdair MacIntyre, *After Virtue: A Study in Moral Theory*, 3rd edn (2007) ©1981, 1984, and 2007 by Alasdair MacIntyre. Reprinted with permission. Published by Bloomsbury Academic, 36 Soho Square, London, W1D 3QY, UK.

Christopher Stephen Lutz, "Understanding the 'Disquieting Suggestion' " originally published in Kelvin Knight and Paul Blackledge, eds, *Revolutionary Aristotelianism* (Stuttgart: Lucius & Lucius, 2008), special edition of *Analyse & Kritik* 30, no. 1 (June 2008): pp. 91–9. Reprinted with permission. Published by Lucius & Lucius, Verlagsgesellschaft mbH, Gerokstr. 51, 70184 Stuttgart.

ABBREVIATIONS

3RV	*Three Rival Versions of Moral Enquiry: Encyclopaedia, Genealogy, and Tradition*
AV	*After Virtue*
AMEM	*Alasdair MacIntyre's Engagement with Marxism*
CNS	"Epistemological Crises, Dramatic Narrative, and the Philosophy of Science"
DPR	*Dependent Rational Animals*
E&P	*Ethics and Politics*
MacReader	*The MacIntyre Reader*
NMW 1	"Notes from the Moral Wilderness," I
NMW 2	"Notes from the Moral Wilderness," II
RP&Ph	"Relativism, Power and Philosophy"
Tasks	*The Tasks of Philosophy*
TEAM	*Tradition in the Ethics of Alasdair MacIntyre*
ToF:RNT	"The Theses on Feuerbach: A Road Not Taken"
V&P	*Virtue and Politics*
WJWR	*Whose Justice? Which Rationality?*

Introduction

Philosophy in abbreviated and summary form is no longer philosophy. How then to proceed?[1]

Initially published in 1981, Alasdair MacIntyre's *After Virtue* (*AV*) presents a worldview shaped by 30 years of rigorous academic work. My purpose in this introduction is only to crack open the door to that worldview for those who find it foreign, and to offer some starting points for further study. *AV* surveys so many areas in history, philosophy, science, and literature that a thorough reading could provide the framework for an excellent education. Yet, the overall argument of the book has only two parts, and each leads to a fairly straightforward conclusion.

First, the ethics of modern liberal individualism, the ethical theories of Immanuel Kant, John Stuart Mill, and their successors, give us no reason to deny Friedrich Nietzsche's claim that morality is only a mask for the will to power. Likewise, the managerial ideologies of modern bureaucracy fail under the examination of philosophy of science. In sum, the secular theories of ethics and management that contemporary politicians, managers, and opinion leaders rely upon to justify their decisions and policies, and to influence others to accept those decisions and policies, must be seen for what they are, manipulative fictions invented to mask arbitrary impositions of individual choice. This critical argument makes up the first half of *AV*.

Second, while modern ethical theories may have failed, it does not follow that Nietzsche's judgment was correct. It is possible to find some truth about ethics and politics in the qualities of character that enhance human freedom and human agency. If there is any future in philosophical ethics, it will be a future in which moral philosophers focus their attention on the conditions that enable human agents to recognize and choose what is good and best, for themselves and others, as members of the communities to which they belong. The qualities of character shared by those who judge and act most effectively in pursuit of the good comprise the virtues. This constructive argument makes up the second half of AV.

These are the two conclusions of the book: that conventional modern moral and political philosophy is inadequate, and that moral and political philosophy can be renewed only by returning to a study of virtue or excellence in human agency. In the course of these arguments, the book delivers withering critiques of specific moral theories while gathering them into the category of "modern liberal individualism." Even Marxism, Marx's critique of liberalism, eventually finds its way into this bestiary. The characters, texts, and events that constitute the narrative of the book, its two arguments, and its various critiques make AV a remarkably rich text. Some readers have found AV to be a difficult book, and some of its commentators and critics have plainly misunderstood it. The aim of this work is to help readers of AV to form a better understanding of its main arguments and to make sense of some of its more distracting details.

There are some themes and distinctions in AV that MacIntyre approaches subtly or from a perspective unfamiliar to some readers. These topics include the philosophical method that MacIntyre developed through his work in the philosophy of the social sciences, and MacIntyre's relationship with the Marxist tradition, including his debts to Marx's critique of capitalism and his criticism of Marxist politics. This guide to AV begins, therefore, by tracing some of the sources of MacIntyre's method. The first chapter explores MacIntyre's debt to and criticism of Marxism. The second chapter examines the "Disquieting Proposal" of AV's opening chapter. Summaries and commentaries on the two main arguments of the book follow in Chapters 3–6. The seventh chapter summarizes the main achievements of MacIntyre's work since AV and identifies some recent, secondary literature.

Philosophy of science

MacIntyre did considerable work in the philosophy of the social sciences from the 1950s through the 1980s,[2] and the outcome of that work provides the philosophical method employed in *AV*. Summaries of the key achievements of three authors, Karl Popper (1902–1994), Thomas Kuhn (1922–1996), and Imre Lakatos (1922–1974), will serve to introduce the field of the philosophy of science.

Popper's work in the philosophy of science began in 1919 with concerns about the nature of three supposedly scientific theories:

> My problem perhaps first took the simple form, 'What is wrong with Marxism, psycho-analysis, and individual psychology? Why are they so different from physical theories, from Newton's theory, and especially from the theory of relativity?'[3]

The adherents of these three problematic theories were impressed by their "explanatory power"[4] and they had no difficulty verifying these theories in their daily experience.[5] Yet, there was something that distinguished these three theories, which many people already believed to be true, from conjectures like Einstein's theory of relativity, which very few people believed.[6] Popper's concern led him to propose that "the criterion of the scientific status of a theory is its falsifiability, or refutability, or testability."[7] In other words, a theory may be called "scientific" only if one can propose a test that could disprove that theory. A theory that fails such a test is falsified, but a theory that cannot be tested is "irrefutable" in the same sense that astrology is irrefutable. Popper concluded that Marxism was falsified by the failure of its predictions, but became irrefutable when its defenders made its predictions indeterminately vague.[8] He found the two psychological theories untestable, and thus nonscientific.[9]

Popper's work leads to the conclusion that scientific theories are not to be verified, but tested, and in some cases, falsified.[10] Popper's philosophy of science raises difficult questions about the role of subjectivity in the application of theory to experience.[11] If verification does not prove scientific theories, how are we to understand the progress of science?

Kuhn took up this question in *The Structure of Scientific Revolutions* (1962). Kuhn identifies "paradigms"[12] (in the postscript to the second edition, he suggests the term "disciplinary matrix"[13]) as the settings for "normal science."[14] A scientific paradigm includes all the presuppositions that its theories take for granted. Normal science does not prove or verify the paradigm, it presumes the accuracy of its paradigm: "Normal science . . . is predicated on the assumption that the scientific community knows what the world is like."[15] When the presuppositions of the paradigm are called into question, it may lead to a crisis within normal science and then to revolution—to paradigm shift. The shift from geocentric astronomy to heliocentric astronomy provides one classic example of a paradigm shift, the shift from Newtonian mechanics to Einstein's theory of relativity provides another.

Scientific revolutions, according to Kuhn, are not regulated by any external standards.[16] They entail the replacement of standards; thus, rival paradigms are incommensurable.[17] Kuhn therefore cannot treat paradigm shift as a rational determination guided by objective standards of reason; he describes it instead as a kind of conversion:

> I would argue . . . that in these matters neither proof nor error is at issue. The transfer of allegiance from paradigm to paradigm is a conversion experience that cannot be forced. . . . Conversions will occur a few at a time until, after the last holdouts have died, the whole profession will again be practicing under a single, but now a different, paradigm.[18]

Philosophers of science found Kuhn's account of paradigm shifts compelling in many ways, but many balked at the irrational nature of his "conversion experience."[19] Criticizing Kuhn, Lakatos writes, "There are no super-paradigmatic standards. The change is a bandwagon effect. Thus *in Kuhn's view scientific revolution is irrational, a matter for mob psychology.*"[20]

Lakatos proposed an alternative to Kuhn, the methodology of scientific research programs. Lakatos spoke of "research programs" rather than "paradigms." A research program is a cluster of theories in which a band of auxiliary theories explain, apply, and defend a core theory. Research programs may either advance or degenerate. An advancing research program is marked by predictive power, by the use of its core theories to predict completely unexpected results. A degenerating research program is marked by an increasing body of auxiliary hypotheses invented to explain and defend the failures of the core theory.[21] The use of Newtonian theory to explain the irregular motion of Uranus by predicting the discovery of the planet we call Neptune exemplifies predictive power. The introduction of epicycles to Ptolemaic and Copernican astronomy to explain the irregular motions of the planets is a classic example of an ad hoc invention to defend a theory.

Lakatos finds that research programs coexist in competition: "*The history of science has been and should be a history of competing research programmes . . . . but it has not been and must not become a succession of periods of normal science.*"[22] Rival research programs are able to compete because they share standards, and they are able to confirm their core theories, and so defeat their opponents, through their superior predictive power.

MacIntyre bears debts to all three of these philosophers of science, particularly Kuhn and Lakatos. In the preface to *The Tasks of Philosophy* (*Tasks*) (2006), MacIntyre explains that his 1977 essay, "Epistemological Crises, Dramatic Narrative, and the Philosophy of Science" ("CNS")[23] "marks a major turning-point in my thinking." "It was elicited by my reading of and encounters with Imre Lakatos and Thomas Kuhn and what was transformed was my conception of what it was to make progress in philosophy."[24] This turning point provided MacIntyre with a new philosophical method.

Method

The method of *AV* follows from MacIntyre's account of philosophical progress in "CNS."[25] There MacIntyre explains that we make sense of our world with narratives, a category that includes autobiography, history, doctrine, myth, and scientific theory, among other things. When one of these narratives fails, when we find that we are wrong about ourselves and our relationships, our history, the nature of God, or the structure of the world, we may be plunged into a period of uncertainty and confusion, an epistemological crisis. What is one to do when one's narratives fail? MacIntyre's answer is central to his subsequent approach to philosophy:

When an epistemological crisis is resolved, it is by the construction of a new narrative which enables the agent to understand *both* how he or she could intelligibly have held his or her original beliefs *and* how he or she could have been so drastically misled by them. The narrative in terms of which he or she at first

[handwritten margin notes:] What is one to do when one's narrative fails? A new narrative that explains the old & also how it was deficient. Continuous w/ the past & open to improvement.

understood and ordered experiences is itself now made into the subject of an enlarged narrative.[26]

One cannot move forward into a better narrative or theory unless one comes to terms with one's previous failure, and the outcome of this process, if one is fortunate, is to discover that the new narrative is itself only "a best account so far"[27] and that it may be supplanted by some more adequate theory or narrative in the future. MacIntyre uses the differences between Shakespeare's *Hamlet* and Jane Austen's *Emma* to distinguish two approaches to philosophy. Hamlet's confusion makes it difficult to determine precisely how to interpret his experiences and leaves provisional answers open to improvement. Emma's clear-minded replacement of error with truth excludes the possibility of further improvement. "Philosophers have customarily been Emmas and not Hamlets," MacIntyre notes, because "the history of epistemology, like the history of ethics itself, is usually written as though it were not a moral narrative, that is, in fact, as if it were not a narrative."[28]

MacIntyre's narrative will not resemble conventional epistemologies. It cannot be a private exercise of Descartes' "contextless" doubt[29] because that kind of exercise, carried through with honesty and conviction, can only lead to David Hume's disease.[30] MacIntyre's narrative must examine the philosophical resources of the community in a history that is informed by the philosophy of science. MacIntyre, like Lakatos, rejects the discontinuity of Kuhn's account of scientific revolutions,[31] Kuhn's reticence to seek truth through science, and Kuhn's consequent reduction of normal science to "puzzle solving."[32] MacIntyre's account of epistemological crises and their resolution retains Kuhn's notion of incommensurability, without importing its irrational notion of discontinuous conversion, and in this sense, it synthesizes the theories of Kuhn and Lakatos into a new account of philosophical progress:

> I am suggesting, then, that the best account that can be given of why some scientific theories are superior to others presupposes the possibility of constructing an intelligible dramatic narrative which can claim historical truth and in which such theories are the continuing subjects of successive episodes.[33]

Epistemological crises, as Kuhn describes them, are real, but their resolution may be rational, insofar as they are continuous with the past and open to improvement in the future. This is the kind of narrative that MacIntyre presents in *AV*.

AV is a book about rival interpretations of historical events and rival ways of judging action and virtue that flow from differing conceptual schemes. When conceptual schemes are extended through time and history, MacIntyre calls them "traditions."[34] The conceptual schemes of *AV* sometimes function like the paradigms or disciplinary matrices of Kuhn's philosophy of science. They can be incommensurable and untranslatable, and their differences can be so great that rival conceptual schemes appear irrational and unintelligible. In these cases, the only way to examine the world in terms of a rival conceptual scheme would be to adopt it in some provisional way, like learning a foreign language. But the transfer of allegiance from one conceptual scheme to another could never be as irrational for MacIntyre as a Kuhnian paradigm shift.[35] At other times, these conceptual schemes are less radically opposed, so that they may communicate with their rivals as readily as Lakatos's research programs are able to communicate with one another.

Traditions appear to be more like Lakatos's research programs than Kuhn's paradigms. Traditions progress or fail to progress, at the level of cosmology and anthropology, in terms of their ability to make sense of the world, to predict the unexpected, and to guide human action reliably in pursuit of the goods of communities. The Aristotelian tradition is, in this sense, a research program, as are the modern liberal individualist tradition and the Marxist tradition. For MacIntyre, philosophical theories are to be tested, not just verified, and, as with Lakatos's research programs, the best way to test a research program may be through critical engagement with its rivals. The outcome of these tests can be rational, because the world itself, which we investigate and describe through our more or less adequate narratives and theories, stands as the measure of our attempts to describe it.

Reading *AV*

AV covers an enormous swath of Western intellectual and political history, much of it in passing, in order to present an interpretation of the whole that departs from conventional readings of that history on several important points. The book speaks across specializations; it addresses authors from 2,500 years of philosophical literature, and covers contemporary topics in history, metaphysics, anthropology, ethics, politics, and the social sciences. To those who are already familiar with all of this material, MacIntyre offers a way of reading that leads out of the wilderness of modern liberal individualism, into a more human land of shared deliberation enabled by virtue. It is unlikely, however, that there are very many of these people, even among professional philosophers and historians of philosophy, as our specializations drive us toward comprehensive knowledge of particular fragments, at the expense of the study of the whole.

To the rest of us, MacIntyre's *AV* stands as an invitation to discover the broader history of our culture by investigating all the unfamiliar topics and figures we encounter in the course of the book. For those who choose to take up this invitation, the internet is an invaluable companion. Books available only in the finest university research libraries in 1981 are now accessible online as pdf files, so that, for example, one may peruse John Adam's personal copy of Hume's *History of England* from any computer on earth with an adequate internet connection.[36] There is a vast collection of Marxist literature hosted at www.marxists.org. The complete works of Thomas Aquinas are hosted in Latin at the Corpus Thomisticum website[37] and the Washington, D.C. Dominican House of Studies hosts many of them in English translation.[38] The Massachusetts Institute of Technology's Internet Classics Archive hosts English translations of a wide array of classical texts.[39] These and other internet databases make it possible to discover a new author or a new problem and to read some of the relevant primary literature without even leaving one's desk. Online encyclopedias, some of them with excellent editorial standards, make it possible to distinguish Jacobins from Jacobites, to become acquainted with William Cobbett, and to discover the Glorious Revolution of 1688 and the inequities of the British enclosures. Readers who have access to online databases like J-Store through their libraries have all the secondary literature that a world-class research library could offer wherever they are able to log in.

Such a reading of *AV* could guide an excellent education and it would take many years to complete. The present volume offers something in the interim. My main goals in writing this guide to *AV* are to provide a summary of MacIntyre's argument, to make some of his points more explicit, to explain some of his literary allusions, and to give clear reference points for additional research. Along the way, I intend to flag some of the book's main controversies, to explain the errors in the text that MacIntyre has acknowledged and to refer the reader to relevant secondary literature. Finally, since *AV* is, as MacIntyre admits in the postscript to the second edition, "a work in progress," it is necessary for the present volume to place *AV* in the broader picture of MacIntyre's career, tracing the trajectory of his constructive work since the mid-1980s. On this last point, particularly, the present volume takes up a different task than my earlier work, *Tradition in the Ethics of Alasdair MacIntyre (TEAM)*. I hope it serves as a useful guide to what remains MacIntyre's most important and influential book.

Two notes on notation

First, since this book is intended to serve as a guide to *AV*, page references to *AV* will be given parenthetically. All other references will be given in endnotes. This should prove helpful to any reader who is working with both books at the same time.

Second, *AV* has been published in three editions. The second edition (1984) adds a postscript (pp. 264–78), but leaves the rest of the book, including its front matter, unchanged. The third edition (2007) adds a prologue (pp. ix–xvi), which repaginates the original preface (formerly pp. ix–xi and now xvii–xix). For this reason, to avoid confusion for those who are working with the second edition, citations of the prologue will specify the third edition, and citations of the preface will give page numbers for both second and third editions.

Notes

1 Alasdair MacIntyre, "Politics, Philosophy and the Common Good," first published in Italian in *Studi Perugini* 3 (1997), published in English in Kelvin Knight, ed., *The MacIntyre Reader* (Notre Dame,

IN: University of Notre Dame Press, 1998), hereafter *MacReader*, pp. 235–52, at 235.

2 See Stephen P. Turner, "MacIntyre in the Province of the Philosophy of the Social Sciences," in Mark C. Murphy, ed., *Alasdair MacIntyre* (Cambridge University Press, 2003), pp. 70–93; see also *TEAM* (Lanham, MD: Lexington Books, 2004), pp. 47–52, and "Alasdair MacIntyre's Tradition Constituted Rationality: An Alternative to Relativism and Fideism," *American Catholic Philosophical Quarterly* 83, no. 3 (Summer 2011): 391–413.

3 Karl Popper, "Science: Conjectures and Refutations," in *Conjectures and Refutations: The Growth of Scientific Knowledge* (New York: Harper and Row, 1963), pp. 33–65, at 34.

4 Ibid., p. 34.

5 Ibid., p. 35.

6 Ibid., p. 34.

7 Ibid., p. 37, emphasis in original.

8 Ibid.

9 Ibid., pp. 37–8.

10 See Thomas Kuhn, *The Structure of Scientific Revolutions*, 2nd edn (Chicago: University of Chicago Press, 1970), p. 146.

11 See Popper, *Conjectures and Refutations: The Growth of Scientific Knowledge*, p. 35.

12 Kuhn, *The Structure of Scientific Revolutions*, 2nd edn., pp. 43–51.

13 Ibid., p. 182.

14 Ibid., pp. 23–34.

15 Ibid., p. 5.

16 Ibid., p. 114.

17 Ibid., p. 148.

18 Ibid., pp. 151–2.

19 See Imre Lakatos, "Falsification and the Methodology of Scientific Research Programmes," in John Worrall and Gregory Currie, eds, *The Methodology of Scientific Research Programmes* (Cambridge, UK: Cambridge University Press, 1978), pp. 8–101, at 9.

20 Ibid., p. 91.

21 Imre Lakatos, "Science and Pseudoscience," in *The Methodology of Scientific Research Programmes*, pp. 1–7, at 5.

22 "Falsification and the Methodology of Scientific Research Programmes," p. 69, emphasis in original.

23 Alasdair MacIntyre, "CNS," *The Monist* 60, no. 4 (October 1977): 453–72, reprinted in *Tasks* (Cambridge, UK: Cambridge University Press, 2006), pp. 3–23.

24 MacIntyre, *Tasks*, pp. vii–viii.

25 CNS, p. 5.

26 Ibid.

27 Ibid., p. 6.

28 Ibid.

29 Ibid., p. 8.

30 Ibid., pp. 12–13, 23.

31 Ibid., p. 17.

32 Ibid., p. 21; see also "Normal Science as Puzzle-Solving," in Kuhn, pp. 35–42.

33 Ibid., p. 22.

34 MacIntyre uses "tradition" in several distinct senses in *AV*. The third-level definition of virtue uses the word "tradition" in an unusual sense; this is not tradition in the sense of a conceptual scheme or worldview, but tradition in the sense of the inherited circumstances of life that constitute one's moral starting point.

35 The reason that MacIntyre's changes in conceptual schemes cannot be as irrational as Kuhn's paradigm shifts has to do with the difference between knowledge and belief and their differing relationships with the intellect and will. A person's choice to view the world provisionally in terms of a conceptual scheme that he or she does not accept is like the choice to follow along with a child's description of the world. It might make the judgments of that rival scheme more intelligible on their own terms, but it would not make the decision to accept that scheme a rational one. The rational decision to accept a rival conceptual scheme becomes possible only when the standpoint provided by that hitherto alien conceptual scheme reveals compelling reasons to reject one's old worldview and to adopt this new one as one's own.

36 www.archive.org/details/historyofengland08hume

37 www.corpusthomisticum.org

38 http://dhspriory.org/thomas/

39 http://classics.mit.edu/index.html

1

MacIntyre and Marxism

Marxism has two distinct components, a "critique of the economic, social, and cultural order of capitalism"[1] and a progressive, socialist, political project. MacIntyre remains "deeply indebted" to the Marxist critique of capitalism, as he notes in the preface to the third edition of *After Virtue* (*AV*).[2] Elements of that critique play visible roles in the critical argument of *AV*, and two of the most important essays in MacIntyre's mature work, "Three Perspectives on Marxism,"[3] and "The *Theses on Feuerbach*: A Road Not Taken"[4] ("ToF:RNT"), demonstrate his continued engagement with the critical element of the Marxist tradition.

MacIntyre's work with the other element of Marxism, its progressive socialist political project, has always been more critical because of that project's troubled origin in nineteenth-century determinist social science. MacIntyre's first book, *Marxism: An Interpretation* (1953), published when he was 24 years old, already takes issue with the predictive scientific claims of Marxist theory. MacIntyre's 1957 essay, "Determinism,"[5] questions the very premises of the social sciences. *Marxism and Christianity* (1968)[6] sharpens the critique of Marxist social science and lays most of the blame for its errors at the feet of Friedrich Engels. *AV* completes MacIntyre's critique of Marxist politics with its conclusion "that Marxism is exhausted as a *political* tradition" (p. 262).

AV is a development of MacIntyre's critique of Marxist social science, which draws some of its resources from Marx's critique of capitalism. So we would do well, at the outset, to consider the relationship between Marxism and social science, and briefly to examine MacIntyre's critique of that relationship.

Action versus behavior

MacIntyre's criticism of Marxist politics has nothing to do with any defense of capitalism. MacIntyre's objection, like Popper's, has to do with Marxist claims to have discovered a scientific account of human history and behavior. The terms "human action" and "human behavior" are often used synonymously, since both can be used to describe the things that humans do. This is not the case in *AV*. In the context of *AV*, these terms are opposites rooted in conflicting presuppositions and conflicting conceptual schemes. This conflict pits what we may call the Aristotelian standpoint of human action against what we may call the modern scientific standpoint of human behavior.

The standpoint of human action sees human acts as freely chosen means to ends pursued by agents. This is the ethical perspective of Aristotle,[7] Thomas Aquinas,[8] Gertrude Elizabeth Margaret Anscombe,[9] and MacIntyre.[10] From the standpoint of human action, it appears that an event like the migration of people from their various homelands to the United States in the late nineteenth century should be a story of *immigration*. From this perspective, one looks at US immigrants as people who believed that they could better themselves and their families by going to the United States, and whose actions express those beliefs.[11] After deliberating about the means, these immigrants struggled to travel great distances over land and sea, even crossing oceans, so that they might establish themselves and their families in the United States. From the standpoint of human agency, human acts are "uncaused" in the modern scientific sense, although in the Aristotelian sense, it could be said that the "final causes" of human acts are to be found in the ends or goals that agents pursue through their actions. In this case, the final causes of the immigrants' actions are to be found in their beliefs about the good life and their desires for freedom and opportunity. From the standpoint of human action, ethics is the study of human action; it investigates the goods people seek to gain through their choices, and the conditions that affect people's abilities to judge and to act effectively in that pursuit.

The standpoint of human action does not assert that human freedom to desire goods, to choose goods, and to act in pursuit of goods is somehow absolute. It may happen that human weakness, ignorance, foolishness, or psychological illness may weaken an agent's freedom or impair an agent's judgment.[12] From the standpoint of human action, these restrictions on free agency do not destroy our freedom. These shortcomings only show that human freedom is limited and difficult in a variety of ways. They point to the importance of learning how to improve and enhance human freedom and agency, and they make these improvements and enhancements central concerns for philosophical ethics.

The standpoint of human behavior opposes that of human action. Mid-twentieth-century social scientists like B. F. Skinner rejected the Aristotelian conception of human ends and rational deliberation in their studies of human behavior. Rather than seeking the causes of human action in agents' beliefs about the ends and purposes that they seek, behaviorist social scientists looked for the causes of human behavior—determinate causes in the modern scientific, Humean, sense—in the circumstances that determine our responses.[13]

B. F. Skinner (1904–1990) exemplifies what I am calling the standpoint of human behavior in his popular overview of behaviorism, *Beyond Freedom and Dignity* (1971).[14] Skinner's work belongs to the same tradition of determinist social science that MacIntyre began to criticize in the 1950s. This is the tradition of eighteenth-century philosophers like Baron D'Holbach (1723–1789) and nineteenth-century pioneers of the social sciences like August Comte (1798–1857) and Friedrich Engels (1820–1895). As MacIntyre pointed out in his 1960 review of Neal Wood's book, *Communism and British Intellectuals*,[15] it is also the tradition of "H. G. Wells, Sir Richard Gregory, Sir Julian Huxley, and countless others" who imagined futures in which scientists would manage and control society.[16]

From the standpoint of human behavior, human migration to the United States is initially a story of *emigration*. Migrants who came to the United States were reacting to "push factors" in their homelands, like war, famine, economic distress, and government repression, and they were drawn to the United States by "pull factors," like the promise of adequate food, housing, employment, and cultural freedom. To confirm this interpretation, social scientists examine the demography of migratory events, seeking statistical regularities among them that they can compare to demographic data about US immigrants. Determinist social scientists found that they did not need to delve into the hopes and dreams of particular migrants to predict general trends in migration. Studying the push and pull factors that appear to drive migration has proved sufficient for their purposes. Similar studies have satisfied social scientists' curiosity about many other behaviors as well.

The standpoint of human behavior conflicts with the standpoint of human action in two ways. First, it seeks determinate causes that trigger behaviors, instead of investigating the goods that agents pursue through their choices and actions. Second, the standpoint of behavior treats "the literature of freedom," with its concern for the ends and purposes of human actions, as a peculiar tool for operant conditioning. According to Skinner, "the literature of freedom . . . does not impart a philosophy of freedom; it induces people to act."[17] So this literature simply belongs to the larger category of things that induce behaviors, the category that behaviorists need to investigate and understand. From what I am calling the standpoint of human behavior, the denial of human freedom is presupposed, because determinism is a precondition of the possibility of any social science.[18]

B. F. Skinner explains his rejection of human freedom in the opening chapter of *Beyond Freedom and Dignity*:

> Physics did not advance by looking more closely at the jubilance of a falling body, or biology by looking at the nature of vital spirits, and we do not need to try to discover what personalities, states of mind, feelings, traits of character, plans, purposes, intentions, or other perquisites of autonomous man really are in order to get on with a scientific analysis of behavior.[19]

From Skinner's perspective, the anthropology of autonomous man seemed superfluous and outdated. For Skinner, the study of behavior was a physical study, not unlike the study of chemistry or physics:

> The task of a scientific analysis is to explain how the behavior of a person as a physical system is related to the conditions under which the human species evolved and the conditions under which the individual lives.[20]

Skinner's behaviorism is materialist and determinist, and on these points, it is in keeping with a long tradition of causal determinism whose modern proponents include the twentieth-century Stalinists who were the original target of MacIntyre's critique.

MacIntyre explained the connection between determinist social science and his defense of free human agency especially clearly in his review of *Communism and British Intellectuals*. MacIntyre marked a sharp distinction between the bureaucratic Marxism of Stalinism and the classical Marxism of Karl Marx. MacIntyre saw Marx, as he saw Trotsky,[21] as a champion of human freedom and agency. MacIntyre saw Stalinism, as Trotsky had, as a betrayal of Marxism and the victory of bureaucracy over human freedom.[22] The opposition between classical Marxism and Stalinism was most apparent in their contrary relationships to the claims of determinist social science:

> According to this doctrine, there are objective causal laws both of nature and of history, knowledge of which enables men to control their own destiny. So far as social life is concerned, the manipulation of society is possible to those who possess the secret of these laws. As Marx saw it, this doctrine implies the sharpest of divisions in society between those who know and those who do not, the manipulators and the manipulated. Classical Marxism stands in stark contrast to this: it wants to transform the vast mass of mankind from victims and puppets into agents who are masters of their own lives. But Stalinism treated Marxist theory as the discovery of the objective and unchangeable laws of history, and glorified the party bureaucrats as the men who possessed the knowledge which enabled and entitled them to manipulate the rest of mankind.[23]

In Marxism's internal disputes between Marx's theories and Stalin's politics, MacIntyre sided with Marx's critique of capitalism and his concern to enable human agency. MacIntyre's mature work continues to pursue these ends.

In the critical argument that makes up the first half of *AV*, the distinction between the standpoint of behavior and the standpoint of human action is the key both to the critique of modern moral philosophy and to the critique of overreach on the part of behaviorist social science. The problem with modern moral philosophy is that it should investigate the whole rich subject of human action, but it limits itself to a study of the criteria for judging human behavior. MacIntyre had already recognized this problem in the "Notes from the Moral Wilderness" ("NMW") (1958–1959).[24] Modern moral philosophy would impose standards for choices about behavior without explaining how those standards serve human action, or how the decision to adopt those standards could constitute a human action. Instead, modern moral philosophy would impose standards for free human action that explicitly denied any connection to agents' goals and thus offered no more than rules for correct behavior.

The problem with overreaching sociological theories is twofold. First, the social sciences lack predictive power. Despite their success in recognizing statistical regularities and trends in human behavior, the social sciences have not discovered any determinate laws of human behavior.[25] Second, the scientists' rational use of determinist social theory to manage and manipulate the irrational behavior of others is incoherent. As Marx himself had pointed out in the third of his *Theses on Feuerbach*, the very notion that some group of social scientists should manage the behavior of others according to determinist laws implies that those social scientists are not governed by those determinist laws.[26] This exceptional view of the free and rational deliberations of scientific managers is incompatible with the determinist theories of behavior that those same managers are supposed to employ to explain, predict, and manage human behavior.

Following the insights of Marx's *Theses on Feuerbach*, MacIntyre took up the study of human agency and social practice at the beginning of his career[27] in the hope of gaining insight into ethics and moral development. He followed that study until it drove him from the Marxist critique of capitalism to the critique of Marx and then through Aristotle to Thomas Aquinas.

The philosophy of the social sciences and the critique of Marxism

MacIntyre began his academic career as a committed and active Marxist, and the Marxist readers of *AV* immediately recognized the book's criticism of the social sciences as a critique of Marxist theory.[28] Marxism was born within the social sciences. Friedrich Engels called Marxism "scientific socialism,"[29] and believed with Marx that society could be understood entirely in terms of economics. According to Engels,

> The materialist conception of history starts from the proposition that . . . production . . . and, . . . exchange . . ., is the basis of all social structure; that in every society that has appeared in history, the manner in which wealth is distributed and society divided into classes or orders is dependent upon what is produced, how it is produced, and how the products are exchanged. From this point of view, the final causes of all social changes and political revolutions are to be sought, not in men's brains, not in men's better insights into eternal truth and justice, but in changes in the modes of production and exchange. They are to be sought, not in the *philosophy*, but in the *economics* of each particular epoch.[30]

Scientific socialism—Marxism—understood itself as a science, not as a philosophy. The goal of Marxist social science was to discover laws of human behavior and history that would allow Marxists to release human creativity and renew morality. Stalinists sought these laws to manage the social, economic, and industrial development of the Soviet Union, just as industrial engineers use the laws of mechanics and of thermodynamics to manage industrial production.

To gain a sense of Marx's intentions, consider two of his fundamental complaints. (1) The industrial revolution made traditional craft techniques obsolete, and in so doing, undermined much of the human development that enabled people to gain excellence not only as craft workers but also as human beings. The new industrial labor reduces the skilled craft worker to a proletarian servant of a machine. (2) The boom and bust cycles of the economy are a consequence of the unmanaged competition of capitalists. Marx saw the solutions to both of these problems in a revolution that would lead to the education of the proletariat, common ownership of industry, and rational management of the economy. Scientific socialism promised to bring the wealth generated by industry and the economy itself to the service of the people. These are very positive aspirations; the question is whether or not it is possible for science to achieve them.

Marxists got a chance to test their theories when the Communist Party took power in Russia in the October Revolution of 1917.[31] Though immense in land and resources, the Russian Empire was remarkably undeveloped. Though it had many people, it had little industry; its nations were largely agricultural and much of its farming was still powered by animals. The new Communist leadership would apply Marxist theory to consolidate its power and to transform the new Soviet Union as quickly as possible into a modern industrial state.

Consolidating power in the vast expanses of Soviet territory during a civil war proved to be incompatible with the Marxist vision of the transformation to communist society. Marx's prediction of democratic self-rule gave way to Max Weber's characterization of a bureaucratic government controlled by professional managers. Shortly after Lenin died in 1924, Josef Stalin assumed the leadership of the Soviet Union and increased the power of the central bureaucracy, which answered to him alone. For the next three decades, Stalin oversaw the social, economic, and industrial transformation of the Soviet Union, which he imposed through the despotic methods that have come to be known as Stalinism. Leon Trotsky, Stalin's chief opponent, saw the economic transformation of the Soviet Union as a powerful verification of Marxist methods,[32] even as he condemned Stalin's bureaucratic police state as a betrayal of the revolution.[33]

The origins of *AV* in the moral critique of Stalinism

The 1981 preface to *AV* begins with a puzzling statement referring to an essay MacIntyre had written in 1958: "ever since the days when I was privileged to be a contributor to that most remarkable journal *The New Reasoner*,[34] I had been preoccupied with the question of the basis for the moral rejection of Stalinism."[35] This statement is more important than it may seem; it is at the root of the book's fundamental questions. It is a statement that takes the entire critical argument to justify adequately, and once MacIntyre's preoccupation with this problem is justified, it takes the whole constructive argument to propose a solution.

What, precisely, is Stalinism? I asked MacIntyre what is at issue in the critique of Stalinism in *AV*, and he replied:

I take it that Stalinism has five salient characteristics.

Stalinists (1) believed in the possibility of "socialism in one country", rather than in the making of socialism as a world-revolutionary enterprise; (2) made the working class serve the needs of the party and the bureaucracy rather than vice versa; (3) were guilty of "the cult of personality"; (4) believed that the end of achieving communism justified unlimited terror and unlimited deceit as means; (5) accepted Stalin's crude mechanistic versions of dialectical materialism and historical materialism.[36]

MacIntyre's description digests decades of internal Marxist debates over Stalin's ideology. "Socialism in one country" was an approach to communism adopted by Stalin in 1923 that abandoned the Marxist imperatives for a worldwide revolution. Leon Trotsky vocally opposed Stalin's "socialism in one country"[37] and his "bureaucratism"[38] until Stalin had him assassinated in 1940. Nikita Khrushchev denounced Stalin's "cult of personality" in the "Secret Speech" to the Politburo in 1956.[39] The fourth point addresses Stalin's barbaric methods. The fifth point has to do with the Stalinists' view of Marxism as a social science.

For Marxists in the British New Left of the late 1950s, including Edward Thompson and MacIntyre, the fifth point of MacIntyre's description, "Stalin's crude mechanistic versions of dialectical materialism and historical materialism," represented Stalinism's most important theoretical break with Marxism. Where Marx had taught that socialism would free people from false consciousness, renew human nature, unfetter human agency, and bring about the brotherhood of man, Stalinism had subjected human agency to the harsh demands of Soviet economic development. Thompson described the result in his 1957 essay, "Socialist Humanism: An Epistle to the Philistines":

Thus the concept of human agency, of the "educators and the educated," became lost in a determinism where the role of consciousness was to adapt itself to "the objective logic of economic evolution." . . . Hence Marx's common-sense view that man's freedom is enlarged by each enlargement of knowledge . . .

is transformed into the mystique of man's freedom consisting in his recognising and serving "the objective logic of economic evolution": his "freedom" becomes slavery to "necessity."[40]

Where Marx had sought to liberate human nature from all dogmatism by examining and living human history through the lens of materialism,[41] Stalin exerted "a despotic authority upon the nation's intellectual and cultural life" which bred "dogmatic orthodoxy as a matter of course."[42]

For those less familiar with Stalinist theory, the "unlimited terror and unlimited deceit" of MacIntyre's fourth point remain its most memorable attributes. Stalin's political apparatus murdered 20 million people as it seized private property, collectivized Soviet agriculture, centralized political power, and defended Stalin's regime against all rivals and opponents. Between 1932 and 1933, Stalin's government starved 7 million people in the Ukrainian famine or "*Holodomor*." In 1939, Stalin's army invaded Poland and transported 25,000 Polish social, military, ecclesial, and economic leaders to reeducation camps in the Soviet Union. Stalin had them slaughtered in 1940 after they resisted reeducation and refused to work for the revolution.[43] After World War II, Stalin reduced the countries of Eastern Europe to a ring of Soviet satellite states. The political ideology that bears Stalin's name continued after his death. Stalinist Soviet leaders suppressed the Hungarian Revolution of 1956 and the Prague Spring of 1968. North Korea remains a repressive Stalinist state in 2012.

It is not only easy but also imperative to condemn the ideology that rationalized the crimes of the Stalinist regime. So how could "the question of the basis for the moral rejection of Stalinism" present a problem at all, much less one that could *preoccupy* MacIntyre's mind for two decades? To find the answer to this question and to understand how the critical argument of *AV* justifies MacIntyre's concern, we need to return to the groundbreaking article MacIntyre published in *The New Reasoner* in 1958.

MacIntyre opened "NMW" with a statement that reflected one of the biggest intellectual challenges of the New Left: "A position which we are all tempted into is that of moral critic of Stalinism."[44] The problem of the moral critique of Stalinism had gained urgency in the wake of the suppression of the 1956 Hungarian Revolution, but the problem was not new. Albert Camus had questioned the morality of Stalinism in his 1951 book, *The Rebel*,[45] only to be condemned by Jean-Paul Sartre who ridiculed Camus for his moralism; Sartre defended Stalinism and dismissed what he called Camus's "anachronistic conception of Absolute Justice."[46]

MacIntyre saw the moral criticism of Stalinism as a temptation, not as an imperative, because he could find no ethical theory that could vindicate the moral rejection of Stalinism on rational grounds. Certainly, Stalinism must be rejected, but it must be rejected for a reason. It would not do to reject the irrationalism of Stalinism by imposing some contrary set of irrational demands. The rejection of Stalinism must have a rational basis, it must be founded upon the discovery of some criterion that does not depend on any human choice, and MacIntyre spent the next two decades looking for that criterion.

Paul Blackledge and Neil Davidson provide an excellent, detailed account of the history of the New Left and MacIntyre's involvement in it in the introduction to *Alasdair MacIntyre's Engagement with Marxism* (*AMEM*).[47] Kelvin Knight describes the importance of "NMW" in MacIntyre's whole career in the introduction to *MacReader*,[48] and provides a full history of MacIntyre's development in the fourth chapter of *Aristotelian Philosophy: Ethics and Politics from Aristotle to MacIntyre*.[49] I have traced some of the main lines of MacIntyre's progress in the first chapter of *TEAM*.[50] Paul Blackledge has summarized the background issues for "NMW" in "Morality and Revolution: Ethical Debates in the British New Left."[51] Readers who want a more complete picture would do well to consult these works. For the limited purpose of this chapter— exploring the problem of the moral condemnation of Stalinism—a sketch of the issues that relate "NMW" to *AV* will suffice.

"NMW" is MacIntyre's contribution to a debate within the New Left movement in Great Britain. The New Left was made up of committed Marxists who had abandoned the "old left" of the Soviet-leaning Communist Party and the Washington-leaning Labour Party, who had joined together in the Campaign for Nuclear Disarmament (1959–1961).[52] *The New Reasoner* chronicled the early years of the New Left as they sought to chart a new course for Marxist politics.

The background discussion to which "NMW" replies began in the first issue of *The New Reasoner* with Thompson's "Socialist Humanism: A Letter to the Philistines." Thompson remained committed to a Marxist revolution, but rejected Stalinism as an ideological distortion of Marxism. Thompson proposed a return to the sources of socialist humanism in Marx that could guide a more humane revolution for Great Britain.

Harry Hanson dismissed Thompson's aims in *The New Reasoner*'s second issue, writing, "This is not Marxism; it is romanticism."[53] Hanson asserted that "the essence of the Marxist ethic . . . is its futurism."[54] Hanson saw that Marxists looked forward to justice, democracy, and a "'really human' morality" when the revolution was complete, but accepted what they took to be the necessity of "a battlefield morality" and "militancy" until that time.[55] Hanson notes that "the bureaucrats of King Street," the headquarters of the Communist Party of Great Britain, are "very nice chaps" and "agree with" Thompson in principle, "Yet they remain solidly, immovably Stalinist. . . . Because they have convinced themselves that the horrors perpetrated by Stalin were unavoidable steps along the road to a communist society."[56] Hanson had abandoned Stalinism, and any aspiration to revolution in Great Britain along with it, because he judged it better to work within the existing political system to improve British democracy.[57]

Charles Taylor also replied to Thompson's essay. He agreed with Thompson's assessment of Stalinism and its crude mechanism:

> The metaphorical characterization of Stalin as "the driver of the locomotive of industry" is very revealing, as is Stalin's definition of the writer as "the engineer of the soul." What man is to do to nature, according to Marx, the Stalinist bureaucrats are to do to their unfortunate subjects.[58]

Like Thompson, Taylor saw the centralization of power and authority in the Party's bureaucracy to oppose rather than advance Marx's stated aims. But Taylor also takes issue with Marx himself, identifying two equivocations in Marxism that lend themselves to Stalinism. First, Marx values the human person for her or his achievements, "man creates that for which he is to be valued," and it seems to follow that those who do not join the work of the revolution may therefore lack human dignity. On this point, Taylor concludes that Marxist humanism is incomplete until it accepts "that man is of value as man, irrespective of the part he plays or fails to play in the development of human potentialities."[59]

Taylor finds a second equivocation arising from the historical realities that face revolutions. "Marx sees the Communist society as the return of man to himself . . . But this return to the self will also represent the return of man to his fellow, the realization of the brotherhood of man."[60] Taylor finds these two aims—return to oneself and return to one's fellow—to conflict when Marxists find themselves struggling for power against those who reject their plans. In these circumstances, Marxists have historically set aside the brotherhood of man for the sake of the return to oneself, the liberation of Promethean man. Taylor concludes, "Marxist Communism is at best an incomplete humanism." Taylor finds that the critique of Stalinism remains unfinished unless it calls Marxism into question as well.

When MacIntyre joined this critical discussion of Stalinism, he focused his attention on the moral question: What is the basis for the moral condemnation of Stalinism? From the atheist, materialist perspective of Marxism, it could not be any divine decree. Nor could it be human rights. Marx had specifically rejected the notion of natural human rights as a fiction created to rationalize the autonomy and moral isolation of the individual:

> Above all, we note the fact that the so-called rights of man, the *droits de l'homme* as distinct from the *droits du citoyen*, are nothing but the rights of a *member of civil society*—i.e., the rights of egoistic man, of man separated from other men and from the community.[61]

From the perspective of Marx, there is nothing more to human rights than the arbitrary demands of individuals. Indeed, from the materialist perspective of Marxism, morality can never represent anything but the choices of individuals. So, MacIntyre asks in "NMW":

> Why do the moral standards by which Stalinism is found wanting have authority over us? Simply because we choose that they should. The individual confronting the facts with his values condemns. But he can only condemn in the name of his own choice.[62]

To see that modern morality lacks authority is to recognize an ultimatum in philosophical ethics that amounts to a secular humanist reduction of Plato's *Euthyphro* problem:[63] either we say that certain things are right and wrong simply because we choose to say so, or we say so because they really are right and wrong. Either morality is nothing but the imposition of will or morality responds to some truth that we can discover through the study of nature.

The choice between the rejection of arbitrary moralism and the discovery of some new basis for morality is an ultimatum between will and nature. In 1958, MacIntyre saw this ultimatum as a choice between the moral wilderness and Marx. Choosing Marx, MacIntyre proposed developing "a Marxist morality" that would reassert "moral absolutes" against Stalinism and reassert the roles of "desire and of history"—essential elements of the standpoint of human action—against liberal individualism.[64]

MacIntyre's quest for a Marxist morality was always somewhat Aristotelian. MacIntyre's essay "Freedom and Revolution" (1960) is a Marxist essay, yet its discussion of "the achievement of freedom" has a great deal in common with Aristotle's treatment of moral formation in the second and third books of the *Nicomachean Ethics* and with Thomas Aquinas's discussions of habits and acquired virtues in the *Summa Theologiae*.[65] For MacIntyre in 1960, freedom is not merely political freedom from external forces, more importantly, it is moral freedom, gained through formation in community, to recognize and pursue what is truly choice-worthy:

> Because the individual exists in his social relations and because the collective is a society of individuals, the problem of freedom is not the problem of the individual against society but the problem of what sort of society we want and what sort of individuals we want to be. Then unfreedom consists in everything which stands against this.[66]

An Aristotelian could make a very similar statement, substituting "virtue" for "freedom." When MacIntyre was ready to offer a rational "basis for the moral rejection of Stalinism," he returned to the same ultimatum between will and nature that he had considered in "NMW." In *AV*, this ultimatum is the choice between Nietzsche and Aristotle.

Marx and MacIntyre versus individualism

MacIntyre's debt to Marx is more apparent in his critique of individualism. MacIntyre claims that "the individual exists in his social relations,"[67] but the modern individual is alienated from his social relations. This point of the Marxist critique of modern capitalist politics plays an important role in the critical argument of *AV*.

MacIntyre finds late modernity to be populated by individuals who have learned to understand themselves not in terms of their social backgrounds, relationships, or commitments, but in isolation from all of these. These are Feuerbach's abstract individuals living in Hegel's "civil society," which constituted the focus of Marx's philosophical work up to 1844.[68] Three examples, not used by MacIntyre, may help to illustrate his meaning. The first two come from Thomas Hobbes and Jean-Jacques Rousseau; Jean-Paul Sartre provides the third.

Writing in 1651, in the wake of the English Civil War and the execution of Charles I, Hobbes asks the readers of *De Cive* to imagine how unrelated individuals in the state of nature might come to govern themselves:

> Let us return again to the state of nature, and consider men as if but even now sprung out of the earth, and suddainly (like Mushromes) come to full maturity without all kind of engagement to each other.[69]

These mushroom people have no natural relationships. They are individuals, and the first problem that confronts each of them after they spring forth from the earth is to ensure their own safety against one another in a world where self-defense is the only law.

Writing in 1755 to the educated subjects of European monarchies, Rousseau, like Hobbes, asks the readers of his *Discourse on the Origin of Inequality Among Men* to imagine human beings in the state of nature. Rousseau's natural man lives for generations as a solitary, meeting other human beings only accidentally, and never forming any lasting community with anyone, even for the sake of family life.[70] Rousseau's individuals are equal, until human progress emphasizes differences in people's skills, causing some to grow wealthier than others, and allowing some to manipulate their fellows more effectively than others and to gain power over them.

Hobbes and Rousseau ask their readers to imagine these situations so that we may consider what remains of the human agent when everything superfluous is stripped away. The mushroom person or the natural man is neither a citizen nor a family member, and her or his freedom is not constrained by any law except that of staying alive. Given Hobbes's general goal in *De Cive*, that his readers "will no longer suffer ambitious men through the streames of your blood to wade to their owne power,"[71] the mushroom people serve a specific rhetorical purpose: they allow readers to imagine what it might be like to engage in practical deliberation without the prejudices or ideological commitments of their contemporary political systems. The natural man serves a similar rhetorical purpose for Rousseau, enabling the reader see the arbitrariness of aristocratic ranks and royal privileges. Both of these isolated individuals already embody the ideology of modern liberal individualism that defines the individual against the community and against the state.

A third example of the modern individual comes from Jean-Paul Sartre's lecture, *Existentialism is a Humanism* (1946). Sartre recalls a student of his who sought advice during World War II. The student had to decide whether to remain at home and care for his widowed mother or to escape from France through Spain so that he might join the Free French Forces in England. Sartre pointed out that the decision ultimately belonged to the student. Even if the student followed the guidance of a trusted advisor, the student would first have to choose the advisor, knowing the advisor's political position, so that in choosing the advisor he would also be choosing the advice.[72] Sartre uses his student to exemplify the moral isolation—the "abandonment"[73]—of what MacIntyre calls "the peculiarly modern self, the emotivist self" (p. 34).

These three examples are related to the history that MacIntyre presents in *AV* in two ways. First, the states of nature presented by Hobbes and Rousseau are both manipulative fictions. The purpose of Hobbes's state of nature, in *De Cive* and again in *Leviathan*, is to emphasize what he took to be the essentially arbitrary character of political power, so that people might choose to get along with whatever government they had, rather than join revolutionary political causes that oppose the state in the name of justice. Rousseau's state of nature also emphasizes the arbitrariness of government, but in this case, his goal is to undermine any claims of natural authority on the part of the monarchy, the aristocracy, or the Church. In both cases, the authors present a fictional caricature of human nature and human history in order to gain support for a political judgment. Neither Hobbes nor Rousseau argues his point by presenting a truthful anthropological theory or an even remotely plausible account of natural history. They endeavor instead to win their audience's support through rhetoric; in this sense, they prefigure what MacIntyre would label modernity's "culture of emotivism."

The example from Sartre is related to MacIntyre's history in a second way. Given the ultimatum between will and nature, between Nietzsche and Aristotle, Sartre chooses will and Nietzsche. What distinguishes Sartre's existentialism from the culture of emotivism is only Sartre's ideological self-awareness. Where Sartre is aware of his atheism and committed to its logical consequences, the culture of emotivism is neither. Practically but unreflectively agnostic, the culture of emotivism maintains elements of traditional morality selectively and justifies its moral commitments fictionally. MacIntyre had the British culture of emotivism in mind when he wrote, "The creed of the English is that there is no God, and that it is wise to pray to him from time to time."[74] Reflectively atheistic, Sartre accepts Nietzsche's view of the human predicament and counsels his student to do the same.

What all three examples have in common is the status of the individual in society. In all three examples, the individual is fundamentally autonomous. Joining society is a choice. Remaining in society is a choice. Belonging to any human community is a choice. Deciding between mother and nation is a choice. Hobbes, Rousseau, and Sartre present their individuals from the standpoint of what Adam Ferguson, and later Georg Hegel, called "civil society." MacIntyre discusses "the standpoint of civil society" in "ToF:RNT."[75]

The individual from the standpoint of civil society is to be distinguished from and contrasted with the set of social relationships into which she or he has chosen to enter. Those relationships, often understood as contractual, are on the one hand a means to the attainment of each individual's ends and on the other a system so constructed that by entering it each individual becomes a means for the attainment by others of their ends.[76] ... The conceptions informing thought within civil society about human relationships are therefore those of utility, of contract, and of individual rights. And the moral philosophy which gives expression to the standpoint of civil society consists of a continuing debate about those concepts and how they are to be applied.[77]

The standpoint of civil society, the standpoint that informs all modern moral and political philosophy, sees the individual as a singular who joins together with others only by choice.

From the standpoint of civil society, there is no common good in the traditional sense of the term. From the standpoint of civil society, the good of any individual is only one small element of the aggregate collective good of society. From what we may call "the standpoint of the common good," the standpoint of Plato, Aristotle, and Thomas Aquinas, the common good is not an aggregation of private interests, and it is not a formal or procedural good like justice or the right to due process. From this ancient and medieval standpoint, the common good is a substantive good that we can seek for ourselves only through participation in the life of the communities to which we belong; it is a good for each of us that we can all share, but only if we seek it together. This ancient and medieval standpoint of the common good views the human person as a political animal who belongs to a community neither by choice nor by accident, but by nature.[78] Unlike the "peculiarly modern self of *After Virtue*," this ancient and medieval individual truly does "exist in his social relationships."[79]

Lacking any common good in the older sense of the term, modern moral and political philosophy places a sharp distinction between egoistic and altruistic actions. It opposes actions done for one's own good against actions done for the good of others or for the good of society. This affects the way that modern people reason about their choices. The reasons for pursuing one's own good are prudential and pragmatic, but not necessarily moral. The reasons for pursuing the goods of others or of society are moral, and they may conflict with prudential reasoning. The language of rights regulates the pursuit of private goods and sets limits on the moral and legal demands that society can make on the individual. Consider how these three kinds of reasons relate to feeding the hungry from the modern liberal individualist perspective of John Locke: One ought to feed oneself for prudential reasons and one ought to feed the hungry for moral reasons, although one has a right to store up property so that one might feed oneself in the future. The hungry have a right to demand surplus perishable food from those who have more than they can use, and those who have surplus perishable food have no right to refuse to feed the hungry with it. Yet, the wealthy have an inalienable right to their accumulated wealth, and neither the poor nor the government have any right to take it from them, as that would violate the purposes for which the government was formed.[80] The wealthy should be praised, however, if they go beyond the demands of morality and feed the poor at their own expense. These are commonplace ideas in modern liberal individualist politics, which views all individuals from the standpoint of civil society.

"Liberalism," Marxism, and Aristotle

AV uses the term "liberalism" in a way that many contemporary readers find misleading. US readers associate "liberalism" with the politics of the Democratic Party, with the welfare state, and with legislative agendas that include progressive taxation, universal health care, and gun control. MacIntyre uses the term in an entirely different way, and to miss the difference between the common contemporary political use of the word "liberalism" and MacIntyre's use of the term, "modern liberal individualism" is to consign oneself at the outset to misunderstanding the central issues of *AV*.

The terms "liberalism" and "modern liberal individualism," as used by MacIntyre in *AV*, come from the Marxist critique of the seventeenth-, eighteenth-, and nineteenth-century political ideology associated with capitalism. MacIntyre's philosophical critique of that ideology remains heavily indebted to the Marxist tradition in which he had worked for the first two decades of his career, but MacIntyre then brings that same critique against Marxist

politics, and leads his readers to consider a new starting point for
contemporary moral philosophy in the ancient ethics and politics
of Aristotle.

Modern liberal individualism—the ideology of Hobbes, John
Locke, Adam Smith, Kant, and Mill; the Glorious Revolution; the
Enlightenment; and later the American and French Revolutions
(although each in a distinct form)—rebels against traditional
forms of moral and political authority. It displaces the Church
from its traditional role in the Christian polis. It rejects mon-
archism and aristocracy in politics. It overturns what it takes to
be the oppressive practices of traditional cultures. It declares the
freedom of all citizens, and it reduces the role of government to
the maintenance of public order or to the protection of private
property.[81] Modern liberal individualism treats human beings as
autonomous individuals who enter "civil society" by choice.[82]
Modern liberal individualism seeks to replace appeals to traditional moral authority with appeals to universal reason, to
replace the commands of God with the rules of universal morality, and to replace the old social structures of medieval feudalism
with democratic structures in which all people may enjoy freedom and prosperity.[83]

Kant declares, *Sapere aude.* 'Have courage to use your own
reason!'—that is the motto of enlightenment."[84] Like Kant, the
modern liberal individualist ridicules the laziness of having "a
book which understands for me, a pastor who has a conscience
for me, a physician who decides my diet, and so forth."[85] The individualist abandons such "self-incurred tutelage"[86] to become the
rational author of her or his own decisions. Modern liberal individualism asserts that neither the Church, nor the state, nor my
brother is my keeper.[87] Liberalism liberates the strong to succeed,
but it often abandons the weak to fail.

Understood in this way, contemporary representatives of modern liberal individualism in the United States include both conservative Republicans and liberal Democrats (p. 222 and chapter
seventeen). Conservative Republicans uphold liberal individualism in their concern to liberate business from the regulatory bur-
dens of government by appeals to rights—to property rights, the
right to contract, the right to work, or to the Tenth Amendment's
protection of rights not surrendered by the states to the Federal
Government under the *Constitution of the United States.* Liberal

Democrats uphold liberal individualism in their work to defend the natural rights of individuals to do whatever they wish, so long as they harm no one else.

In the classical sense that MacIntyre uses the term "liberal," the radio personality Rush Limbaugh, who treats "rugged individualism" as a central tenet of his political creed, is a modern liberal individualist, while the policies Limbaugh decries as "liberal"—welfare, progressive taxation, universal health care, and gun control—are not liberal at all. Limbaugh defines himself as a "conservative" but as MacIntyre points out in the latter part of *AV*:

> modern conservatives are for the most part engaged in conserving only older rather than later versions of liberal individualism. Their own core doctrine is as liberal and as individualist as that of self-avowed liberals (p. 222).

What contemporary conservatives and liberals share at the level of political ideology are their concerns for individual autonomy and their rejection of the tradition of the virtues, although each focuses her or his concern and rejection on different areas of human conduct.[88]

In order for modern liberal individualism to justify its moral and political claims, it must show that it is more than secularized Christian morality. It must show that it is more than the secularized moral habits of people raised as Western Christians who have rejected the Christian faith. It must show that its "rights" are real, and explain their existence. It must show that its notions of justice are rooted in reality. As a secular, materialist, positivist philosophy, modern liberal individualism, as it stands today, simply lacks the capacity to address these problems, much less to solve them, and inasmuch as it cannot justify its moral claims, those moral claims are exposed as the selectively Christian, and sometimes un-Christian morality of an arbitrary post-Christian ideology.

Marxism presents an alternative to modern liberal individualism. Marxism influences a great deal of contemporary political "liberalism" and progressivism inasmuch as those ideologies champion the redistribution of wealth through progressive taxation and government welfare programs. Marxism sought to abolish private property, to foster educational and economic development, and to end nationalism and religion through a worldwide communist revolution, and its theorists believed that their ideology was justified by a properly scientific understanding of the world.

In his early work,[89] Marx was a trenchant philosophical critic of the standpoint of civil society, beginning with its individualist notion of the human essence. For Marx, we cannot discover the human essence by studying isolated individuals, for the human essence is social. MacIntyre summarizes Marx:

> Human beings who genuinely understand what they are essentially will have to understand themselves in terms of their actual and potential social relationships and embody that understanding in their actions as well as in their theories.[90]

Marx's notion of the social nature of the human person is a materialistic notion. As MacIntyre does in *AV*, Marx theorizes teleology socially.

Against the standpoint of civil society, Marx proposed "the standpoint of social practice."[91] From the standpoint of social practice, educators would not impose values on society, but enable the members of a community to discover what is good and best through the pursuit of goods internal to their practices.[92] MacIntyre finds an example of this kind of life "in the account given by Thompson in *The Making of the English Working Class* of the communal life of the hand-loom weavers of Lancashire and Yorkshire."[93] Marx, Thompson, and MacIntyre agree that the loss of such communities through industrialization and proletarianization reduces communities of skilled workers engaged in crafts to collections of unskilled laborers performing tasks. They also agree that this process of proletarianization affects the moral and social development of the members of those communities.

Marx never developed the notion of a revolutionary practice that he mentioned in *Theses on Feuerbach* in a systematically philosophical manner, and neither has later Marxist philosophy.[94] Marxist philosophers have followed two paths: the road of Engels and Plekhanov and the road of Lukács. Marxist theorists took no interest in the standpoint of social practice as a resource for ethics because they viewed it as an expression of the arbitrary "attitudes and interests of those involved in practices."[95] For MacIntyre, however, the standpoint of social practice is the road not taken that leads through the study of human action to the discovery of objective conditions for excellence in human agency.

"ToF:RNT" (1994) presents a suitable counterpoint to MacIntyre's first book, *Marxism: An Interpretation* (1953). In that first book, MacIntyre recognizes the potential of the *Theses on Feuerbach* and laments Marx's abandonment of it; in this mature essay, MacIntyre summarizes the key achievements that he has been able to make, building on the foundation laid but abandoned by Marx. It was Marx's "revolutionary practice" that opened the way to *AV*'s definition of virtue in terms of action, practice, and social identity.

MacIntyre accepts Marx's materialist critique of enlightenment natural rights—modern, secular, and liberal individualist natural rights. When pressed to justify its moral and political claims, liberalism fails because it is incoherent. But Marxism has its problems too, and when pressed to justify the claims of its progressive, socialist political program, it too fails because it, too, is incoherent.

The implicit critique of Marxism presented in the first half of *AV* is subtle to readers unfamiliar with Marxism, but came across very clearly to MacIntyre's Marxist readers. Marxism claims that its theories are scientific, that its determinist understanding of human behavior is correct, and that the revolution it envisions, with all its benefits, is inevitable. But all of this hinges on the status of the kind of social sciences that Marxism represents. If the scientific status of Marxist determinism cannot be justified, then Marxism cannot claim to be a science.

Popper saw the progressive socialist political theory of Marx transformed from a scientific theory falsified by the failure of its predictions to a pseudoscientific theory protected from falsification by untestable vagueness.[96] Imre Lakatos spoke of this in his 1973 radio address, "Science and Pseudoscience":

Has, for instance, Marxism ever predicted a stunning novel fact successfully? Never! It has some famous unsuccessful predictions. It predicted the absolute impoverishment of the working class [under Capitalism]. It predicted that the first socialist revolution would take place in the industrially most developed country. It predicted that socialist countries would be free of revolutions. It predicted that there will be not conflict of interests between socialist countries. Thus the early predictions of Marxism were bold and stunning but they failed. Marxists explained all their failures: they explained the rising living standards of the working class by devising a theory of imperialism; they even explained why the first socialist revolution occurred in industrially backward Russia. They explained Berlin 1953, Budapest 1956, Prague 1968. They explained the Russian-Chinese conflict. But their auxiliary hypotheses were all cooked up after the event to protect Marxian theory from the facts. The Newtonian programme led to novel facts; the Marxian lagged behind the facts and has been running fast to catch up with them.[97]

For Lakatos, Marxism provides a prime example of a degenerating, pseudoscientific research program.

The failure of social science to meet the criteria set by the philosophy of science or even to make good on its promise to discover determinate, predictive laws of human behavior entails the collapse of Marxism as a social scientific political project. MacIntyre's critique of the social political, pseudoscientific abuse of the social sciences in *AV* does not mention Marxism or the politics of the Left explicitly, but MacIntyre's Marxist and post-Marxist friends had no question about its intended object.[98]

Marx Wartofsky pointed out these implications of *AV* in an insightful book review published in 1982:

> The hidden agenda of MacIntyre's critique is also the failure of the socialist revolution to usher in that new moral age which it promised, and the failure of Marxist theory to provide any more coherent or soundly based theory of the good life than that which it condemned as "ideology."[99]

If Marxist political theory is not a science, it is a pseudoscience and what had appeared to be the scientific predictions of its progressive, socialist, political program are exposed as the wishful thinking of a party of like-minded revolutionaries.

With its scientific authority undermined, the progressive socialist political project of Marxism collapses, but this has no impact on Marx's critique of capitalism. Industrialization does change the nature of work and employment, proletarianization does undermine the formation of human agency, and both pose difficulties for the development of human communities. MacIntyre finds enduring value in this part of Marx's interpretation of the world, but MacIntyre proposes a different way to change it.

Notes

1 *AV*, 3rd edn, p. xvi.
2 Ibid.
3 Alasdair MacIntyre, "Three Perspectives on Marxism" (Introduction), in *Marxism and Christianity*, revised edition (London: Gerald Duckworth and Company, Ltd, 1995), reprinted in *Ethics and Politics* (*E&P*), pp. 145–58.
4 Alasdair MacIntyre, "ToF:RNT," in Carol C. Gould and Robert S. Cohen, eds, *Artifacts, Representations, and Social Practice: Essays for Marx Wartofsky* (Dordrecht: Kluwer Academic Publishing, 1994), reprinted in Kelvin Knight, ed., *MacReader* (Notre Dame, IN: University of Notre Dame Press, 1998), pp. 223–34.
5 MacIntyre, "Determinism," *Mind*, 66 (1957): 28–41.
6 MacIntyre, *Marxism and Christianity* (New York: Schocken Books, 1968).
7 See Aristotle, *Nicomachean Ethics*.
8 See Thomas Aquinas, *Summa Contra Gentiles*, book III, and *Summa Theologiae*, I–II, questions 1–21.
9 See G. E. M. Anscombe, *Intention* (1957; reprinted by Cambridge, MA: Harvard University Press, 2000).
10 See MacIntyre, "Freedom and Revolution," *Labour Review* 5, no. 1 (February–March 1960): 19–24, reprinted in Paul Blackledge and Neil Davidson, eds, *AMEM* (Leiden: Brill Academic Publishing, 2005; republished in paperback, Chicago: Haymarket Books, 2009), pp. 123–34. See also MacIntyre, *Dependent Rational Animals* (*DPR*) (Chicago: Open Court, 1999).
11 See MacIntyre, "A Mistake about Causality in Social Science," in Peter Laslett and W. G. Runciman, eds, *Philosophy, Politics and Society* (second series) (Oxford: Basil Blackwell, 1962), pp. 48–70, at 51.
12 See Aristotle, *Nicomachean Ethics*, book 3, chapter 5; and book 7.
13 For MacIntyre's early critique of determinist social science, see "Determinism," pp. 28–41.
14 B. F. Skinner, *Beyond Freedom and Dignity* (1971; reprinted, Indianapolis: Hackett, 2002).
15 MacIntyre, "Communism and British Intellectuals," in *AMEM*, pp. 115–22.

16   "Communism and British Intellectuals," p. 119.
17   Skinner, *Beyond Freedom and Dignity*, p. 30.
18   See "Determinism," p. 29.
19   Skinner, *Beyond Freedom and Dignity*, p. 15.
20   Ibid., p. 14.
21   See "Breaking the Chains of Reason," in *AMEM*, p. 166.
22   See Leon Trotsky, *The Revolution Betrayed*, trans. Max Eastman (Garden City, NY: Doubleday, Doran, & Co., 1937; reprinted, Mineola, NY: Dover Publications, Inc., 2004).
23   Alasdair MacIntyre, "A Review of Neal Wood, Communism and British Intellectuals," in *AMEM*, pp. 115–22 at p. 119.
24   "NMW I," *The New Reasoner* 7 (Winter 1958–1959): 90–100. Reprinted in Knight, *MacReader*, pp. 31–40 and in Blackledge and Davidson, *AMEM*, pp. 45–57; "NMW II," *The New Reasoner* 8 (Spring 1959): 89–98. Reprinted in *MacReader*, pp. 41–9 and in *AMEM*, pp. 57–68. See "NMW," part 2/§III; Knight, *MacReader*, p. 41; Blackledge and Davidson, *AMEM*, p. 58.
25   See *AV*, chapter 8.
26   Ibid., pp. 84–5; see also "Communism and British Intellectuals," pp. 118–19.
27   See MacIntyre, *Marxism: An Interpretation* (1953). Karl Marx, *Theses on Feuerbach*, in Lewis S. Feuer, ed., *Marx & Engels: Basic Writings on Politics and Philosophy* (New York: Anchor Books, 1959).
28   See Marx Wartofsky, "Virtue Lost or Understanding MacIntyre," *Inquiry* 27 (1984): 235–50.
29   See Friedrich Engels, *Socialism: Utopian and Scientific* http://www.marxists.org/archive/marx/works/1880/soc-utop/index.htm
30   Friedrich Engels, *Socialism: Utopian and Scientific* (1880), trans. from the French by Edward Aveling in 1892 (authorized by Engels) http://www.marxists.org/archive/marx/works/1880/soc-utop/ch03.htm, retrieved April 7, 2011.
31   For a book-length account of the Russian Revolution, see E. H. Carr, *The Russian Revolution from Lenin to Stalin 1917–1929*, 2nd edn (Basingstoke, UK: Palgrave Macmillan, 2004); for a more thorough account, see E. H. Carr, *The Bolshevik Revolution 1917–1923*, 3 vols (New York: W. W. Norton & Co., 1985).
32   Trotsky, *The Revolution Betrayed*, chapter 1.
33   Ibid., chapter 3, section 2, and chapter 5.
34   Alasdair MacIntyre, "NMW," in two parts: I, *The New Reasoner* 7 (Winter 1958–1959): 90–100; II, *The New Reasoner* 8 (Spring 1959): 89–98; reprinted in Kelvin Knight, ed., *MacReader*, pp. 31–49; also reprinted in Paul Blackledge and Neil Davidson, eds, *AMEM*, pp. 45–68.

35 MacIntyre, *AV*, 2nd edn, p. ix; 3rd edn, p. xvii.
36 MacIntyre, e-mail correspondence, April 14, 2010.
37 See Trotsky, *Permanent Revolution* (1931) and *The Revolution Betrayed* (1937).
38 See Trotsky, "Ch. 3: Socialism and the State," in *The Revolution Betrayed*, pp. 35–49.
39 Khrushchev's speech is available online: http://www.marxists.org/archive/khrushchev/1956/02/24.htm
40 Edward P. Thompson, "Socialist Humanism: An Epistle to the Philistines," *The New Reasoner* 1 (Summer 1957): 105–43, at 134.
41 Materialism is the atheistic doctrine that there is nothing in existence except matter and energy; it is a rejection of any kind of divine, spiritual, or ideal reality.
42 Thompson, *The New Reasoner*, p. 109.
43 The Katyn massacre of 4,000 Polish military officers in a Russian forest in 1940 is the best-known part of the mass killings of 25,000 Polish prisoners from the Kozelsk, Starobelsk, and Ostashkov prisoner camps that year.
44 Knight, *MacReader*, p. 31; Blackledge and Davidson, *AMEM*, p. 45.
45 Albert Camus. *L'Homme Révolté* [*The Rebel*] (Paris: Gallimard, 1951); trans. Anthony Bower, *The Rebel: An Essay on Man in Revolt* (New York: Vintage Books, 1956).
46 Emile Perreau-Saussine, "The Moral Critique of Stalinism," in Paul Blackledge and Kelvin Knight, eds, *Virtue and Politics* (*V&P*) (Notre Dame, IN: University of Notre Dame Press, 2011), pp. 134–51, at 137.
47 Blackledge and Davidson, *AMEM*, pp. xx–l.
48 Knight, *MacReader*, pp. 1–27.
49 Kelvin Knight, *Aristotelian Philosophy: Ethics and Politics from Aristotle to MacIntyre* (Cambridge, UK: Polity, 2007).
50 Christopher Stephen Lutz, *TEAM*.
51 Paul Blackledge, "Morality and Revolution: Ethical Debates in the British New Left," *Critique* 35, no. 2 (August 2007): pp. 211–28.
52 Blackledge and Davidson, *AMEM*, p. xx.
53 Harry Hanson, "An Open Letter to Edward Thompson," *The New Reasoner* 2 (autumn 1957): 79–91, at 87.
54 Ibid., pp. 80–1.
55 Ibid., p. 81.
56 Ibid., p. 83.
57 Ibid., p. 86.
58 Charles Taylor, "Marx and Humanism," *The New Reasoner* 2 (autumn 1957): 92–8, at 94.
59 Ibid., p. 97.
60 Ibid.

61 Karl Marx, *On the Jewish Question* [by Bruno Bauer, 1843],
    Deutsch-Französische Jahrbücher (February 1844); http://www.
    marxists.org/archive/marx/works/1844/jewish-question/index.htm,
    retrieved April 7, 2011.

62 Knight, *MacReader*, p. 34; Blackledge and Davidson, *AMEM*,
    pp. 48–9.

63 See Plato, *Euthyphro*, 10a.

64 Knight, *MacReader*, p. 47; Blackledge and Davidson, *AMEM*, p. 66.

65 See Aquinas, *Summa Theologiae*, I–II, questions 49 through 66.

66 MacIntyre, "Freedom and Revolution," in Blackledge and Davidson,
    AMEM, p. 129.

67 Ibid.

68 See "ToF:RNT," pp. 223–8.

69 Thomas Hobbes, *De Cive*, chapter 8, http://www.constitution.org/th/
    decive08.htm, accessed June 11, 2009.

70 See Jean-Jacques Rousseau, *Discourse on the Origin of Inequality*,
    part 1, paragraph 25, and part 2, paragraph 2.

71 Hobbes, *De Cive*, "Author's Preface to the Reader," http://www.
    constitution.org/th/decive00.htm, accessed June 12, 2009.

72 Jean Paul Sartre, *Existentialism is a Humanism*, trans. Carol
    Macomber (New Haven: Yale University Press, 2007), pp. 30–3.

73 Ibid., p. 30.

74 Alasdair MacIntyre, "God and the Theologians," in *Against the Self-
    Images of the Age* (Duckworth, 1971; reprinted by University of Notre
    Dame Press, 1978), pp. 12–26, at 26. For a more extensive treatment
    of this subject, see MacIntyre, "The Debate about God: Victorian
    Relevance and Contemporary Irrelevance," in Alasdair MacIntyre
    and Paul Ricoeur, *The Religious Significance of Atheism*, Number 18
    Bampton Lectures in America Delivered at Columbia University, 1966
    (New York: Columbia University Press, 1969), pp. 3–55.

75 MacIntyre, "ToF:RNT," pp. 223–34.

76 Ibid., p. 223.

77 Ibid.

78 See Aristotle, *Politics* I, 2 [1253a3], trans. Benjamin Jowett, in
    Richard McKeon, ed., *The Basic Works of Aristotle* (New York:
    Random House, 1941), pp. 1113–16; see also Thomas Aquinas,
    Commentary on Aristotle's Politics, trans. Richard Regan
    (Indianapolis: Hackett, 2007), book 1, comment 20, p. 16.

79 MacIntyre, "Freedom and Revolution," in Blackledge and Davidson,
    AMEM, p. 129.

80 See John Locke, "Second Treatise of Government" (chapter 5, at
    §§31, 46, 50), in *Two Treatises of Government* (1698). Ed. Peter
    Laslett. (Cambridge: Cambridge University Press, 1992).

81 Ibid., §3.

82 MacIntyre, "ToF:RNT," in *MacReader*, p. 223.

83 MacIntyre, "Some Enlightenment Projects Reconsidered," in *E&P*, pp. 172–3.

84 Immanuel Kant, "What is Enlightenment," in *Foundations of the Metaphysics of Morals*, trans. Lewis White Beck, Library of Liberal Arts (New York: Macmillan, 1990), p. 83.

85 "What is Enlightenment," p. 83.

86 Ibid.

87 Gen. 4.9.

88 In his remarks on the penultimate draft of the manuscript of this book, Ron Beadle notes the connection that Ayn Rand found between the freedom and the values of liberals and conservatives. Rand held that liberals and conservatives value freedom in the things they value least, while they regulate the things they value most.

89 MacIntyre distinguishes Marx's early philosophical work up to 1844 from his subsequent economic and social scientific work in "ToF:RNT," p. 224.

90 "ToF:RNT," p. 229.

91 Ibid., p. 230.

92 Ibid., p. 231.

93 Ibid. See Edward Thompson, *The Making of the English Working Class* (New York: Pantheon, 1964), pp. 269–313.

94 "ToF:RNT," p. 232.

95 Ibid., p. 233.

96 In addition to "Science: Conjectures and Refutations," Karl Popper also addresses this problem in *The Poverty of Historicism* (London: Routledge & Kegan Paul, 1966).

97 Lakatos, "Science and Pseudoscience," pp. 5–6.

98 See Marx W. Wartofsky, "Virtue Lost or Understanding MacIntyre," *Inquiry: An Interdisciplinary Journal of Philosophy* 27, no. 1 (1984): 235–50, and MacIntyre's reply in the same issue: Macintyre, "*After Virtue* and Marxism: A Response to Wartofsky," *Inquiry* (1984): 251–4.

99 Ibid., p. 237.

2

Understanding the "Disquieting Suggestion"

From Voluntarist Nominalism to Rationalism to Chaos:
Alasdair MacIntyre's Critique of Modern Ethics[1]

One question that can lead a person into the history of philosophy and ethics is, "How did we get here from there?" This question demands immediate attention to two other questions: What is
"here"? and what was "there"? MacIntyre's *AV* offers answers to
all three of these questions. According to *AV*, "here" is a culture in
which discussions of morality—both academic and popular—tend
to be incoherent, and strangely disconnected from discussions of
practical wisdom; "there" was a culture in which discussions of
human action were at the same time both moral and practical; and
the process that brings us "here from there" centers around the
cultural turn from teleological practical reasoning to voluntarist
moral reasoning. This process is dramatically summarized in the
opening chapter of *AV* with its "Disquieting Suggestion" that our
moral culture bears the consequences of an unrecognized catastrophe that has led to the culture of emotivism. The precise meaning and reference of that story is not always clear to its readers;
nevertheless, the attentive reader can recognize and reconstruct
the events of the analogous philosophical catastrophe through a

careful reading of the book, and the reader who realizes that the catastrophe is not just a broad metaphor holds a powerful tool for the interpretation of MacIntyre's critique of modernity.

The "Disquieting Suggestion"

AV begins with "A Disquieting Suggestion":

> Imagine that the natural sciences were to suffer the effects of a catastrophe. A series of environmental disasters are blamed by the general public on the scientists. Widespread riots occur, laboratories are burnt down, physicists are lynched, books and instruments are destroyed. Finally a Know-Nothing political movement takes power and successfully abolishes science teaching in schools and universities, imprisoning and executing the remaining scientists.[2]

MacIntyre tells us that after some passage of time, "enlightened people" pick up the pieces, a collection of fragments of descriptions lacking any of the comprehensive theories that constitute the research programs of the sciences as we know them. These enlightened people would believe that they were doing science again but, in fact, they would not be, and they have no way of recognizing that they were not. Were they, like us, to have the rational resources of analytical philosophy, phenomenology, and existentialism, MacIntyre says they would remain incapable of recognizing their own condition, because none of these approaches would help them to recognize the differences between the pieces of scientific knowledge that they hold and memorize, and the practice of science as it had been before its destruction.

This is an interesting story, it is fascinating to imagine what might pass for science in such a culture, but the real "Disquieting Suggestion" itself soon follows:

> The hypothesis which I wish to advance is that in the actual world which we inhabit the language of morality is in the same state of grave disorder as the language of natural science in the imaginary world which I described. What we possess, if this

view is true, are the fragments of a conceptual scheme, parts which now lack those contexts from which their significance derived. (p. 2)

The point of MacIntyre's story is that an event occurred in our past that suspended the rational investigation of morality and practice, and that modern efforts in moral philosophy are nothing but faulty attempts using broken tools to resuscitate a study that had once been dead.

This is an amazing claim, and MacIntyre anticipates the obvious complaint, writing, "Yet our history lies open to view, so it will be said, and no record of any such catastrophe survives" (p. 3). In response, he presents another striking supposition:

Suppose it were the case that the catastrophe of which my hypothesis speaks had occurred before, or largely before, the founding of academic history, so that the moral and other evaluative presuppositions of academic history derived from the forms of the disorder which it [i.e., the catastrophe] brought about. . . . For the forms of the academic curriculum would turn out to be among the symptoms of the disaster whose occurrence the curriculum does not acknowledge. (p. 4)

In other words, modern history does not record the catastrophe because the catastrophe is invisible to it, because modern history is itself one of the fruits of the catastrophe.

The "Disquieting Suggestion" comes down to this: even though any professional philosopher can recount the history of philosophy, at least in broad strokes, from Thales to Derrida, there is a catastrophic event hidden from view within that history, the effects of which render modern efforts at moral philosophy incoherent at best, but this event and its effects are invisible to the modern academy, even as we suffer their consequences. MacIntyre writes: "One way of stating part of the hypothesis is precisely to assert that we are in a condition which almost nobody recognizes and which perhaps nobody at all can recognize fully."[3] It is, MacIntyre acknowledges, an implausible theory, but its very implausibility he takes to be evidence that it might be true.

The "Disquieting Suggestion" is a difficult passage for several reasons, including the fact that the historical narrative that unfolds through the rest of the book does not openly identify any events in our history with the calamities, the riots, or the "Know-Nothing political movement" described in that opening paragraph. What, then, is the catastrophe?

Recognizing the catastrophe

To find the catastrophe in the text, we must begin by returning to chapter one to find out what kind of thing we are looking for. MacIntyre writes:

> We shall have to look not for a few brief striking events whose character is incontestably clear, but for a much longer, more complex and less easily identified process and one which by its very nature is open to rival interpretation. (p. 3)

The catastrophe is not any singular event; it is a series of events stretched out over several centuries; and it is not recorded as a catastrophe because it is not typically interpreted as such. In all likelihood, it is familiar to us, but is ordinarily seen as a great achievement, or at least as a positive development. Where, then, do we see such a process described in *AV*?

There are four places where MacIntyre indicates most clearly what he takes the catastrophe of the "Disquieting Suggestion" to be. The first place is in chapter four. After describing the incoherence of moral language in our post-catastrophe "culture of emotivism" in chapters two and three, MacIntyre turns in chapter four to a discussion of the predecessor to the culture of emotivism, namely the culture of the enlightenment. But here, MacIntyre begins by drawing a very peculiar picture of the enlightenment. It is not the French enlightenment of Rousseau and Voltaire, but a specifically Anglo-Scottish-German enlightenment of Hume, Smith, and Kant; and MacIntyre gives very specific reasons for drawing this peculiar picture:

> What the French lacked was threefold: a secularized Protestant background, an educated class which linked the servants of government, the clergy, and the lay thinkers in a single reading public, and a newly alive type of university exemplified in

Königsburg in the east and in Edinburgh and Glasgow in the west. . . .

Hence what we are dealing with is a culture that is primarily Northern European. Spaniards, Italians, and the Gaelic and Slavonic-speaking peoples do not belong to it. (p. 37)

In short, what gives birth to the culture of emotivism in *AV* is the enlightenment as it played out in the Protestant countries of northern Europe. This might be taken—mistakenly—to identify the catastrophe with the Protestant Reformation, but it certainly does indicate that the Protestant Reformation is an episode in the process that constitutes the catastrophe.

MacIntyre clarifies the identity of the catastrophe in a second place, in chapter five:

Suppose that the arguments of Kierkegaard, Kant, Diderot, Hume, Smith and the like fail because of certain shared characteristics deriving from their highly specific shared historical background. . . .

. . . Whence did they inherit these shared beliefs? Obviously from their shared Christian past compared with which the divergences between Kant's and Kierkegaard's Lutheran, Hume's Presbyterian, and Diderot's Jansenist-influenced Catholic background are relatively unimportant. (p. 51)

The focus here is on the peculiarities of the theologies of Luther, Calvin, and Jansen; all three were theological voluntarists, that is, all three posited the divine will as the primary principle of existence. Where Thomas Aquinas, in his synthesis of Christian Neo-Platonism[4] and Aristotelian hylomorphism,[5] always maintained the priority of the intellect in creation,[6] theological voluntarists asserted the priority of the divine will, and this had far-reaching consequences for philosophy and theology. So after summarizing some points of agreement among medieval Christian, Jewish, and Muslim thinkers who shared an Aristotelian view of nature and reason, MacIntyre writes:

This large area of agreement does not however survive when Protestantism and Jansenist Catholicism—and their immediate late medieval predecessors—appear on the scene. For they embody a new conception of reason. (p. 53)

MacIntyre's catastrophe is not the Protestant Reformation, nor is it Protestantism combined with Jansenism, rather it is the whole process of that turn from natural teleology to theological voluntarism and nominalism—the foundation of which is typically attributed to William of Ockham—that leads to the voluntarist theologies of Luther, Calvin, and Jansen.

This identification of the catastrophe is confirmed in a third place in *AV*, when MacIntyre sketches twelfth-century Christian efforts to work out the apparent conflicts between the philosophical tradition that honored the moral excellence of the cardinal virtues and the Christian theological tradition that mandated obedience to the divine law. This gets at the real difference between classical and contemporary notions of morality. If I were to formulate the moral question that Aristotle answers in the *Nicomachean Ethics*, it would be, "How can I become the kind of a person who has the practical wisdom to recognize what is good and best to do and who also has the moral freedom to act on that judgment?" Thus understood, ethics is about developing a rich, natural understanding of living well. This ceases to be the case when morality is reduced to rule-following. Here MacIntyre looks into Peter Abelard's *Ethics* and finds an approach to moral philosophy that centers on questions about obedience and sin. In this kind of morality, MacIntyre writes:

> Everything turns on the character of the interior act of the will. Character therefore, the arena of virtues and vices, simply becomes one more circumstance, external to will. The true arena of morality is that of the will and of the will alone. (p. 168)

For Abelard, the central human question, and the central question of his *Ethics*, is about salvation and damnation: What constitutes sin? In his *Ethics*, Abelard identifies consent, which we list among the acts of the will,[7] as the essential character of sin, distinguishing it both from vicious dispositions to sin and from other acts that either precede consent or follow upon it.[8] The reduction of morality to consent to obey impoverishes ethics and opens the door to the rejection of nature as a source of moral norms. Morality as a rich understanding of living well is replaced by morality as a meeting of two wills, and all other factors begin to fall into the periphery.

This medieval emphasis on the act of the will is not just the product of biblical interpretation; MacIntyre notes that it is also the fruit of the Stoic tradition. Stoicism reduces virtue from a complex account of the functioning of the powers of the soul to a singular perfection of the will, and Stoicism abandons the teleological notion of moral excellence as the perfection of the rational and appetitive powers of the free human agent, affirming instead only the unconditional goodness of the will that obeys moral law (pp. 168–9).

Intellectually, then, voluntarism seems to be an outcome of the Christian and Stoic traditions, but there is another factor that brings Stoicism to prominence from time to time, namely political change. When radical political change overturns shared conceptions of the common good, one is left with a culture in which morality appears to demand real personal sacrifice for no other end than obedience to the law. Looking back into the collapse of community life that originally led to Stoicism, MacIntyre writes: *impact on the "rule of law"*

> any intelligible relationship between the virtues and law would disappear. There would be no genuine shared common goods; the only goods would be the goods of individuals. And the pursuit of *any* private good, being often and necessarily in these circumstances liable to clash with the goods of others, would appear to be at odds with the requirements of the moral law. Hence if I adhere to the law, I will have to suppress the private self. The point of the law cannot be the achievement of some good beyond the law; for there now appears to be no such good. (p. 170)

The political circumstances that brought about Stoicism in the first place are not unique in history, and so MacIntyre proposes that similar circumstances are likely to bring about recurrences in Stoicism whenever they arise.

The identification of the catastrophe with the turn to voluntarism and nominalism is confirmed again in a fourth place in *AV*:

> I have suggested that a great part of modern morality is intelligible only as a set of fragmented survivals from that

[Aristotelian] tradition, and indeed that the inability of modern moral philosophers to carry through their projects of analysis and justification is closely connected with the fact that the concepts with which they work are a combination of fragmented survivals and implausible modern inventions. (p. 257)

The rejection of the Aristotelian tradition with its natural teleology and the transition to voluntarist morality is the philosophical event that corresponds to the destruction of science in the "Disquieting Suggestion."

The events of that historical process are familiar to us, whether we are moderns, postmoderns, or Thomists. We are familiar with the medieval rediscovery of Aristotle, and its rejection; we know about the Black Death and the other complex circumstances that brought medieval culture into decline; we know about the Renaissance and the Reformation; and we know about the secularization that came with the Enlightenment. The difference MacIntyre is proposing is one of interpretation: While these events are commonly read as the history of progress toward individual freedom, they are also moments in the history of the turn to voluntarism that gave birth to the modern culture of emotivism that tyrannizes those traditional moral communities that it does not dissolve.[9]

Moral action and human action

The outcome of the rejection of Aristotelian natural teleology in ethics was the establishment of a morality in which obedience to moral norms can be conceived only as an end in itself. The voluntarism of Luther, Calvin, and Jansen made their accounts of moral norms, like their accounts of reward and punishment, essentially arbitrary. Kant's rejection of the moral worth of heteronomy, of doing good for any reason except respect for duty[10] gives voluntarist morality a new philosophical expression, but does not change its character. Mill's affirmation that the "readiness" to serve "the happiness of others by the absolute sacrifice of his own . . . is the highest virtue that can be found in man"[11] sounds noble, but only renews the stoic denial of the private self in a social arena that lacks shared conceptions of the common good.

Taken together, the emphasis on law, the rejection of teleology, and the denial of the private self establish an approach to morality and moral action in which both morality and moral action become unintelligible, for moral action, thus conceived, cannot be accounted for as human action. This is a problem in modern moral philosophy that MacIntyre had already been working on for nearly 20 years when he wrote *AV*. In "NMW II," MacIntyre wrote:

> We make both individual deeds and social practices intelligible as human actions by showing how they connect with characteristically human desires, needs and the like. Where we cannot do this, we treat the unintelligible piece of behavior as a symptom, a survival, or a superstition.[12]

Human action is so inherently teleological that the normal human response to actions that do not seem to make sense is to ask "what are you doing?" and "why are you doing that?" To disconnect freedom and obedience from salvation, as Luther, Calvin, and Jansen do, to propose that morality should be pursued without an end in view, as Kant does, or to affirm that readiness to act in ways that serve the pleasure of others through utter self-destruction is a sign of moral excellence, as Mill does, is to make it impossible to answer these normal human questions in any satisfying way. The answers leave the questions unanswered.

Every human act worthy of the name is pursued for an end, and sound practical rules are nothing but wise counsels, directing the complex web of human actions toward the common good. But when the common good is no longer understood, the rules survive only as social habits, as material survivals of a culture that is formally lost. When European explorers encountered these kinds of unintelligible moral habits among Polynesian people, they took these taboo rules to be a sign of primitiveness, but as MacIntyre pointed out, first in "NMW," and again in at least four subsequent works,[13] what they had failed to recognize when they made that harsh judgment was that their own moral rules had already become social habits of the same kind.

MacIntyre's critique of modernity has two main points: The first is that modernity has lost its capacity to understand the real practical wisdom of its traditional morality, and has formulated an approach to moral thinking that is unintelligible, unjustifiable, and ultimately arbitrary. The second is that morality, formulated in this modern fashion, can be used, and has been used, as a tool for social manipulation (p. 110). Late modernity, what MacIntyre has called "the culture of emotivism" is an essentially manipulative culture. It does not seek the truth about morality because it has systematically cut itself off from the intellectual resources required to express moral truth, much less to seek it. Consequently, modern moral discourse ceases to be anything but a manipulative tool. MacIntyre writes:

> What is the key to the social content of emotivism? It is the fact that emotivism entails the obliteration of any genuine distinction between manipulative and non-manipulative social relations. . . .
>
> If emotivism is true this distinction is illusory. . . . The sole reality of distinctively moral discourse is the attempt of one will to align the attitudes, feelings, preference and choices of another with its own. Others are always means, never ends. (pp. 23–4)

These are the main themes of MacIntyre's critique of modernity,[14] and they help to frame up the constructive project that has followed upon it.

Moving forward: History, realism, and tradition

MacIntyre's critique of modernity, summarized in the metaphor of the catastrophe, is a valuable resource for the contemporary philosopher. MacIntyre's critique of modernity focuses on ideological blindness and lack of self-knowledge, exposing the pretensions of those modern thinkers who claim a tradition-independent approach to the truth. Consequently, MacIntyre's critique challenges the contemporary philosopher to investigate three things: history, realism, and tradition. First, by questioning the modern academic historian's understanding of modern history, MacIntyre is challenging the contemporary philosopher to recognize and question the interpretative preconceptions of modern history.[15]

Second, MacIntyre's criticism of modern voluntarism and nominalism indicates the shortcomings of non-realist approaches to philosophy. MacIntyre's later Thomistic work, particularly *Three Rival Versions of Moral Enquiry (3RV)* and his *Aquinas Lecture*, show the promise of realism for any investigation of our world that does seek truth. Finally, the plight of the fictional pseudoscientists in MacIntyre's story indicates something about the fragility of a tradition and the possibility of losing large portions of the tradition-dependent substantive rationality of a community; thus, it challenges contemporary philosophers to work diligently to comprehend their own traditions, even as they seek to transcend the limitations of those traditions while doing the work of philosophy within a limited human perspective.

Notes

1 Previously published in Kelvin Knight and Paul Blackledge, eds, *Revolutionary Aristotelianism* (Stuttgart: Lucius & Lucius, 2008), special edition of *Analyse & Kritik* 30, no. 1 (June 2008): 91–9.

2 Alasdair MacIntyre, *AV*, 2nd edn (Notre Dame, IN: University of Notre Dame Press, 1984), p. 1.

3 Ibid.

4 "Christian Neo-Platonism" characterizes the theology of Augustine of Hippo and his successors, who used elements of the philosophy of Plotinus to describe the created world. According to Christian Neo-Platonism, ideas in the divine intellect are exemplars for all created things. See Aquinas, *Summa Theologiae*, I, question 15; see also Augustine of Hippo, *Confessions*, book 7, chapter 9.

5 "Hylomorphism" is Aristotle's physical theory that each substance is a composite of matter and form. See Aquinas, *Summa Theologiae*, I, question 4.

6 See Thomas Aquinas, *De Potentia Dei*, question 3, article 15, 3rd argument.

7 Aquinas lists consent *among* the acts of the will; in *AV*, MacIntyre describes it as *the* act of the will.

8 Peter Abelard, *Ethics: Or Know Thyself*, trans. R. McCallum, in Arthur Hyman and James J. Walsh, eds, *Philosophy in the Middle Ages* (Indianapolis: Hackett, 1973), pp. 188–202.

9 This summarizes a point MacIntyre made in an interview first published in Italy in 1991. See Giovanna Borradori, "Nietzsche or

Aristotle," in *The American Philosopher* (Chicago: University of Chicago Press, 1994), reprinted in *MacReader*.

10 See Immanuel Kant, *Foundations for the Metaphysics of Morals*.

11 John Stuart Mill, *Utilitarianism*, chapter 2.

12 "NMW II," *The New Reasoner* 8 (Spring 1959): 89–98, reprinted in Kelvin Knight, ed., *MacReader*, pp. 41–9.

13 See "NMW II"; "Some More About 'Ought,'" in *Against the Self-Images of the Age*, pp. 166–7; "Can Medicine Dispense with a Theological Conception of Human Nature?," pp. 30–1; *AV*, pp. 111–13; *3RV*, pp. 27–8, 178–89.

14 Those who are familiar with Anscombe's essay, "Modern Moral Philosophy" (*Philosophy* 33 (1958): 1–19), will recognize the parallels between that work and MacIntyre's approach to ethics. MacIntyre cited that work in an article published in 1959 ("Hume on 'Is' and 'Ought,'" *Philosophical Review* (1959), reprinted in *Against the Self-Images of the Age*, p. 124) and acknowledged his debt to—as well as his difference from—Anscombe in *AV* (p. 53).

15 In "An Interview for *Cogito*," *Cogito* 5, no. 2 (1991), reprinted in *MacReader*, pp. 267–75, MacIntyre said: "Any adequate narrative of my life would have to emphasize a radical change in it around 1971. . . . In that same period, after 1971, I had occasion to rethink the problems of rational theology, taking seriously the possibility that the history of modern secularization can only be written adequately from the standpoint of Christian theism, rather than vice versa."

3

Summary of the critical argument

The works of Aristotle usually begin by surveying the opinions of his predecessors in order to identify the problems to be solved. Thomas Aquinas's disputed questions begin similarly. Thomas begins by laying out the strongest objections against his own opinions, in order to lay out the problems he must solve and the questions he must answer when he argues his position.

The critical argument of *AV* that forms the first half of the book serves the same purpose. The constructive argument in the second half of the book will make the case that ordinary people can recover the standpoint of the virtues through rational action, involvement in practices, and attention to their social identities. But before we can approach that solution, we need to understand the questions that it addresses; revealing these questions is the task of the critical argument.

Overview of the critical argument

MacIntyre's argument in chapters one through nine shows that the ethical theories of modern liberal individualism are simply incoherent, and that the social sciences have yet to discover the kinds of law-like generalizations about human behavior that could give scientific justification to the decisions of bureaucrats and managers. Recognition of the incoherence of modern ethics and the failure of determinist social theory leads to a choice between the alternatives presented in chapter nine, "Nietzsche or Aristotle." MacIntyre finds that Nietzsche's critique of ethics overturns both the rational determinations of the moral theorist and the scientific calculations of the bureaucratic manager, for in the absence of any compelling justification of the theories that are said to support those determinations and calculations, both are revealed as arbitrary impositions, as manifestations of the will to power.

MacIntyre then asks if it was a mistake for modernity to abandon Aristotle's ethics. For Aristotle, ethics studies human action and the virtues necessary for effective practical reasoning and deliberate human agency. Unlike modern moral philosophy, Aristotelian ethics does not treat morality as something distinct from the pursuit of personal happiness, but as a necessary part of that pursuit. Unlike modern moral philosophy, Aristotle does not view human moral freedom as a given, but as an achievement. In Aristotle's ethics, the excellent or virtuous human agent is the one who judges well about what is good and best to do, and follows through on that judgment; thus for Aristotle, moral freedom is identical with virtue. MacIntyre proposes that we consider whether it is possible to recover Aristotle's conception of practical reason, and consider whether it is possible to justify Aristotle's contention that virtue enables the pursuit of the good life. MacIntyre suggests that recovering Aristotle's notions of human action and practical reasoning may open the path to real progress in moral philosophy.

The narrative of the critical argument moves backward in history because it follows the order of discovery. Examination of contemporary morality reveals the culture of emotivism. Examination of the roots of the culture of emotivism leads to modern moral philosophy. A study of the roots of modern moral philosophy leads to the voluntarist and nominalist theologies of the fourteenth, fifteenth, and sixteenth centuries. Those theologies began with a rejection of what they took to be Aristotelian determinism.[1] After peeling away these layers of history, MacIntyre comes to Aristotelian philosophy with its ethics of human action, and asks whether this alternative way of understanding ethics and virtue may provide a more fruitful path for our future.

Summaries of each chapter follow.

Chapter one: A "Disquieting Suggestion"

MacIntyre begins his critical argument with a story and a suggestion. The story describes a culture that had abandoned the natural sciences, lost its cultural memory of the practices that had constituted the natural sciences, and then sought to resurrect the natural sciences by gathering fragments of texts and charts which they memorized and recited. Since the practices of the sciences had been lost, the generation that would resurrect them would have no substantive way to judge their success. No logical examination of their neo-scientific endeavors would reveal their shortcomings, for the only way to learn how to do scientific research properly is to be trained in the practice as an apprentice is trained by a master, and no masters in the practice of science remain. Consequently, their neo-science is utter nonsense, and they have no way to recognize that.

MacIntyre suggests that the language and methods of contemporary moral philosophy are deeply incoherent, and that mainstream modern and postmodern academic moral philosophy is blind to this problem. This incoherence would be the outcome of a crisis in our history that modern academic history does not recognize. The tools of modern analytic philosophy are limited to judging the logical consistency of philosophical claims; they allow us to judge philosophy formally, but they do not enable us to judge substantive claims. Trapped by this limitation, MacIntyre proposes that modern formal philosophy coexists with the deep substantive incoherence of modern ethics without recognizing it. MacIntyre argues that the language of contemporary moral philosophy is very much like the neo-scientific language in his story.

Chapter two: The nature of moral disagreement today and the claims of emotivism

Moral disagreements today (e.g. debates over the justice of war, the legality of elective abortion, and public funding for education and health care) are characterized by three things. (a) These contending moral positions cannot resolve their differences by argument because the contending positions are based on radically different presuppositions about the issues involved (these differences are incommensurable); (b) all parties to these disputes appeal to objective, impersonal standards to support their claims; and (c) the contending groups draw the parts of their arguments from varying historical origins, often ignoring the broader cultural issues, beliefs, and philosophical theories that had originally shaped and justified those parts of their arguments.

These three common characteristics suggest three problems. (a) The contending views of the facts in each case suggest that the apparent truth of the contending position is relative to the perspectives of those who advance them. (b) The standards may not be as objective or impersonal as their users maintain. (c) When the contending parties construct their arguments by picking and choosing their principles, it appears that their rational arguments are arbitrary constructions created to defend irrational decisions that have already been made. These three characteristics of contemporary moral disagreement raise questions about the way moral language is used. MacIntyre will characterize the pragmatic use of moral language as emotivist.

Emotivism was a theory about the *meaning* of evaluative judgments (especially moral judgments) that developed among the students of G. E. Moore, particularly by C. L. Stevenson,[2] in the early twentieth century. According to emotivism, the *meaning* of an objective judgment like "this is right" is really only the subjective statement, "I approve of this, do so as well"; or even "Hurrah for this" (p. 12). But most people have rejected this *theory of meaning*, and accept that moral judgments mean what their authors say they mean—even if those authors are wrong. MacIntyre reinterprets this false *theory of meaning* as a "cogent *theory of use*." According to MacIntyre's reinterpretation, many people *use* moral judgments— whatever their words may mean—to express arbitrary choices and preferences, and to encourage or manipulate others to join them in those arbitrary choices and preferences. MacIntyre argues that this is a fair description of the *use* of moral language in much of contemporary culture, which he calls "the culture of emotivism."

Unlike the discarded emotivist *theory of meaning*, which had claimed that evaluative judgments are always essentially subjective and arbitrary, MacIntyre's emotivist *theory of use* gives a name to the subjective and arbitrary abuse of evaluative language. MacIntyre's distinction between meaning and use suggests that it may be possible to acknowledge and reject the emotivist abuse of moral language, but vindicating evaluative judgments in the culture of emotivism would demand that we find a basis for practical evaluation that is not arbitrary.

Chapter three: Emotivism: Social content and social context

In chapter three, MacIntyre explains how emotivism understands the human agent and how emotivism understands the "reasons, motives, intentions, and actions" that agents pursue through action (p. 23). Emotivism, however, reduces the agent to a ghostly will (p. 32) and it rejects any criteria to judge its choices (p. 33). Emotivism, thus, represents the self-destruction of ethics. Emotivism does away with traditional accounts of the agent that begin with a social identity (pp. 33–4) and it abandons any conception of "a whole human life" that might serve as a *telos* for human action or a standard for the assessment of one's conduct. The abandonment of the human *telos* was "celebrated historically . . . as self-congratulatory gain" (p. 34), but MacIntyre sees it differently, as the turn that led to the culture of emotivism.

Emotivism "entails the obliteration of any genuine distinction between manipulative and non-manipulative social relations" (p. 23). Under emotivism, "The sole reality of distinctively moral discourse is the attempt of one will to align the attitudes, feelings, preference and choice of another with its own" (p. 24). The manipulative character of emotivism does not arise because emotivists are particularly imperious or oppressive; emotivists begin by asserting that "values . . . are created by human choices," and conclude that "All faiths, and all evaluations are equally non-rational; all are subjective directions given to sentiment and feeling" (p. 26).[3] As a consequence, there is no value or principle that exercises any authority over the emotivist; the emotivist exercises authority instead over values and principles by choosing or not choosing to value them.

To the criterionless, emotivist self, moral disagreements are nothing but clashes of wills; hence, there is nothing to do in the event of a moral disagreement except for "one will to align the . . . choice of another with its own."

Emotivist theory is embodied in certain "social characters" in late modern culture—the rich aesthete, the manager, and the therapist, to which MacIntyre has recently added "the conservative moralist" (third edition, p. xv). What these characters have in common is that they never truly engage in shared practical deliberation or moral debate with others. They do not question what they do, they merely do it, and they judge their success by the measurable effectiveness of their efforts to join others to the projects that they manage (p. 30). The rich aesthete manipulates others for entertainment. The manager drives the bureaucracy to achieve its ends without questioning those ends. The therapist helps the patient to become more effective in doing whatever the patient chooses to do, without questioning the patient's goals and purposes. The conservative moralist opposes liberal politicians who use permissive law to transform traditional society, but "conservatism by prohibitive legal enactments now tries to use that same power for its own coercive projects" (third edition, p. xv).

In short, emotivism gains autonomy for the individual at the expense of identity and teleology. "The peculiarly modern self, the emotivist self, in acquiring sovereignty in its own realm lost its traditional boundaries provided by a social identity and a view of human life as ordered to a given end" (p. 34). MacIntyre began this chapter by arguing that "it would generally be a decisive refutation of a moral philosophy to show that moral agency on its own account of the matter could never be socially embodied" (p. 23). Emotivism's account of moral agency—ill-defined agents doing as they choose—cannot be socially embodied, for whenever it is embodied it threatens—rather than fosters—social life.

What then does emotivist culture look like? It is a collection of autonomous individuals who struggle to balance individualism and collectivism, liberty and oppression, and chaos and control. They seek a rational basis for this balance, but they agree that moral choices are either essentially or effectively arbitrary. Each individual has her or his own arbitrary ends, and the state has another set of arbitrary ends; so questions about individualism and collectivism become questions of power, thus besides the options of autonomy and state control, there is no third option. In the culture of emotivism, even the decision to seek practical wisdom could be interpreted only as an arbitrary choice. The presuppositions of the culture of emotivism lead its inhabitants to view shared deliberation about means as a form of collectivism.

Chapter four: The predecessor culture and the enlightenment project of justifying morality

As the chapter title suggests, MacIntyre holds that the culture of emotivism followed upon the collapse of the enlightenment project of justifying morality. This project sought to produce a rational apologetic for the external practices of Christian morality when secular modern thinkers denied that its moral rules should be accepted as the commands of God, while they maintained that those rules were morally necessary. The predecessor to emotivist culture is the secularized Protestant culture of Northern Germany and Great Britain, and includes certain similar groups in other parts of Western Europe (p. 37). In these places, voluntarist Christian moral theology (a theology that held the arbitrary will of God to be the only source of moral law) had taught a morality of arbitrary divine commands, and had thus separated moral judgment from practical reasoning and denied that we may discover what is right through any consideration of natural inclination or desire.[4] Secular modern moral philosophers steeped in the culture of this theology denied that morality proceeded only from divine commands, but they presupposed the rational morality that their new theories would justify would have the same content and form as the Christian morality of their youth. "Kant never doubted for a moment that the maxims which he had learnt from his own virtuous parents were those which had to be vindicated by a rational test" (p. 44). Among the elements of that moral theology that modern moral philosophy retained were the rejection of any fixed goal or *telos* of human life, and consequently, the separation of desire and morality, and the rejection of the moral significance of inclination. The rejection of teleology drove ethical considerations into the new, independent field of "morality" (pp. 38–9).

MacIntyre argues that "morality," as a subject matter distinct from sound practical judgment, good character, or obedience to God, originates in early modernity. The word "moral," as we use it, was not used until the seventeenth century, and there is no word in classical Latin or Greek that approximates its meaning. MacIntyre traces the origin of the term to the period "from say 1630 to 1850," when "'morality' became the name for that particular sphere in which rules of conduct were neither theological nor legal nor aesthetic" (p. 39). So the universal morality that the enlightenment apologists sought to justify was peculiar in two senses: first, it amounted to the practices of Christian morality, and second, this very notion of "universal morality" was both novel and provincial.

MacIntyre illustrates the enlightenment project of justifying morality by summarizing arguments from Kierkegaard's *Enten-Eller* (*Either/Or*, 1842), Diderot's *Le Neveu de Rameau* (*Rameau's Nephew*[5]), Hume's *Treatise of Human Nature*,[6] and Kant's principal ethical works.[7] MacIntyre presents all four as "moral conservatives" who accept, for the most part, the content of traditional Christian morality (p. 47) but find themselves caught between the autonomy of the individual and the authority of moral principles. Of the four, only Kierkegaard, Kant, and Hume are central to the argument.

Kierkegaard presents his views under three pseudonyms in Enten-Eller: In the character of Victor Eremeta, Kierkegaard presents the writings of A and B, which offer the alternatives of aesthetic and ethical ways of life. The choice to be made is a radical one: "The choice between the ethical and the aesthetic is not the choice between good and evil, it is the choice whether or not to choose in terms of good and evil" (p. 40). MacIntyre denies that Kierkegaard endorses either position, and concludes that Kierkegaard treats the choice of the ethical life, the choice of first principles, as an ultimate and criterionless choice: "the principles which depict the ethical way of life are to be adopted *for no reason*" (p. 42). MacIntyre argues that such an arbitrary choice cannot instill any authority into the principles it chooses, and that Kierkegaard thus fails to justify morality.[8]

In making this argument against what he took to be Kierkegaard's justification of morality, MacIntyre disagreed both with Kierkegaard's autobiography and with contemporary Kierkegaard scholars who found Kierkegaard's endorsement of the ethical life less ambiguous. From his longer explanation in his Kierkegaard article in the *Encyclopedia of Philosophy*, it is clear that MacIntyre does not see Kirkegaard's judgment to be ambiguous. Rather, like Kant, who sought to make room for belief against the determinist implications of modern science, Kierkegaard seeks to maintain freedom for faith against Hegel's notion of rational progress. To do this, Kierkegaard embraces radical voluntarism. Consequently, for Kierkegaard, "What the individual does depends not upon what he understands, but upon what he wills."[9] This passage generated a considerable response from the Kierkegaardian community.[10]

MacIntyre presents Kierkegaard's notion of a "radical and ultimate choice" (p. 41) as a response to what Kierkegaard took to be the failure of Kant's rational justification of morality. Kant sought to justify morality by "discovering a rational test which will discriminate those maxims which are a genuine expression of the moral law . . . from those maxims which are not" (p. 44). Kant denies that this test can consider either "whether obedience to it would in the end lead to happiness" (p. 44) or "whether it is commanded by God" (p. 44). Kant's philosophy thus distinguishes morality from the pursuit of human happiness and from obedience to God, the rules of morality are rules without purposes, and the test that is to distinguish the true maxims of the moral law from the false is whether or not they are universalizable (p. 45). MacIntyre concludes that Kant's position for the respect of human reason and against manipulation is in keeping with the conclusions of philosophers since Plato, "But Kant gives us no good reason for holding this position" (p. 46). As he had noted earlier in his career,[11] since Kant had separated morality from practical reason—in this case from divine obedience and from the pursuit of happiness—Kant's moral judgment provides no reason that could move one to act. The autonomy of the agent undermines the authority of whatever moral norms she or he might adopt.

MacIntyre uses Diderot's *Rameau's Nephew* (*Le Neveu de Rameau*) to illustrate the problems inherent in any effort to justify morality by appealing to the passions. Since it was not published until 1805, it could not have influenced the development of Kant's moral philosophy. Diderot's *philosophe* defends conventional morality "the rules which the appeal to their basis in desire and passion will vindicate" (p. 47), but this undermines the authority of conventional morality since there are a variety of passions and a variety of ways to order them (p. 48).

MacIntyre treats Kant's moral philosophy as a response to Hume's attempt to justify morality by appeal to the passions. MacIntyre cites three of Hume's works by the shorthand titles, the *Treatise*, the *Enquiry*, and the *History*. These are *A Treatise of Human Nature* (1739), *An Enquiry Concerning Human Understanding* (1748), and *The History of England* (1754–1762).[12] In his earlier work on Hume, MacIntyre credited Hume for holding on "at all costs to the internal connection between morals and desires,"[13] but noted that Hume was already aware of the weakness of resting moral theory on desires that could be "modified, criticized, rejected, developed, and so on."[14] For Hume, the rules of morality were to be justified, "by showing their utility in helping us to attain those ends which the passions set before us" (p. 48). But given the range of passions that may drive human action, Hume's account must identify some set of passions as "normal," and MacIntyre uses the moral narrative of Hume's *History* to determine what this is: "The normal passions are those of a complacent heir to the revolution of 1688"[15] (p. 49).

Hume's identification of "normal" with those like himself seems to reduce his ethical argument to a simple projection, but MacIntyre finds another problem with it. In the *Enquiry*, Hume notes that we obey the rules of morality for our long-term interest, and then asks whether one should justly break the rules, if one can get away with it, if it serves one's long-term interest (p. 49). This question shows that Hume's appeal to the passions gives no authority to the rules of morality; as with Kierkegaard and Kant, the autonomy of the individual seems to be incompatible with impersonal and objective moral norms.

Hume, Kant, and Kierkegaard represent three different ways of justifying morality in the absence of a fixed goal for human desire and action. Each approach excludes the other two. Hume argues from the rational pursuit of desires. Kant counters with the rational determination of the will. Kierkegaard abandons both in favor of the arbitrary choice of the will. Given the constraints of enlightenment thought, specifically its rejection of any fixed goal or *telos* of human life, these three approaches seem to exhaust the possibilities, and all three have failed to justify the authority of moral rules over the lives of human agents.

MacIntyre's interpretation of Kierkegaard remains controversial among Kierkegaard specialists, but MacIntyre has not abandoned it. MacIntyre's article on Kierkegaard in the *Encyclopedia of Philosophy* (1967)[16] had already established his interpretation of the role of criterionless choice in Kierkegaard's thought. *AV* draws this interpretation of Kierkegaard into the history of the culture of emotivism. Two decades after the publication of *AV*, some leading Kierkegaard scholars gathered their critiques of MacIntyre's interpretation into a volume called *Kierkegaard After MacIntyre* (2001), and MacIntyre contributed a response.[17] While acknowledging certain shortcomings in the *AV* account, MacIntyre defended the heart of his interpretation.

Chapter five: Why the enlightenment project of justifying morality had to fail

The enlightenment project of justifying morality had to fail because enlightenment moralists refused to treat ethics and human action teleologically. They refused to treat the rules of morality as guides to choosing the best means in the pursuit of a fixed goal or *telos* of human life. Aristotle or Aquinas could judge a desire or an action to be good or evil if it helped or hindered an agent's pursuit of the good. Without a fixed natural *telos*, there is no such measure by which the good or evil of desires and actions could be judged, and the contingent facts about the random desires of individuals would have no clear relationship with moral rules intended only to curb abusive behavior. This separation between the norms of morality and the purposes of human actions left modern moral philosophy with a view of moral rules that did not fit with its notion of human nature (p. 52).

The rational ethics of Plato and Aristotle had three elements. Plato and Aristotle sought to raise the human person from (a) an unperfected condition to (b) a perfected condition (c) by means of moral training. The perfected condition, "human-nature-as-it-could-be-if-it-realized-its-*telos*" (p. 53) is the goal of moral training and human action, and obedience to moral norms was historically understood as a means to pursue this goal.

But teleology in rational ethics suffered two historical challenges. First, Luther, Calvin, and Jansen all denied that reason could genuinely comprehend "man's true end" because "that power of reason was destroyed by the fall of man" (p. 53). Second, secularization and the scientific rejection of Aristotelian natural philosophy combined to eliminate "any notion of man-as-he-could-be-if-he-realized-his-*telos.*"

Two of the three elements of Plato's and Aristotle's rational ethics survived into modernity: untutored human nature and moral rules, but those rules have been "deprived of their teleological context" (p. 55) and there is no notion of human perfection to serve as a goal for the transformation of "untutored-human-nature-as-it-is." Where the classical tradition saw imperfect people seeking human excellence through moral development, modernity sees imperfect people who must obey the rules of morality—period (p. 55). The task of modern moral philosophy was to find a rational basis for the rules of morality without directing those rules to any purpose beyond "morality."

MacIntyre finds three early critics of this project in Hume, Diderot, and Kant. Hume had introduced the "is-ought" problem in the *Treatise* (1739), Diderot puzzled over the same issue in *Rameau's Nephew* (ca. 1761–1772), and Kant accepted the need for a teleological framework in the second *Critique* (i.e. the *Critique of Practical Reason*, 1788). Hume's doubt about moving from is to ought (p. 56) would become the doctrine that one cannot infer an "ought" from an "is," through the influence of Moore's *Principia Ethica* (1903). Moore's "naturalistic fallacy" has become an influential part of modern ethics. Is it possible to overcome the naturalistic fallacy?

Any movement from is to ought presupposes a "functional concept" which is defined "in terms of the purpose or function which . . . [it is] characteristically expected to serve" (p. 58). MacIntyre presents the examples of a watch and a farmer; the watch is good if it keeps time accurately and the farmer is good if he farms well. But the modern concept of the human person is not a functional concept, because modernity abstracts the person from all roles, relationships, and responsibilities (p. 59). This "loss of traditional structure was seen . . . as the achievement by the self of its proper autonomy" (p. 60). But the invention of autonomy and of the individual led to the creation of our emotivist culture (p. 61).

Chapter six: Some consequences of the failure of the enlightenment project

The modern individual is "sovereign in his moral authority," and the "rules of morality" have been "deprived of their teleological character" as rational laws, "and of their even more ancient categorical character as expressions of an ultimately divine law." The task of modern moral philosophy is therefore to devise "some new teleology" or to find "some new categorical status" for the rules of morality so that appeal to them does not "appear as a mere instrument of individual desire and will" (p. 62). But it is impossible to reconcile moral autonomy either with teleology or with categorical moral norms, so every effort to do so fails. Thus, every modern moral theory ultimately may be unmasked as an instrument of individual desire and will.

Every modern moral theory ultimately is an instrument of individual will & desire

Utilitarianism begins with Bentham's and Mill's efforts to devise a new teleology that seeks the greatest happiness of the greatest number, where happiness means pleasure and the avoidance of pain. But what, *precisely*, does the pursuit of the greatest happiness entail? Nothing; and that makes utilitarianism little more than an ideological tool, a deceptive, and perhaps self-deceiving mask for arbitrary choice:

> The notion of the greatest happiness of the greatest number is a notion without any clear content at all. It is indeed a pseudo-concept available for a variety of ideological uses, but no more than that. Hence when we encounter its use in practical life, it is always necessary to ask what actual project or purpose is being concealed by its use. (p. 64)

The philosophical failure of utilitarianism moved through Sidgwick to Moore, whose intuitionism led to the theory of emotivism.

MacIntyre briefly treats Alan Gewirth's *Reason and Morality* (1978) as one of the most recent efforts to offer a philosophically rigorous contribution to modern moral philosophy but ultimately criticizes Gewirth's uncritical use of rights language.

The autonomy of the modern agent leaves us with this quandary: on the one hand, we want to protect our autonomy, and to that end we want to avoid being manipulated. On the other hand, we want to bring others to share in our projects and points of view, but there is nothing objective that we modern agents can point to that might require anyone else to join in our personal preferences and opinions; so if we are to align others to ourselves, manipulation seems to be the only means to do so (p. 68).

MacIntyre treats the modern and postmodern concepts of "rights," "protest," and "unmasking" as three kinds of manipulative tools. The "rights" MacIntyre dismisses are not "those rights conferred by positive law or custom on specified classes of person." MacIntyre dismisses only modern rights "which are cited as a reason for holding that people ought not to be interfered with in their pursuit of life, liberty, and happiness" (pp. 68–9). These "rights" do not exist, except as manipulative tools, and this is why every effort to explain their existence has failed (pp. 69–70).[18] Protest is likewise merely manipulative since it "cannot be *rationally* effective" (p. 71). Even unmasking, the practice of revealing "the unacknowledged motives of arbitrary will and desire" is manipulative, since "unmasking arbitrariness in others may always be a defense against uncovering it in ourselves" (p. 72).

Lacking any firm foundation for their moral claims, the three characters of the culture of emotivism (four with the third edition's conservative moralist) use the language of morality arbitrarily to manipulate others to join their preferences and choices: "they trade and cannot escape trading in moral fictions" (p. 73). This is as true of the therapist's theories, the manager's "effectiveness," and the conservative moralist's "values" as it is of the rich aesthete's schemes. Once this is made clear, "our morality will be disclosed as a theater of illusions" (p. 77).

Chapter seven: "Fact," explanation, and expertise

Facts are artifacts of interpretation. Explanations are artifacts of interpretation. These interpretations are based on culturally developed standards. Facts are not prior to theory; instead, every fact and every explanation presupposes allegiance to some set of presuppositions. Consequently, there is no neutral, impersonal appeal to objective facts, and inasmuch as "expertise" involves knowledge of facts or explanatory theories, it, too, is never truly objective; it is always partisan.

Where Aristotle examined human actions directed to natural ends, modern social scientists examine human behaviors which they take to be determined by the mechanical causes that trigger them. The Aristotelian facts about human action have to do with the ends to which those actions are directed (p. 84). In the modern social sciences, the "facts" about human behavior have been designed to exclude "all reference to intentions, purposes, and reasons for action" (p. 83). The social scientists decided to exclude these in order to support their efforts to establish a mechanistic science of human "behavior." MacIntyre questions the coherence of this project using examples from Quine and from the third of Marx's *Theses on Feuerbach* (pp. 83–4).

The project to establish a mechanistic science of human behavior seeks to discover "invariances specified by law-like generalizations" (p. 82). This goal has not been met, but that has not prevented some social scientists from acting as if it has. Their "social performance . . . disguises itself as such achievement" (p. 85). And government bureaucracies have aided and abetted this social performance in order to justify their own authority through the "expertise" of social scientists.

Chapter eight: The character of generalizations in social science and their lack of predictive power

MacIntyre asserts that the authority of managerial expertise needs to be vindicated by the social sciences. The social sciences, in turn, need to be justified by "providing a stock of law-like generalizations with strong predictive power," but so far those sciences have not discovered "any law-like generalizations whatsoever" (p. 88). It follows that the social sciences have yet to be justified as sciences; consequently, it also follows that inasmuch as managerial expertise borrows its authority from the social sciences, that authority has yet to be vindicated.

MacIntyre explores this problem by presenting four examples of "law-like generalizations" generated by the social sciences and identifying "three notable characteristics" that they share. The four examples are (a) a theory about conditions that cause revolutions, (b) a theory about the relationship of the height of high-rise buildings to criminal behavior, (c) a theory considering the differences between policemen's and courts' understanding of law, and (d) a theory about the relationship of the political and social stability of a society to its degree of modernization. The studies from which MacIntyre takes these examples are listed in the bibliography (pp. 279–81). What characteristics do these law-like generalizations share?

> First of all, they all coexist in their disciplines with recognized counterexamples. (p. 90)
>
> Second . . . they lack not only universal quantifiers but also scope modifiers. That is, . . . we cannot say of them in any precise way under what conditions they hold. (p. 91)
>
> Third, these generalizations do not entail any well-defined set of counterfactual conditionals in the way that the law-like generalizations of physics and chemistry do. . . . Thus they are not laws. (p. 91)

They cannot even be described accurately as "probabilistic generalizations." (p. 91). The social sciences have failed to establish law-like generalizations, not because they "are still young sciences" but because their task is not suited to their subject matter; they are trying to make laws to predict what is systematically unpredictable.

source of systematic unpredictability in human affairs

MacIntyre lists "four sources of systematic unpredictability in human affairs": First, "radical conceptual innovations," new inventions and new ideas, can change cultures and societies in completely unexpected ways (pp. 93–5). Second, the outcomes of choices that we have not yet made are not predictable (pp. 95–7). Third, game theory teaches us that it is difficult to predict the choices and actions of people engaging in competitive activities who benefit from deception and misinformation. These difficulties for prediction are only compounded in real-life circumstances where the hidden interests of individual players multiply the

number of games being played. Another kind of difficulty arising from game theory appears when we realize that the kinds of
events that game theorists study may not appear as such to their
real-life participants, as Robert E. Lee could not have known that
he was involved in the Battle of Gettysburg until the fight was well
under way (pp. 97–9). MacIntyre identifies a fourth source of systematic unpredictability in human affairs as "pure contingency"
(pp. 99–101).

MacIntyre finds that what is predictable in social life is comparatively limited. The agreed schedules of a community or a society are predictable. "Statistical regularities" are predictable, but
are independent from "causal knowledge" (p. 102). "Knowledge
of causal regularities in nature" constrains "human possibility"
in predictable ways, as does "knowledge of causal regularities in
social life" (p. 103). Yet, these predictable features of human life
do not challenge the "pervasive unpredictability of human life"
(p. 103).

If the social sciences cannot be vindicated, then neither can the
authority of the manager. Thus, MacIntyre lists the manager as a
character of the culture of emotivism:

> The realm of managerial expertise is one in which what purport
> to be objectively-grounded claims function in fact as expressions
> of arbitrary, but disguised, will and preference. (p. 107)

MacIntyre's critique of the social sciences concerns the kinds of
appeals to social theory that governments and other large institutions use to justify large-scale actions and policy directives. It
is directed, implicitly, against the claims of Marxist and Stalinist
social scientists. MacIntyre notes that many real managers might
object that their own claims to specialized knowledge are very
modest, and that they are themselves unlike his emotivist character. MacIntyre agrees with them but denies that their claim
counters his; the appearance that it does only serves as a deceptive apologetic against MacIntyre's argument. The manager who
stands as a character in the culture of emotivism is the bureaucratic
manager who claims her or his authority on the basis of a knowledge of the science of management, rather than on any practical or
prudential knowledge of the practices engaged by the people she or
he manages.

Chapter nine: Nietzsche or Aristotle?

MacIntyre brings the critical argument to its conclusion in chapter nine. The central issue in the critical argument is that there is a gap between the meaning and the use of moral language, that the *meaning* of moral language has become obscured by events in the history of ideas, and that traditional moral rules that once had authority over the lives of people because they were taken to be the commands of God, now have no authority over modern secular thinkers who continue to obey them out of habit or choice. Morality's loss of authority over secular modern individualists, however, has not prevented these same people from imposing traditional rules on others in a selective fashion, and from developing new moral injunctions, *using* traditional moral terms, to impose their will on others through what amounts to quasi-moral manipulation. The main concern of the critical argument comes into sharp focus in this passage:

> If moral utterance is put to uses at the service of arbitrary will, it is someone's arbitrary will; and the question whose will it is is obviously of both moral and political importance . . . What I need to show to accomplish my present task is only how morality has become available for a certain type of use and that it is so used. (p. 110)

The culture of emotivism is a manipulative culture, and in its hands, moral language is little more than a manipulative tool.

MacIntyre compares secular modern morality to the taboo rules of Polynesia encountered by Captain Cook during his third voyage (1776–79). Polynesian culture once had a set of "background beliefs in the light of which the taboo rules had originally been understood" but those beliefs "have not only been abandoned but forgotten" (p. 112); so Kamehameha II repealed the taboo rules in 1819 with little controversy. If imaginary Polynesian analytic philosophers were to have studied "taboo," they might have tried to define it in the same ways that modern analytic philosophers have tried to define the terms of morality. So MacIntyre asks: "And why should we not think of Nietzsche as the Kamehameha II of the European tradition?" (p. 113).

This leads to the ultimatum: Nietzsche or Aristotle. The theological rejection of Aristotle by late medieval Nominalists and by

[Handwritten margin note at top:] Can we so conceive a human telos such that through virtue (habit) applied to human actions we can establish & enable good judgment that will allow us to understand the authority & function of the rules

Luther, Calvin, Jansen, and the communities they founded, created the voluntarist moral theology that the enlightenment rejected. It was the secular rejection of that theology that led to "the Enlightenment project of discovering new rational secular foundations for morality" that Nietzsche repudiated (p. 117). Nietzsche's repudiation of that secular project is compelling, but it opens a new question: "was it right in the first place to reject Aristotle?" (p. 117).

The rest of the book argues that the rejection of Aristotle was a mistake. In place of a modern morality in which rules are primary and virtues serve rules, MacIntyre proposes a recovery of the Aristotelian account of human action and of the role of the habits—the virtues—in establishing and enabling good judgment that may allow us "to understand the function and authority of rules" (p. 119). Returning to an ethics of virtue means returning to teleology; thus, one of the central challenges of the constructive argument of chapters ten through eighteen is to propose a teleology that is amenable to contemporary thought, an account that begins from experience rather than from metaphysical assertions about Aristotelian forms.

This is another controversial turn in the argument of *AV*, because the defense of any teleology in human action that transcends the chosen ends of the agent demands a metaphysical account of the Good, which, in the view of secular, materialist, modern philosophy, would amount to a theology of the Good. As the critical argument has already shown, without a *telos* that transcends the ends that an agent chooses, moral rules can only be imposed by some person's will; they cannot be discovered.

[Handwritten margin note:] w/o a telos that transcends the end an agent chooses (i.e. a metaphysical acct of the good) moral rules can only be imposed by some persons will. They cannot be discovered

Hobbes clearly understood that without a fixed *telos*, every measure of morality and justice must be essentially arbitrary, imposed by a will. His *Leviathan*, which rejects any shared natural end for human activity, "any common rule of good and evil,"[19] insists as a consequence that there can be no sin, either in desire or in action, until there is a promulgated law given by an accepted lawgiver.[20] For Hobbes, this is also the case with divine law, as Abraham's obedience to God's command began with God's covenant with Abraham.[21] Many readers of Hobbes consider him an atheist,[22] MacIntyre's colleague, Peter Geach, has argued that Hobbes was a Socinian Christian,[23] but in either case, Hobbes's nominalism, materialism, and determinism reduced what he called the laws of nature to strategies of self-preservation.[24]

In the prologue to the third edition, MacIntyre admits that *AV* had unacknowledged metaphysical presuppositions (p. xi). He says that he had "presupposed the truth of something very close to the account of the concept of good that Aquinas gives in question 5 in the first part of the *Summa Theologiae*" (p. xi). Such a conception of the good is necessarily at odds with the "anti-theological presuppositions" of the secular modern philosophy that MacIntyre had only questioned at the end of "Epistemological Crises" in 1977.[25]

Notes

1 According to Heiko Oberman, medieval Christians were concerned by the apparent causal determinism of Aristotelian natural philosophy, particularly in the form of Latin Averoism, and responded by defending the freedom of God. See Heiko Oberman, Dawn of the Reformation (Edinburgh: T & T Clark, 1986), p. 6. See also, Heiko Oberman, "Some Notes on the Theology of Nominalism," *The Harvard Theological Review* 53 no. 1 (January 1960): 47–76, at 74.

2 Alasdair MacIntyre cites C. L. Stevenson, *Ethics and Language* (1945), chapter 2. Alasdair MacIntyre's 1951 master's thesis, *The Significance of Moral Judgments*, is a critique of the emotivist theory of G. E. Moore and C. L. Stevenson. The thesis remains unpublished, but is available through the University of Manchester Library; for a summary, see Thomas D. D'Andrea, *Tradition, Rationality, and Virtue: The Thought of Alasdair MacIntyre* (Hampshire, England: Ashgate, 2006), pp. 3–18.

3 MacIntyre quotes and cites R. Aron, "Max Weber," in *Main Currents in Sociological Thought*, trans. R. Howard and H. Weaver (1967), pp. 206–10 and 192.

4 Voluntarism takes its name from the Latin word for the will, *voluntas*. Voluntarist moral theology held that its absolute affirmation of divine sovereignty entailed that God commands because God commands, not because those commands serve what human beings take to be good, or even what God takes to be naturally good for human beings, but simply because God wills it. Early Protestant moral theology, as expressed in Luther's *Bondage of the Will*, Calvin's *Institutes*, and the Canons of the Synod of Dort, teaches that the sin of Adam and Eve recounted in the third chapter of the book of *Genesis* deprives the human person of any effective natural desire for the good.

5 "From internal evidence, it was probably written between 1761 and 1772. So far as is known, however, Diderot did not refer to

it in his letters or other writings, and no contemporary author mentions it." David J. Adams, "*Le Neveu de Rameau*," in *The Literary Encyclopedia* http://www.litencyc.com/php/sworks. php?rec=true&UID=4074, accessed June 24, 2009.

6   Published in 1740.

7   *The Critique of Pure Reason (Der Kritik der Reinen Vernunft)*, published in 1781. *Foundations of the Metaphysics of Morals (Grundlegung der Metaphysic der Sitten)*, published in 1785; *The Critique of Practical Reason (Kritik der praktischen Vernunft)*, published in 1788.

8   MacIntyre had already explained Kirkegaard's strategic use of pseudonyms and Kierkegaard's "doctrine of the primacy of the will" in Alasdair MacIntyre, "Kierkegaard, Søren Aabye," in Paul Edwards, ed., *Encyclopedia of Philosophy* (New York: Macmillan, 1967), vol. 4, pp. 336–40.

9   "Kierkegaard, Søren Aabye," p. 337.

10   See *Kierkegaard After MacIntyre: Freedom, Narrative, and Virtue*, ed. Anthony Rudd and John Davenport (Chicago: Open Court, 2001); *International Kierkegaard Commentary: Either/Or Part II*, ed. Robert L. Perkins (Macon, GA: Mercer University Press, 1995); and Gregory Beabout, "The Silent Lily and Bird as Exemplars of Active Receptivity," in Robert L. Perkins, ed., *International Kierkegaard Commentary: Without Authority* (Macon, GA: Mercer University Press, 2007), pp. 127–46.

11   "NMW" (1958).

12   The history was published serially, beginning with *The History of Great Britain: Volume I, The Reigns of James I and Charles I* (Edinburgh: Hamilton, Balfour, and Neill, 1754). The full history was republished in 1778, 2 years after Hume's death, as *The History of England, from the Invasion of Julius Caesar to the Revolution in 1688*, in eight volumes, a new edition, with the author's last corrections and improvements, to which is prefixed a short account of his life, written by himself (London: T. Cadell, in the Strand, 1778).

13   Alasdair MacIntyre, "Introduction" in *Hume's Ethical Writings: Selections from David Hume* (Collier Books, 1965; reprinted by University of Notre Dame Press, 1979), pp. 9–17, at 16; and "Hume on 'Is' and 'Ought' " *The Philosophical Review* (1959), reprinted in *Against the Self-Images of the Age: Essays on Ideology and Philosophy.* (London: Duckworth; New York: Schocken Books, 1971), pp. 109–124.

14   Ibid.

15   The "Glorious Revolution" of 1688 deposed King James II of England, and replaced him with his sister and her husband, William and Mary. It also brought an end to religious toleration of Catholics in Great Britain, in Ireland, and in the American colony of Maryland.

The revolution of 1688 was a triumph for the modern liberal individualist political ideology of the Whig party, which John Locke discussed in his *Second Treatise of Government.*

16   MacIntyre, "Kierkegaard, Søren Aabye," pp. 336–40.

17   MacIntyre, "Once More on Kierkegaard," in *Kierkegaard After MacIntyre*, pp. 339–55.

18   The political language of the Catholic Church has put great emphasis on the protection of human rights for nearly 50 years, but in its appeal to human rights, the Church emphasizes the theological origins of these rights. MacIntyre's critique focuses on the natural rights of autonomous individuals theorized by secular, materialist philosophers.

19   Thomas Hobbes, *Leviathan*, chapter 6, paragraphs beginning with "And because the constitution of a man's Body" and "But whatsoever is the object of any man's Appetite or Desire."

20   *Leviathan*, chapter 13, paragraph beginning "It may seem strange to some man."

21   *Leviathan*, chapter 40.

22   For example, Douglas M. Jesseph, "Hobbes's Atheism," *Midwest Studies in Philosophy* 26 (2002): 140–66.

23   Peter Geach, "The Religion of Thomas Hobbes," *Religious Studies* 17, no. 4 (December 1981): 549–58.

24   *Leviathan*, chapters 14–15.

25   In 1977, MacIntyre writes "our anti-theological presuppositions may make us uncomfortable" with "the notion of an underlying order" in the universe (*The Monist*, p. 470). He revised this in 2006 to read, "their anti-theological presuppositions may make some of our contemporaries uncomfortable" (*Tasks*, p. 22).

4

Commentary on the critical argument

The critique of modern moral philosophy that makes up the first nine chapters of *AV* examines the kinds of arguments that people today use to convince one another to do things. MacIntyre finds these arguments to be of two kinds: one kind appeals to abstract and impersonal moral standards and the other appeals to objective facts. In both cases, the purpose of these arguments is to give some sort of authority or necessity to choices and decisions that is independent of anyone's personal preferences. Political hawks claim that maintaining a nuclear deterrent is necessary because of the facts of world politics. Peace activists say that nuclear warheads are indiscriminate weapons and that their use could never be just. In the debate over universal health coverage in the United States, those in favor of the new legislation have appealed to the justice of caring for everyone and condemned the injustice of leaving the poor to fend for themselves. Those opposed have decried the injustice of forcing people to buy health insurance or predicted violations of individual rights that would follow if the government were to control our health care decisions. When we argue about what to do, we appeal to the authority of justice, morality, rights, or objective facts, and this is necessary for us because we completely reject the arbitrary imposition of one person's will upon others. For us, commands are only suitable for children; we are free people, and we respect each other's right to decide what to do for ourselves.

MacIntyre finds two general reasons to question the authority that is imputed to these moral standards and objective facts. On the one hand, an examination of the *use* of moral standards and scientific facts to influence moral and political decisions reveals that they are used inconsistently and eclectically in a way that suggests that we create some of these arguments only after we have decided arbitrarily what to do (chapters two to four). On the other hand, the best efforts to justify the objectivity and authority of modern philosophical principles have failed, while careful study reveals that "objective facts" are interpretations, and therefore have a subjective element (chapters five to eight). So MacIntyre concludes that the standards and facts do not rule the choices of those who invoke them; rather, those people's moral and political choices determine the principles that they will use to defend those choices. In the "culture of emotivism," "moral utterance" has indeed been "put to uses at the service of arbitrary will" (p. 110). Emotivists use moral terms to manipulate the opinions of others; moral terms that once had their authority on the basis of natural law or divine command are transformed into moral fictions to be used at the discretion of emotivist ethicists. As the putative authority of these standards and facts begins to disappear, MacIntyre writes, "To a disturbing extent our morality will be disclosed as a theater of illusions" (p. 77).

For MacIntyre, discovering of the culture of emotivism leads to a dilemma: either there really is nothing more to ethics and morals than arbitrary choices and impositions of the will to power (Nietzsche) or there is something fundamentally insufficient in the modern liberal individualist account of human agency, and we need to investigate an entirely different approach to ethics and politics that sees the criteria for moral decision making arising from the requirements of human excellence (Aristotle). MacIntyre finds compelling reasons to follow Aristotle rather than Nietzsche, but following Aristotle demands that we take an approach to moral philosophy very different from that of our leading contemporaries.

Conventional moral philosophy

The central problems of conventional moral philosophy today have to do with the existence of objective moral norms and human knowledge of those norms. When students sign up for ethics courses in colleges, they expect to learn theories that will help them to know what is right and wrong, to know what justice demands, and to know the extent of our natural human rights. As they work through those courses, however, they discover a wide variety of disagreements about the scope, content, and even the existence of the norms and rights that their ethics courses were supposed to explain.

One finds this kind of disagreement, for example, in *The Elements of Moral Philosophy*, a popular college ethics textbook by James Rachels, first published in 1986 and now in its posthumous fifth edition. "Moral philosophy," Rachels writes at the beginning of the book, "is the attempt to achieve a systematic understanding of the nature of morality and what it requires of us." Thirteen chapters later, after surveying and criticizing the leading positions in contemporary moral philosophy, Rachels concludes that none of them provides a complete and sufficient ethical theory.

What Rachels suggests instead, in the closing chapters, is eclectic. It borrows elements from a variety of theories to create what Rachels calls "Multiple-Strategies Utilitarianism,"[1] and he proposes that students use this approach to establish a "best plan" for life:

> At any rate, there is some combination of virtues, motives, and methods of decision making that is best *for me*, given my circumstances, personality and talents—"best" in the sense that it will optimize the chances of my having a good life, while at the same time optimizing the chances of other people having good lives. Call this optimum combination *my best plan*. The right thing for me to do is to act in accordance with my best plan.[2]

"My best plan" is the best that Rachels can offer, but given the range of things that may be included in "good lives" in contemporary culture, coupled with the flexibility of these "multiple strategies," it is difficult to see how Rachels's "best plan" differs from the relativism and subjectivism that Rachels had examined and rejected in the opening chapters of his book. The use of "multiple strategies" that rely on contradictory theoretical foundations leaves the appearance that Rachels is teaching students to use the language of ethics to justify whatever decisions they *have made*, rather than helping them to discover a sound theoretical basis for *making* their decisions.

From the standpoint afforded by MacIntyre's *AV*, we should say that Rachels's "attempt to achieve a systematic understanding of the nature of morality and what it requires of us" has been transformed, in the course of Rachels's book, into an attempt to understand how to *use* the terms of morality for our own ends. By the standards set out at the beginning of Rachels's book, his effort to understand the nature of morality has failed, and it has failed precisely because "the nature of morality" that he investigates is a false subject. For just as there is nothing left to discover in a systematic study of the nature of "taboo" (pp. 111–13) so neither is there anything left to discover through the study of modern liberal individualist "morality." Modern morality has no nature beyond the content of its rules. If MacIntyre is correct, modern morality is little more than selected practices of Western Christian morality, divorced not only from the natural teleology of Aristotle and Aquinas that had once informed its practices, but also from the divine command ethics of Ockham and his Nominalist successors that had maintained its categorical status, and it has thus been reduced to a rationally opaque collection rules. In this sense, it has become rationally equivalent to taboo (p. 112). Consequently, the little ethics textbook that begins with an argument against relativism ultimately undermines that argument, and the author who promised to teach his readers *The Elements of Moral Philosophy*, trains them instead in the practices of the culture of emotivism.

In the face of the culture of emotivism, MacIntyre recommends that we stop trying to justify moral judgments and managerial decisions by appealing to moral fictions that exercise no authority over our choices. Instead, he proposes that we learn to make decisions instead through shared deliberation about ends and means. If we want to find real standards for moral and political judgment, MacIntyre says that we should step away from moral theories and look instead into the demands of the good life that are discovered only through engagement in practice. It is through the pursuit of excellence in practices that we may rediscover the kind of telos that the predecessors to the culture of emotivism abandoned on their way to modernity.

This move from theory to practice, a move suggested by Marx in the *Theses on Feuerbach*,[3] has been central to MacIntyre's ethical and political work from the beginning of his career. It was one of the main themes of *Marxism: An Interpretation* (1953)[4] and it drove a series of essays reprinted in *Against the Self-Images of the Age* (1970),[5] including "What Morality is Not" (1957).[6] The *Theses on Feuerbach* figure prominently in MacIntyre's 1960 essay, "Breaking the Chains of Reason,"[7] and play an important role in the argument against the ideological abuse of the social sciences in *AV* (pp. 84–5). MacIntyre's more recent essay, "ToF:RNT" (1994)[8] reveals the importance of this 11-paragraph work of Marx over MacIntyre's entire career.

Marx's insight about the relationships among moral knowledge, moral education, and the capacity for moral leadership appears in the third of the *Theses on Feuerbach*: "The coincidence of the changing of circumstances and human activity can be conceived and rationally understood only as *revolutionary practice*."[9]

The philosophical Marx of 1845 argues that one does not determine the course of the revolution a priori in theory and then apply it. Instead, one sets out to change things and discovers in the process what must be done and how it must be done, and it is through this work that one becomes the kind of person who can do such things and teach others to do the same. The demands of the revolution were not to be determined theoretically in some philosopher's study, but discovered practically in the revolutionary practices of the community in daily life. For Marx, this insight became "A Road Not Taken" because Marx abandoned philosophy and turned to the social sciences in his work with Friedrich Engels,[10] but for MacIntyre, this insight was to illuminate a way to philosophical progress.

MacIntyre's purposes in *AV* differ from those of most contemporary ethical writers. He is not trying to show us how to overcome relativism or how to reform political life or how to recognize abstract moral principles to govern our private lives; he is showing that all three of those projects are responses to false questions. What he proposes instead is a new point of view, a different conceptual scheme, which treats the shared pursuit of goods, and shared deliberation about means to ends as the only philosophically proper approaches to practical and political decision making. For MacIntyre, the pursuit of justice is an interested pursuit of substantive goods, and for this reason, moral excellence—excellence recognized and developed through involvement in communities engaged in practices—is a necessary qualification for moral and political leadership.[11]

Relativism?

Some of MacIntyre's readers have claimed that his rejection of conventional moral theories amounts to moral relativism, just as Rachels's failure to overcome relativism in *The Elements of Moral Philosophy* might be taken to support moral relativism. Is this the case? And if not, why not? There are two ways to consider these questions. One considers relativism as a sincerely experienced impediment to philosophical progress. The other considers relativism as it appears in the culture of emotivism and examines its use as a moral fiction. In this part of the commentary, we will consider the use of relativism as a moral fiction. We will turn to MacIntyre's treatment of sincere philosophical relativism at the end of the commentary on the constructive argument.

Moral relativism asserts that the truth of any moral judgment is relative to some non-moral, variable factor, like culture, perspective, circumstances, or personality, so that no moral judgment is ever simply true. Taking food from a market, for example, may be condemned as unlawful theft under any conditions in one culture, while it might be justified in another if the food taken was needed to feed a family. The Thomist may claim that what *seemed* just to one community or culture *was in fact* unjust, and that the other community *rightly judged* that taking food to feed a family was justified. The cultural relativist has no use, however, for such distinctions between seeming and being. She or he simply claims that one thing was true in one culture, and the opposite was true in the other. The subjectivist might make the further claim that the same things were true for the agents in both examples, but their truths differed from the truths of the communities that condemned them.

Many college students claim to be relativists. Open a discussion about "right and wrong" in an undergraduate ethics class and certain patterns of discussion will invariably follow. Always some student, Sam, will confidently assert some uncontroversial moral norm, and always a classmate, Pat, will respond just as confidently that Sam's moral norm reflected only what was right for Sam, and that Sam would be seriously mistaken if Sam were to claim that the same judgment was necessarily true for Pat, or for anyone else. This kind of relativism is quite commonplace.

But is relativism really the problem? Notice that Pat's relativist claim implies a universal moral judgment that it is always wrong to impose one's private moral judgment on others. A thoroughgoing moral relativist would hold that no moral judgment is abstractly and universally true—even the judgment that one should never impose one's own opinion. But no one seriously holds this. When we see gross injustice, we react with confidence, we punish those who harm others, and we do it because we are sure that doing so is right, not just legally right, but morally right—and not just morally right from our own peculiar point of view.

It was this moral confidence that demanded the prosecution of war criminals at the Nuremburg trials after World War II and justified the acts of civil disobedience in the United States Civil Rights movement. It was this moral confidence that left so many Marxists disillusioned by the Soviet invasion that ended the Hungarian Revolution of 1956 and by the revelations of Stalinist atrocities in the Soviet Union following Stalin's death. If moral relativism really is the problem underlying contemporary moral and political disputes, it is a very selective kind of moral relativism.

If the underlying problem in contemporary disputes were relativism, the disputes might be less acrimonious. A culture of true relativism would be a culture of tolerance, if only because it would be a culture of moral paralysis. It is the intolerance of this contemporary pseudo-relativism that reveals the culture of emotivism. The problem as it manifests itself is not really relativism but disagreement, including disagreement in our most confident beliefs about what justice demands, what constitutes gross injustice, and what should be punished and what should not. These are serious disagreements, backed by serious arguments advanced by respected scholars, clergy, legislators, and jurists. When these people advance their arguments, they appeal to rational standards and respected authors; yet, the disagreements generally remain. What are we to make of this kind of disagreement? The first half of *AV* investigates this question.

Practical reasoning and moral judgment

The intractable moral and political disagreements that MacIntyre lists at the beginning of chapter two (the justice of war, the legality of elective abortion, and the appropriateness of public funding for education and medical care) are irresolvable because they are construed primarily as moral disagreements. As moral disagreements, (1) the choices involved are taken to be moral rather than practical, so that their resolution is bound up in questions about *what ought to be done*, questions of what is right and just, rather than in questions about *what the agents involved are trying to achieve*, and (2) they are treated as conflicts about the kinds of principles that should govern the resolution of these disagreements.

These intractable disagreements help to reveal the separation between practical and moral reasoning in modern moral and political philosophy. They also shed light on the closely related problem of the role of human desire in ethics. Both the separation of practical from moral reasoning and the separation of desire from ethics have been the themes in MacIntyre's writing since the 1950s.[12] These themes are not always explicit in *AV*, but they are implicit in MacIntyre's treatment of the history of the word "moral" (p. 38), his discussion of Polynesian taboo in chapter nine, and his use of the term "practical reasoning" in a variety of places where many readers might expect to read about "moral reasoning." These two separations—practical from moral reasoning and desire from ethics—play an important role in the critical argument. What is practical reasoning, and how does it differ from moral reasoning?

Whenever ordinary adults approach a complicated task, we begin more or less with the method Aristotle described in the third book of his *Nicomachean Ethics*: We consider what we are trying to do, and then we deliberate, choose, and employ what we take to be the best means to reach our goal. This process of determining a goal, deliberating about means, and then employing the means to reach our goal, is practical reasoning.

In the minds of classical philosophers like Plato, Aristotle, Augustine, and Aquinas, practical reasoning always has a moral dimension, because practical decisions affect an agent's freedom. Classical philosophers did not treat human freedom as a given, but as an achievement. Freedom was not just being "free from being hindered by opposition,"[13] as it was for Thomas Hobbes. It was the freedom to live up to one's nature. Servais Pinckaers discussed the difference between these two contrary notions of freedom in *The Sources of Christian Ethics*, calling the Nominalist view of freedom advanced by the tradition of Ockham and Hobbes, "freedom of indifference" and the older view of freedom maintained by Aristotle and Aquinas, "freedom for excellence."[14] Freedom for excellence, the ability to recognize and pursue what is good and best, could be developed or damaged[15] through one's choices; thus, practical and moral reasoning were not separate concerns for Plato, Aristotle, Augustine, or Aquinas; the practical goal of liberation and happiness was identical with the moral goal of virtue.

Neither was morality separated from desire in classical thought. Plato speaks of the role of eros in the moral life in the *Symposium*.[16] Aristotle speaks of the good life as a life of "*eudaimonia*," which is usually translated as "happiness." Augustine writes of the soul's desire for God in the opening prayer of his *Confessions*.[17] Aquinas speaks of people seeking ultimate "*felicitas*," which, like Aristotle's *eudaimonia*, is translated as "happiness." For the modern reader, the idea that the good life is directed to happiness may seem problematic because modern thought takes happiness to be subjective and identical with pleasure,[18] but for Plato, Aristotle, Augustine, and Aquinas, happiness is objective, and distinct from pleasure; it is flourishing according to one's nature.

[margin: happiness is flourishing according to one's nature]

For Aristotle, three things are worthy of choice: the noble, the useful, and the pleasant, and there are three things that should be avoided: the base, the harmful, and the painful.[19] These two lists imply a hierarchy of goods and evils. A noble but painful act may be worthy of choice when it is prudent, while a pleasurable but base act should always be avoided. For Aristotle, learning to recognize what is truly desirable or choice-worthy[20] and what is not requires training in virtue. The happiness of the good life is pleasurable, but it is not simply a life of pleasure; for a life directed to the pursuit of pleasure is almost certain to devolve into dissolution, dissipation, and vice. The distinction between happiness and pleasure makes it possible to connect practical reasoning with moral reasoning in classical ethics.

Aristotle discusses the connection between practical and moral reasoning in *Nicomachean Ethics*, book three, chapter four, when he asks whether the true good, or merely some apparent good, is "the object of wish," that is, the goal of human action. This passage is crucial to the unity of practical and moral reasoning. Successful practical reasoning involves obtaining the things I pursue, it means getting what I want. Successful moral reasoning involves choosing what is good and best, or choosing what I should want. To identify practical reasoning with moral reasoning is to claim that getting what I want entails choosing what I should want. To ask Aristotle's question in *Nicomachean Ethics* 3.4 is to ask whether moral judgment and practical judgment coincide, or whether moral philosophy is possible at all. Does deliberation begin with a single, true good, or with various apparent goods?

Aristotle begins his answer by noting the difficulties involved in the question: whoever claims that the goal of human action is always the true good must be prepared to tell the one who chooses wrongly that he is not doing what he wants to do. On the other hand, whoever claims that the goal of human action is never more than the apparent good severs any connection between practical reasoning and moral reasoning. Aristotle concludes that the goals that appear to be good or choice-worthy to a person depend on that person's character: "that which is in truth an object of wish is an object of wish to the good man, while any chance thing may be an object of wish to the bad man."[21] Since Aristotle had already linked happiness to the pursuit of the true good earlier in the *Nicomachean Ethics*,[22] the discussion in book three implies that one's ability to pursue happiness depends on one's character; it depends on one's habits of judgment and action.

This connection between practical and moral reasoning is generally absent from modern thought. MacIntyre traces this change to early modernity's dependence on the Nominalist and voluntarist presuppositions of its predecessors. Within the constraints that modernity inherited from late medieval and Protestant divine command theory, modern ethicists take moral rules to have no essential relationship to the ends that individuals seek, while moderns take practical reasoning to have no higher standard or measure than the agent's subjective desires. Modern thinkers from Hobbes to Kant to Mill have made the reduction of happiness to pleasure explicit in their writings. Hobbes asserts the subjectivity of good and evil in *Leviathan*;[23] Kant identifies happiness with the satisfaction of subjective desire in the *Critique of Pure Reason*,[24] and Mill defines happiness as "pleasure and the absence of pain" in *Utilitarianism*.[25] Where Aristotle had held that good people seek the true good, "while any chance thing may be an object of wish to the bad man,"[26] the moderns hold that "any chance thing may be an object of wish" for anyone, good or bad, for there is no true good to desire.

The early christian moralist & followed by te liberal moral Philosophers seperated a man's individual Desires from first God's divine commands & then from an objective & impersonal rational std of morality both of which we've designed to set up commands intenda to restrict the unbridle pursuit of known personal happiness

Because modern moral philosophers hold, therefore, that practical reasoning is merely pragmatic, they have followed their late medieval and Protestant forbearers in drawing a sharp distinction between this merely pragmatic reasoning on one hand and properly moral reasoning on the other. For late medieval Nominalist and Protestant Christian moral theologians, moral reasoning determined what obedience to divine commands required. For modern moral philosophers, moral reasoning would determine what was required by the objective and impersonal rational standards of morality. In either case, the desire for personal happiness that motivated and regulated classical ethical accounts of practical reasoning is replaced by a set of commands intended to restrict the pursuit of personal happiness.

Modern secular moral philosophers, like the Nominalist and Protestant Christian moral theologians who preceded them, see practical reasoning as a purely pragmatic exercise because they identify the pursuit of happiness with the pursuit of pleasure. They recognize that subjective desires often run contrary to the demands of morality, and so conclude, and rightly so, that when this happens, the agent must be prepared to follow morality, rather than desire.[27] What makes modern moral philosophy different from Nominalist and Protestant Christian moral theology is modernity's insistence that the commands of morality are independent of the divine will, and that they may be known, without God's help, through reason. But the modern moral philosopher's task of explaining what the demands of morality are, how they exist, and how they are known has proved problematic; modern moral philosophy has never generated any consensus about how these universal demands of morality exist,[28] much less how they are known.

What makes Modern liberal Moral Philosophy different from te prior Christian morality is that it trys to make te command of morality indepeneden of divine will

Contemporary work in modern moral philosophy focuses on two standard theories, the ethics of Kant and the utilitarianism of Mill. Kant presented his moral theory in a series of works over the last two decades of a long career. The principal works include his *Critique of Pure Reason* (*First Critique*, 1781), the *Groundwork for the Metaphysics of Morals* (1785), and the *Critique of Practical Reason* (*Second Critique*, 1788). A central concern for Kant, a contemporary of the materialist, determinist philosophers of the enlightenment, was to defend the freedom of the human will and to distinguish it from the material impulses of our bodily nature.[29] So Kant judged that human excellence demanded the development

The Problem Is modern liberal moral philosophy has never generated concensus on how universal demands exist or how they are known of a will freed from impulse, desire, and inclination, a will that decided its actions on the basis of reason, rather than passion, out of respect for duty.[30] This will determines its duty through the categorical imperative. The first formulation of the categorical imperative, "Act only according to that maxim by which you can at the same time will that it should become a universal law,"[31] is equivalent to the second formulation, "Act so that you treat humanity, whether in your own person or in that of another, always as an end and never as a means only."[32] For Kant, one could not determine one's duty by obeying other people or even God, since obedience might follow interests that are not rational; so the third formulation emphasizes the need for moral judgment to proceed from an autonomous, rational, will: "the Idea of the will of every rational being as a will giving universal law."[33] Kant's effort to separate free human moral judgment from mechanistic accounts of human behavior was admirable (p. 82),[34] but Kant's critics have never found it compelling as an account of the origin of moral obligation.

The chief complaint against Kant's ethics is that Kant's autonomous agent gives the universal moral law to herself or himself. Anscombe dismisses Kant's notion of "legislating for oneself," in "Modern Moral Philosophy," her famous critique of consequentialism. She called it "as absurd" as the unanimous decision of a democracy of one, "The concept of legislation requires superior power in the legislator." Kant's theory, on the contrary, makes the law's subject the master of the law.[35] MacIntyre notes his debt to Anscombe (p. 53), and on this point, his critique is similar. MacIntyre stresses the criterionlessness (p. 33) of the choice that Kant's modern agent is to make, since Kant denies any natural telos for human life and action, and denies the moral worth of actions that pursue ends,[36] the agent alone determines what maxims can and cannot be universalized (pp. 45–6).

Mill's utilitarianism stands with Kant's ethics as the other standard theory in contemporary moral philosophy. Mill's theory affirms much of the practical content of Kant's ethics, but Mill claims that moral rightness is truly measured by what brings the greatest happiness to the greatest number of people. Mill emphasizes that his theory rejects the private pursuit of personal pleasure: "That standard is not the agent's own greatest happiness, but the greatest amount of happiness altogether."[37] Unlike Kant's a priori rational judgment about duty, Mill proposes an a posteriori empirical judgment that presupposes an education that enables one to judge the relative merits of various kinds of pleasures and pains. In both cases, however, personal happiness is excluded from the ends of moral reasoning. As with Kant, MacIntyre's critique of Mill focuses on the criterionlessness of the judgment Mill's modern agent must make. "The greatest happiness of the greatest number" is so vague a notion that it could justify almost anything. "It is a pseudo-concept available for a variety of ideological uses, but no more than that" (p. 64).

Moral reasoning in either Kantian or Utilitarian ethics does not evaluate *what the agent wants*, it determines *what should be done*. It applies apparently objective and impersonal moral standards, but at best, those standards only mask the criterionless choices of sovereign modern individuals; hence, the objective principles of modern moral philosophy are truly moral fictions. At worst, those standards actually gain authority over agents who become estranged from their own goals in life, and thus become easy prey for those who would press them into the service of an ideology.

Contemporary debates and disagreements

This is the setting for the examples MacIntyre introduces at the beginning of chapter two. What the debates over just war, legal restrictions on abortion, and government support for health care and education have in common is that all of the parties to those contemporary debates carry them out in terms of moral, rather than practical reasoning. They do not tell us how to achieve a given end; rather, they tell us how our choices are constrained by the standards of morality.

MacIntyre identifies three "salient characteristics" that "these debates and disagreements share" (p. 8). First, in all three debates, each contending position is logically coherent, but rational discussions between the opposed positions are impossible, for the positions are incommensurable. They are incommensurable because they differ substantively on what counts as a rational basis for the argument.[38] What counts, substantively, as a good reason or a good premise on one side, does not count as a good premise or a good reason on the other. MacIntyre notes that the parties to these disputes usually come to these debates as committed partisans rather than as open-minded enquirers, so that these ethical disputes that present themselves as clashes of rational arguments appear to mask clashes of wills (p. 9).

The second salient feature of the three debates is that each side claims to be making impersonal arguments appealing to objective rational standards. That is, all of the parties are engaged in moral rather than practical reasoning. Yet, in light of the first salient characteristic, it appears that the contending sides are marshalling these impersonal rational arguments in the service of very personal and irrational clashes of wills; thus, their use of these objective terms seems like a masquerade, and leaves MacIntyre asking, "Why *this* masquerade?" (p. 9).

The third salient characteristic of these contemporary debates is that they are theoretically eclectic. This eclecticism comes across in two ways. First, the competing parties in contemporary moral and political disputes display no obvious concerns about the broader theoretical and historical contexts that produced the bits of moral rhetoric that they use as arguments to support their claims. Second, these parties carry out this work of rhetorical assembly to support particular parts of their agendas without any obvious concern for inconsistencies and contradictions between the arguments that support those various parts.[39] The outcomes of this are policy agendas that appeal to stunningly incoherent sets of beliefs.

Returning to the examples MacIntyre sets out at the beginning of chapter two, consider the platforms of the major US political parties in 1980. The Republican Party's policy toward the Soviet Union exemplified the pragmatic position that viewed war and even nuclear war as necessary options for defense policy; it also endorsed pro-life moral and political positions that appealed to fairness and viewed abortion as murder; on education and health, it advanced a policy of individual rights, albeit not as extreme as the one MacIntyre described (pp. 6–7).[40] The Democratic Party took opposing positions on each of these issues. In both cases, the parties justified the various planks of their platforms with rational arguments that (1) seem irreconcilable with arguments that backed other planks or (2) appeal to principles that seem to be valued only pragmatically for the rhetorical support they lend to particular agenda items. Both of these characteristics appear to confirm the view that these platforms are based on arbitrary choices, and that the rational arguments used to defend them are chosen strategically, pragmatically, ex post facto.

Like MacIntyre's post-catastrophe pseudoscientists who memorized bits and pieces of scientific theory and deployed them in ways unimaginable to the real scientists who had originally developed them, contemporary moral and political thinkers have entirely transformed the principles they employ. Arguments and principles pried loose from "those intricate bodies of theory and practice which constitute human cultures" (p. 10) are used to support the contending positions in these contemporary debates in a way that only amplifies the appearances of arbitrariness.

What seems to emerge from MacIntyre's consideration of the three salient characteristics of these contemporary debates is a gap between meaning and use, between the meanings of moral terms in these contemporary debates and the ways those terms are used. The meanings of the terms are taken at face value, even though their full significance is obscured by their extraction from their conceptual homes, and there is nothing uncertain about the ways those terms are used. As we look more closely, the whole picture begins to resemble an adversarial courtroom, in which the competing advocates in the case are committed only to effective prosecution and defense, and evidence is sometimes presented selectively with a mind to success. The outcome is what MacIntyre calls "the distinctively modern standpoint,"

> which envisages moral debate in terms of a confrontation between incompatible and incommensurable moral premises and moral commitment as the expression of a criterionless choice between such premises, a type of choice for which no rational justification can be given (p. 39).

The problem for the contemporary agent is to recognize that this distinctively modern standpoint is peculiar, that it reflects the peculiar outcomes of our history, and that there may be another way to approach these issues of human agency and social life.

The accuracy of MacIntyre's assessment of conventional contemporary moral philosophy is confirmed by the popularity and success of Rachels's *Elements of Moral Philosophy* as a

[handwritten margin note: The arguments may proceed rationally from their premises but the choice of a particular set of premises is irrational & often incoherent b/w sets.]

college ethics textbook, for Rachels's eclectic "Multiple Strategies Utilitarianism" not only describes the ethics of the culture of emotivism with remarkable clarity—albeit entirely unwittingly—it also presents emotivism as the goal of the study of ethics.

Emotivism in the gap between meaning and use

Emotivism was a theory advanced by C. L. Stevenson and some of his contemporaries to explain the *meaning* of evaluative, especially morally evaluative statements. Emotivists claimed that these kinds of statements do not mean what they appear to mean, that they actually express nothing but our attitudes and feelings. According to Stevenson, statements like "This is morally right" really *mean* "I approve of this; do so as well" (p. 10). As a theory of the *meaning* of sentences, emotivism was soon rejected and discarded, and MacIntyre summarizes some of the reasons for doing so, but in his definition and criticism of the theory of emotivism, he draws attention to the real gap between the meaning and use of evaluative statements that the emotivist theory had tried to address.

Once MacIntyre has identified the gap between the meaning and use of morally evaluative language, he proposes that we reinterpret emotivism as a theory of the *use* of evaluative statements:

> even if the meaning of such sentences were quite other than emotivist theorists supposed, . . . in using such sentences to *say* whatever they mean, the agent was in fact *doing* nothing other than expressing his feelings or attitudes and attempting to influence the feelings and attitudes of others. (p. 14, emphasis in original)

The emotivists made unsupportable claims about the *meanings* of people's words, and so their theory fails; but MacIntyre proposes that we take a hard look at the underlying empirical observations they made about the *use* of moral speech.

The shift from meaning to use allows us to distinguish between the emotivist theory of meaning and the emotivists' observation about the use of moral language. The emotivists had studied ethics at Cambridge with Moore after the publication of Moore's *Principia Ethica* in 1903, and continued to talk about morality with their friends in the Bloomsbury group in London. From their own accounts of those discussions of morality, it was plain that they were engaging in moral manipulation rather than moral philosophy, and MacIntyre proposes that the emotivists overgeneralized their experience of these manipulations:

> It is not implausible to suppose that they did in fact confuse moral utterance at Cambridge . . . after 1903 with moral utterance as such, and that they therefore presented what was in essentials a correct account of the former as though it were an account of the latter. (p. 17)

So it was a mistake to propose emotivism as a general theory about the *meaning* of evaluative language. But that does not mean that it was not an insightful description of a peculiar misuse of language, a misuse that commonly arises at a certain stage in the decline of a culture, when thoughtful people recognize that objective moral language has become available for subjective use (p. 19). By distinguishing the observation from the theory, and reinterpreting emotivism as a theory of use, rather than of meaning, MacIntyre is able to transform emotivism into a very useful tool for the investigation of contemporary ethics.

From epistemology to action

The shifts from meaning to use and from theory to practice take a decisive step away from the problems of modern philosophy by turning from epistemology—the study of knowledge—to action. Modern philosophy is said to begin with Descartes' account of his quest for the foundation of knowledge. Descartes had lost confidence in the things he had learned in school and decided to doubt everything he thought he knew, until he could find some epistemological first principle that he could not doubt, so that he could rebuild his knowledge on that principle. For Descartes, this principle was the *cogito*, "I think therefore I am" and it became the first principle of his epistemology.

Epistemology investigates knowledge, its origins, and the existence of truth. For Descartes, for his contemporaries, and for their successors, modern philosophy begins with epistemology, and for some moderns and postmoderns, philosophy is nothing but epistemology. For Descartes, the central task of philosophy was to sort out knowledge from opinion; from that point on, epistemology held so central a place in modern thought that survey courses in early modern philosophy are best structured as surveys of the epistemological theories of Descartes, Hobbes, Locke, Berkeley, Hume, and Kant, and the consequences of their epistemological theories for other subdisciplines of philosophy, including ethics.[41] This transformation of philosophy transformed ethics into moral epistemology, a study concerned principally with knowing what one should do.

The study of human action, not moral epistemology, is at the center of MacIntyre's ethics. This is something he shares with Aristotle and Aquinas, but it is rooted, in part, in his Marxist background. Writing as a Marxist in the "Notes from the Moral Wilderness," MacIntyre asserts, "the concept of human action is central to our enquiry."[42] A few years later, in "Breaking the Chains of Reason," MacIntyre writes:

> Human action can only be understood in terms of such concepts as purpose and intention. To know what someone is doing is to know what ends he is pursuing, what possibilities he is realising. Human history is a series of developing purposes, in which through the exercise of reason in the overcoming of conflicts freedom is attained.

Where the modern ethical theorist asks the epistemological question, "How can I know what I should do?" MacIntyre asks about action: What are we trying to do as human beings who are members of a community? How can I learn to recognize and pursue my own ends? How can we accomplish our shared ends?

Moral relativism is an epistemological theory. It is a theory about the existence of moral truth and the human capacity for moral knowledge. The relativist looks at contemporary moral disagreements and concludes that each party to the dispute has a different truth. This is a very troublesome claim for a variety of reasons, but MacIntyre leaves the whole question of relativism behind when he moves from epistemology to action. When MacIntyre looks at those same disagreements, he concludes that the discussion has broken down; as evidence, he shows that the contending parties are using rational arguments to advance claims for which they have no rational basis. This diagnosis allows the quest for truth to continue and raises at least two kinds of questions that may reshape that quest.

First, consider the difference between relativism and MacIntyre's theory of the emotivist use of moral language in the light of *Nicomachean Ethics* 3.4. Aristotle realized that if the apparent good were the object of wish, the link between practical reasoning and moral reasoning would be broken, and he concluded that the true good is the object of wish for the good agent, and that "any chance thing" could be the object of wish for a bad agent. Relativism contradicts Aristotle; if relativism were true, whatever any group or individual wanted would be that group or person's true good. MacIntyre's theory of the emotivist *use* of moral language, however, does not contradict Aristotle, for the emotivist observation speaks only of people's preferences; it does not evaluate those preferences, and it does not judge their motivation. The culture of emotivism refers only to the way the culture uses—or misuses—moral language. The term can describe arguments promoting acts of virtue as well as acts of vice. When MacIntyre describes moral arguments as emotivist, the truth of their moral claims remains a separate issue.

Second, if we treat emotivism as a theory of use, it demands that people consider what they are doing when they use moral language. If moral language is really so broken that contemporary moral debates are masks for arbitrary choices, then any philosophical question about the truth of moral norms must be set aside, at least for the time being, so that we can ask more fruitful questions. We need to begin instead by asking what we are doing and whether our actions are consistent with our goals. We need to ask what kinds of habits we are building or shaping in ourselves and in our society through our actions and whether these actions are consistent with our goals. These are the questions of practical reasoning, and when answered, they promise to provide us with practical and prudential norms that are not subject to the divorce between practical and moral reasoning that gave birth to the culture of emotivism.

We need to begin by asking what are we doing & whether our actions are consistent w/ our goals

MacIntyre's theory of emotivist use is quite different from Stevenson's false emotivist theory of meaning. MacIntyre's emotivism does not entail that moral judgments made in the culture of emotivism are false. It only entails that moral language can be an obstacle to authentic practical reasoning, and that in the hands of clever and unscrupulous people, moral language may serve as a powerful, and potentially destructive, manipulative tool.[43] Unlike this theory of use, the emotivist theory of meaning denies that moral judgments may be true in any objective sense whatsoever. According to the emotivist theory of meaning, all contemporary moral language is essentially ideological; consequently, what are important about contemporary ethical debates are neither their terms nor their contents, but the ends that those arguments serve, and the ways that ideologues craft those arguments as tools to influence the opinions of others.[44]

Four characters from emotivist culture

To illustrate the culture of emotivism in chapter three, MacIntyre presents three emotivist characters: the Rich Aesthete, the Manager, and the Therapist. In the prologue to the third edition, MacIntyre adds a fourth character, the Conservative Moralist (third edition, p. xv). What do these four characters have in common? They are united in the way that they approach cooperative human action. In the culture of emotivism, shared deliberation among peers about the best means to the true good will have no place, for no good is true and no means is best. In emotivist culture, one agent takes the lead as an arbitrary judge, ruling things according to personal preference, and it becomes that agent's task to motivate subordinate agents to join, endorse, and participate in the views, policies, and actions that she or he has chosen.

This is the approach to cooperative human action that we find in the four characters of the culture of emotivism. The rich aesthetes in Henry James's novel, *The Portrait of a Lady*, manipulate others for personal pleasure (p. 24). The manager of Max Weber's work on bureaucracy marshals the forces of labor in pursuit of "values . . . created by human decisions,"[45] and the authority of that manager is based on nothing but her or his success in using that power (p. 26).

[Handwritten margin note at top: In all four emotivist characters the model for cooperative human action begins w/ an arbitrary choice that is sold to subordinate agents through influence & persuasion]

Where the manager sets aside questions about the discernment of truth in favor of measurable effectiveness in pursuing arbitrarily chosen ends, the therapist sets aside moral debates and focuses on counseling the patient to become a more effective agent (p. 30). Finally, the conservative moralist sets aside shared deliberation about political goods and seeks to use "the power of the modern state" to pursue her or his "own coercive purposes" (third edition, p. xv). In all four cases, the model for cooperative human action begins with an arbitrary choice that is subsequently sold to subordinate agents through influence and persuasion. These four characters are the masks worn by emotivism (p. 28), and inasmuch as any individual acts as one of these characters, she or he acts as an emotivist.

Practical rules and moral fictions

Chapters four through nine set the stage for the move from theory to practice by exploring the "theatre of illusions" (p. 77) of modern moral philosophy and the culture of emotivism, and by identifying some of the moral fictions that animate it. This passes through two phases. The first phase, chapters four through six, draws on the Marxist critique of liberalism to reject Kant's deontology, Bentham and Mill's utilitarianism, and modern "natural rights" language. The second phase, chapters seven through nine, brings that same Marxist critique against the elements of the bureaucratic structures advanced by Stalinists, especially managerial expertise, and crude deterministic sociological theories. All of these he dismisses as moral fictions because these theories were all invented to create reasons for actions after natural, teleological reasons for action had been rejected.

Aristotle's *Nicomachean Ethics* begins with the claim that every human action and endeavor is directed to some end, goal, purpose, or *telos*:

Every art and every inquiry, and similarly every action and pursuit, is thought to aim at some good; and for this reason the good has rightly been declared to be that at which all things aim.[46]

Aquinas likewise affirms the rational purposefulness of human action when he argues that every agent acts for an end under the aspect of good.[47] Consequently, for both Aristotle and Aquinas, and for the traditions that followed from them, action is ruled ultimately by the good that people seek, and all rules for action, whether political, moral, or technical, are similarly practical. They instruct people in the best ways to pursue goods they already desire, either by nature or by choice. This is what it means to say that norms are teleological, or that Plato, Aristotle, Augustine, and Aquinas all belong to the tradition of teleological ethics.

With the loss of teleology, first in theology and then in natural philosophy, a revived moral philosophy arose to defend morality, independent of religion, in an increasingly secular world. Yet, the task taken up by these moral philosophers was extremely problematic: modern moral philosophers were to affirm the moral sovereignty of the individual and at the same time explain why that sovereign individual was bound to follow the traditional rules of morality (p. 62). Furthermore, modern moral philosophers were to explain the rules of morality without considering either what those rules were meant to produce or what the agent was to gain by following them. So whatever this new appeal to reason was to be, it could hardly be considered an appeal to practical reason.

What modern moral philosophy produced, MacIntyre says, was a series of moral fictions. Utilitarianism is a fiction, because "the greatest happiness of the greatest number" has no precise meaning (p. 64). The Kantian project, even as developed in Alan Gewirth's *Reason and Morality* (1978), is a moral fiction because that project depends on a notion of "natural rights" that is itself a fiction. "The truth is plain": MacIntyre tells us, "there are no such rights, and belief in them is at one with belief in witches and unicorns" (p. 69).[48] Intuitionism is a moral fiction, because it amounts to subjectivism.

The problem with these theories is that they are *ex post facto* apologetics for presupposed conclusions. To borrow a term from Wendell Johnson, they are "plogglie theories." In *People in Quandaries*, a book about scientific reasoning, Johnson introduces the requirements of good scientific theory by telling a story about a bad prescientific one:

> According to this story, there were once two very perplexing mysteries, over which the wisest men in the land had beat

their heads and stroked their beards for years and years. But nothing came of all this. The two mysteries continued to plague everyone.

The mysteries were that whenever anyone wanted to find a lead pencil he couldn't, and whenever anyone wanted to sharpen a lead pencil the sharpener was always filled with pencil shavings.

It was a most annoying state of affairs, and after sufficient public agitation a committee of distinguished philosophers was appointed by the government to carry out a searching investigation and, above all, to concoct a suitable explanation of the outrage.

One can hardly imagine the intensity of the deliberations that went on among the august members of this committee. Moreover, their deliberations were carried out under very trying conditions, for the public, impatient and distraught, was clamoring ever more loudly for results. Finally, after what seemed to everyone to be a very long time, the committee appeared before the Chief of State to deliver a truly brilliant explanation of the twin mysteries.

It was really quite simple, after all. Beneath the ground, so the theory went, lived a great number of little people. They are called plogglies. At night, explained the philosophers, when people are asleep, the plogglies come into their houses. They scurry around and gather up all the lead pencils, and then they scamper over to the pencil sharpener and grind them all up. And then they go back into the ground.

The great national unrest subsided. Obviously, this was a brilliant theory. With one stroke it accounted for both mysteries. The only thing wrong with it was that there were no plogglies.[49]

Johnson finds inventions of plogglies quite common. He holds that gods, demons, fairies and elves are plogglies, and so are luck, fate, heredity, environment, and human nature.[50] What all plogglies and plogglie theories have in common is that they are crafted only to account for what is already known; they have no predictive power and they cannot be falsified. Anomalous events can always be dismissed "by saying, as solemnly as possible, 'Well, that's how it always goes with plogglies.'"[51] The things that MacIntyre calls "moral fictions" are plogglie theories in ethics.

Notice that to describe utility and natural rights as plogglies or as moral fictions does not entail that the moral standards those theories were devised to uphold are necessarily false. To claim that something is false because it has not been proven is to commit the logical fallacy of appeal to ignorance. Someone in Johnson's story was misplacing all those pencils, and someone was letting all those pencil sharpeners fill up with shavings; the problem was that it was not the plogglies. Likewise, there is something deeply appealing about justice, prudence, and self-discipline, the problem is that neither natural rights language nor utilitarianism, nor appeals to Kantian duty can adequately explain what that is.

MacIntyre's rejection of "rights" applies only to the kind of natural rights that were invented along with the notion of human autonomy in modern thought:

> By "rights" I do not mean those rights conferred by positive law or custom on specified classes of person; I mean those rights which are alleged to belong to human beings as such and which are cited as a reason for holding that other people ought not to be interfered with in their pursuit of life, liberty, and happiness. (pp. 68–9)

In his rejection of modern natural rights and in the distinctions he draws between natural rights and political rights, MacIntyre follows the tradition of Marx.

The problem with these rights is like the problem with plogglies. Where do the plogglies live? How do the plogglies exist? To what category of existing things do plogglies belong? None of these questions can be answered for plogglies, and neither can they be answered in modern secular terms for these modern natural rights.

Perhaps the problem of accounting for the existence of natural rights changes if one says that they are God-given rights. Then they could be said to proceed from divine positive law or from the natural law in us that Aquinas took to be the source of all normative human inclinations and the basis of all good human customs. Or they may simply be said to proceed from the dignity of the human person who is made in the image and likeness of God. Jacques Maritain took up this theology of creation to connect the language of natural rights to the theological tradition of the Catholic

Church, and some find his arguments compelling. But this theological approach offers no comfort to anyone who would defend "natural human rights" in secular political thought, because this theological way of explaining human rights only serves to emphasize that human rights have an inescapably religious character—even when those rights are advanced by atheists. Natural rights are artifacts of interpretation and choice, and whether human rights are willed by God or by human beings, in neither case are they "natural" in the customary, secular, modern sense.

To claim that secular natural rights are discovered rather than willed by those who wield them is to appeal to a moral fiction. Similarly, to speak of "utility" and "the greatest happiness of the greatest number," without establishing some specific meaning for those terms is to appeal to moral fictions.[52] To appeal to these fictions in order to close off shared deliberation about means to ends, or to close debates, or to disqualify opponents from shared deliberation is to embrace the culture of emotivism.

The false promise of a scientific alternative to moral philosophy

If the language of modern moral philosophy is little more than a collection of moral fictions that are put to use to manipulate compliance and to close debates, then we must reject it. But is there another source of authority to regulate our common life? The culture of emotivism seeks an alternative in the objective facts of the social sciences:

> Neither manager nor therapist, in their roles as manager and therapist, do or are engaged in moral debate. They are seen by themselves and by those who see them with the same eyes as their own, as uncontested figures, who purport to restrict themselves to the realms in which rational agreement is possible—that is, of course from their point of view to the realm of fact, the realm of means, the realm of measurable effectiveness. (p. 30)

The alternative to sterile moral debate is the morally neutral appeal to facts, and to the law-like generalizations of the social sciences

(p. 77). The morally neutral authority of managers depends on the success of the social sciences, so if the social sciences fail, the authority of managers falls with them.

In chapters seven and eight, MacIntyre turns his attention to the history of "facts" and the origin of the fact–value distinction, and reveals that this materialistic appeal to objective truth is no less a form of emotivism than the abuse of moral language discussed in the preceding chapters. A careful analysis of the political and managerial use of the social sciences shows it to be only one more stage setting in modern morality's theater of illusions.

Chapters seven and eight draw upon the philosophy of the social sciences to argue three points. First, in chapter seven, the neutral "facts" to which emotivism appeals are not neutral at all, and the notion that they are is just a remnant of a discredited empiricist theory of knowledge. That is what makes " 'fact' . . . a folk-concept with an aristocratic ancestry" (p. 79). The philosophy of science has come to recognize that we interpret our experience with "theory-laden concepts" (p. 79), so that our facts are artifacts of interpretation.

The second point, also in chapter seven, is that modern mechanistic accounts of human behavior stand in direct opposition to the Aristotelian account of human action. Behaviorism originated when Aristotle's account of human action was rejected (p. 82). And as Quine showed that behaviorism could become a science only if it were "formulated in a vocabulary which omits all reference to intentions, purposes, and reasons for action" (p. 83), it follows that if it turns out to be impossible to account for human activity without those references, a human science of behavior is likewise impossible.

Third, in chapter eight, MacIntyre shows that it is impossible to discover the kinds of law-like generalizations that the social scientists sought, because of systematic unpredictability in human affairs (pp. 93–100). MacIntyre concludes that managerial expertise grounded in the social sciences is only one more moral fiction:

> For it follows from my whole argument that the realm of managerial expertise is one in which what purport to be objectively-grounded claims function in fact as expressions of arbitrary, but disguised, will and preference. (p. 107)

There is no arena of contemporary practical discourse, then, that is immune from the problems that face the culture of emotivism; emotivism even finds expression in the language of science.

One of the most striking parts of this last stage in the argument is MacIntyre's treatment of facts and theories. He begins chapter seven by declaring that facts are not what most modern people take them to be. Facts are not objective bits of data to be observed neutrally and then assessed through theory, on the contrary, facts are dependent on the theories through which they are characterized and understood. So MacIntyre concludes this part of the argument, "Theory is required to support observation, just as much as observation theory" (p. 81).

It matters, then, what kind of theory is informing our observations. When an Aristotelian observes human action, she or he sees a person working out means to ends, so that the only way to understand what the agent is doing is to determine what the agent is trying to do. When a modern behaviorist observes human activity, however, she or he sees only behavior; the behaviorist gathers what are taken to be neutrally observed facts about human behavior, which are to be understood in terms of behaviorist theory. Looking at the same people doing the same things, the Aristotelian and the behaviorist make entirely different observations, which are directed to entirely different goals. Where the Aristotelian wants to understand the actions of agents in order to discover the best way to form the agent to pursue the true good, the modern social scientist wants to understand the behaviors of individuals in order to derive law-like generalizations that can enable modern managers, bureaucrats, and politicians to make effective decisions in the absence of any given true good.

The notion that facts are independent of theory, and the idea that science, including social science, is objective and untainted by ideology are indeed deeply held modern prejudices. For the reader who is unfamiliar with the literature on the philosophy of science and the philosophy of social science that informs MacIntyre's argument in these two chapters, these claims may seem troublesome, but it is well worth the effort to wrestle with this passage, for if it is true that theory shapes facts, then two things follow. First, it follows that apparently neutral appeals to facts and putatively neutral theoretical analyses of those facts may conceal arbitrary choice and will. Second, it also follows that such neutral appeals may conceal their arbitrariness not only from those subjected to their conclusions, but even from those who draw those conclusions. The modern conceit that it has transcended tradition is precisely the cause of the ideological blindness that masks the culture of emotivism from those subjected to it (p. 81).

Nietzsche or Aristotle?

MacIntyre's treatment of contemporary moral utterance as a theater of illusions examined moral fictions at work in social, philosophical, and scientific appeals to objective standards in moral and political decision making. MacIntyre's examination of the ordinary social and political use of moral language shows that the inhabitants of the culture of emotivism typically choose whatever moral principles and moral arguments serve their purposes, often with little awareness or regard for the larger bodies of theory from which those principles and arguments had been derived, and the affirmation of which would be required to justify their use. Next, MacIntyre turned to philosophical moral theory and found that it was also compromised; MacIntyre denounced modern liberal individualist natural rights as fictions and showed that Mill's principle of utility was far too undefined to provide any objective guide to moral judgment. In the absence of any given end or fixed teleology for human agency, modern moral and political philosophy must choose its values, and this choice makes its ethics and politics fundamentally arbitrary, all its protestations to the contrary notwithstanding. Finally, even the social sciences are unable to provide objective criteria to guide practical decision making, for a number of reasons, including (1) the human origins of facts and theories, (2) the inherent inadequacy of any theory that would treat human agency as caused behavior, and (3) various factors that make it impossible for behaviorists to establish law-like generalizations about human behavior that have strong predictive power. Thus, the authority claimed by bureaucrats and managers on the basis of these social sciences is unwarranted.

Given the arbitrariness of so much of contemporary moral and political discourse, MacIntyre asserts that there are only two ways to move forward. On the one hand, we can accept the modern denial of teleology, accept that we choose our values, and follow the path of Nietzsche. For the secular philosopher, this is a real and attractive option, and there are many who have chosen it. Yet, the Nietzschean position carries burdensome consequences, for it undermines any rational "basis for the moral rejection of Stalinism" or of any other deceitful, arbitrary, murderous, terrorist political ideology. Nonetheless, the Nietzschean position remains attractive, for so long as moral philosophy is held to be a study that determines the rules that should guide behavior irrespective of the purposes of human acts, Nietzsche's philosophy will appear to provide the obvious natural conclusions to every argument in secular ethics.

On the other hand, if we look beyond the rules of morality, to consider their purpose as guides to practical reason, we may renew ethics, both secular and theistic, as a study of the demands of rational human agency. In chapter nine of *AV*, MacIntyre identifies this option with Aristotle. Given the choice between Nietzsche and Aristotle, MacIntyre chooses Aristotle and builds on Aristotle's account of human action to clear a pathway out of the moral wilderness.

[handwritten margin notes: In M's view rules of morality have a purpose as guides to practical reason — leading to the human good.]

Notes

1 Rachels, *The Elements of Moral Philosophy*, 5th edn (New York: McGraw Hill, 2007), p. 198.
2 Ibid., p. 199.
3 Karl Marx, *Theses on Feuerbach*.
4 MacIntyre, *Marxism: An Interpretation*,
5 MacIntyre, *Against the Self-Images of the Age*.
6 MacIntyre, "What Morality is Not," *Against the Self-Images of the Age*.
7 Alasdair MacIntyre, "Breaking the Chains of Reason," in E. P. Thompson, ed., *Out of Apathy* (1960).
8 MacIntyre, "ToF:RNT," pp. 223–34.
9 Marx, *Theses on Feuerbach*, p. 244.
10 See "ToF:RNT," in Knight, p. 226.
11 See "Freedom and Revolution," pp. 131–4, *DPR*, pp. 87–98, and *E&P*, p. 3.
12 For more on this, see Christopher Stephen Lutz, *TEAM*, pp. 34–9, and MacIntyre, "NMW II," in Knight, ed., *MacReader*, pp. 41–9.

13 Thomas Hobbes, *Leviathan*, chapter 5 [19].

14 Servais Pinckaers, *Sources of Christian Ethics*, trans. Sr. Mary
    Thomas Noble, OP (Washington, DC: Catholic University of America
    Press, 1995), pp. 242, 379–99.

15 See Aristotle, *Nicomachean Ethics*, book 3, chapter 5 [1113b.15–
    1114a.23].

16 Plato, *Symposium*, Diotima's account of the ascent of the soul
    (p. 210).

17 Augustine, *Confessions*, chapter 1.

18 The identification of happiness with pleasure has been part of
    modern thought from the beginning. We find it in Hobbes, *Leviathan*
    (London: The Green Dragon in St Paul's Church-yard, 1651), chapter
    6; Kant, *Critique of Pure Reason* (Riga: Johann Friedrich Hartknoch,
    "A" edition 1781, "B" edition 1787), A806, B834; and John Stuart
    Mill, *Utilitarianism* (London: 1863), ed. Oskar Piest (Library of the
    Liberal Arts), chapter 2.

19 Aristotle, *Nicomachean Ethics*, 2.3 [1004b30–1].

20 This is a term for "good" that MacIntyre used in his presentation in
    Dublin, in March 2009.

21 Aristotle, *Nicomachean Ethics*, 3.5 [1113a25–7], trans. W. D. Ross.

22 Aristotle, *Nicomachean Ethics*, 1.

23 Hobbes, *Leviathan*, chapter 6.

24 Kant, *Critique of Pure Reason*, pp. A806, B834.

25 Mill, *Utilitarianism*, chapter 2.

26 Aristotle, *Nicomachean Ethics*, 3.5 [1113a25–7], trans. W. D. Ross.

27 Aristotle makes a similar point in *Nicomachean Ethics*, book seven,
    when he distinguishes between the moral character of the weak
    and the enduring agent. The weak agent follows passion rather
    than reason and does wrong, but the enduring agent follows reason
    rather than passion and does right. Nonetheless, Aristotle's agent is
    following practical reasoning in pursuit of personal and communal
    goods, and what reason dictates to the enduring agent is the pursuit
    of a higher good than the lower good counseled by passion.

28 In response to MacIntyre's rejection of natural rights in *AV*, Alan
    Gerwirth argues that "rights are normative entities whose existence
    must be established primarily by normative justificatory argument"
    and that "it *is* possible to provide empirical correlates for their
    existence, where 'existence' has the secondary meaning of social
    recognition and legal enforcement" (Alan Gewirth, "Rights and
    Virtues," *The Review of Metaphysics* 38, no. 4 (June 1985): 740).
    Given the range of things that have received social recognition
    and legal enforcement in history, and the novelty of many of the
    "rights" advanced in contemporary culture, it is hard to see how this

establishes that natural rights, construed as secular moderns have construed them, exist.

29 Kant, *Critique of Pure Reason*, pp. A802, B830.

30 Kant, *Groundwork for the Metaphysics of Morals*, pp. 395–401.

31 Immanuel Kant, *Foundations of the Metaphysics of Morals* [*Groundwork*], trans. Lewis White Beck (Macmillan/Library of the Liberal Arts, 1990), p. 44 (421).

32 *Foundations*, p. 46 (429).

33 Ibid., p. 49 (432).

34 *Groundwork*, pp. 455–63.

35 G. E. M. Anscombe, "Modern Moral Philosophy," *Philosophy* 33 (January 1958): 1–19, at 2.

36 *Groundwork*, p. 398.

37 Mill, *Utilitarianism*, p. 16.

38 MacIntyre's way of describing this problem developed considerably over the years since *AV*. In *Whose Justice? Which Rationality?* (*WJWR*), MacIntyre speaks of "any substantive set of principle of rationality" (p. 4) and "rationalities rather than rationality" (p. 9); MacIntyre distinguishes formal and substantive rationality more clearly in *3RV*, p. 11.

39 This second kind of eclecticism is what MacIntyre has elsewhere called "compartmentalization." He discusses this problem in "Social Structures and Their Threats to Moral Agency," in *E&P*, pp. 186–204, especially pp. 196–202.

40 See *AV*, pp. 6–7, positions 1.b, 2.b, 2.c, and 3.b.

41 For a good example of this survey, see the relevant chapters Donald Palmer, *Does the Center Hold?* 4th edn (McGraw-Hill, 2007).

42 *MacReader*, p. 41.

43 See Anscombe, "Modern Moral Philosophy," *Philosophy* 33 (1958).

44 See MacIntyre's remarks about "moral utterance . . . put to the service of arbitrary will," *AV*, p. 110.

45 Aron, *Main Currents in Sociological Thought*, 1967, pp. 206–10, quoted in *AV*, p. 26.

46 Aristotle, *Nicomachean Ethics*, book 1, chapter 1.

47 See *Summa Contra Gentiles* book three, chapters two and three; see also Thomas Aquinas, *Summa Theologiae*, I–II, questions 1–5, 18–19, and question 94, article 2.

48 For Gewirth's reply, see Alan Gewirth, "Rights and Virtues," *The Review of Metaphysics* 38, no. 4 (June 1985): 739–62.

49 Wendell Johnson, *People in Quandaries: The Semantics of Personal Adjustment* (New York: Harper and Brothers, 1946), p. 76.

50 Ibid., pp. 77–9. Scientific studies of genetics, epigenetics, and human development have made great progress since 1946, and

these should not be confused with the plogglie theories of heredity and environment that Johnson condemns. "Human nature," can be a plogglie if it is treated reductively as a cheap false answer to a question, but it can also be treated as the name of a cluster of experiences, questions, and problems, and then it is not a plogglie, because the question is allowed to remain.

51 Ibid., p. 77.

52 In the essay "Toleration and the Goods of Conflict," in *E&P*, MacIntyre discusses the role of "important fictions" in politics. Although we may recognize, for example that "ostensible neutrality on the part of the state" concerning religious and political opinions "is never real, it is an important fiction, and those of us who recognize its importance as well as its fictional character will agree with liberals in upholding a certain range of civil liberties" (E&P, p. 214).

Nietzsche's conclusion is that the ultimate foundation of morality is the will to power.

5

Summary of the constructive argument

In the first half of the book, MacIntyre showed that the language of contemporary social and political life has broken down in a very specific way. Contemporary people use moral and political language to argue what ought to be done, and what must be done, but they do this without appealing to the goals that people pursue or the need to obey any traditional moral authority, instead they appeal to objective and impersonal moral standards or to the facts of social life or to the theories of the social sciences. MacIntyre shows that neither the appeals to moral standards nor the appeals to facts and theories can justify their claims to objectivity, and that both are likely to mask the arbitrary preferences of those who use them. If we are to avoid the conclusion of Nietzsche that the ultimate foundation of morality is the "will to power," we must start over again; we must determine whether the modern rejection of the classical notion of teleology was a mistake, and whether something like the philosophy of Aristotle may provide us with a more fruitful research program in ethics and politics.

To justify a return to Aristotle at this point in the argument is no small task. Having spent the first half of the book attuning his readers to the many ways that our supposedly objective moral arguments—even some of our scientific arguments—may mask arbitrary preferences, MacIntyre needs to show that his interest in a virtue theory like Aristotle's is not similarly arbitrary.

The constructive argument that makes up the second half of the book proposes a way to discover the virtues naturally in terms of a social teleology; it moves through three phases. First, MacIntyre specifies why we should look at Aristotle, and not some broader category like classical thought or Greek philosophy; he shows us what it is in Aristotle that is most interesting to him, and what sets Aristotle against his classical predecessors and his modern successors. Second, MacIntyre develops his own theory of virtue through the three levels of practice, whole human life, and tradition. Third, MacIntyre uses his account of the virtues to interpret the history of ethics and politics since the rejection of Aristotelian teleology, and to consider what might be needed to renew the tradition of the virtues in today's world.

Specifying Aristotle

These chapters set out three characteristics of Aristotle and the Aristotelian tradition of the virtues. First, Aristotle is an heir to the heroic notion that human excellence, as understood by a given community, is a desirable and normative goal for human action. Second, Aristotle is an intellectual successor to that transformation from the heroic competitive virtues to the classical cooperative virtues which made it possible to imagine moral norms that transcend community standards and thus to view Socrates as a moral hero. Third, the heart of Aristotle's theory of virtue is its teleology.

Chapter ten: The virtues in heroic societies

Unlike early modern theorists who wrote fictional accounts of pre-social human beings living in imaginary states of nature,[1] MacIntyre gathers evidence about ancient societies from the early literature that captured their oral traditions. The heroic societies presented in Homer's poems, in Iceland's Sagas, and in Ireland's Ulster cycle may or may not have existed precisely as described. But the stories handed over to the written tradition by Homer, by thirteenth-century Icelanders, and by twelfth-century Irish monks certainly tell us how classical Greek, Icelandic, and Irish cultures

understood themselves. These stories tell us what they valued and
what they honored in moral character and action.

In Homeric, Icelandic, and Irish heroic societies, moral life
and social life were inseparable, for one's social role and status,
one's work and deeds, and one's relationships to family and community were the main elements of personal identity. The Greek
term "aretê," which we translate as "virtue" meant "excellence"
in strength and skill as well as character, and courage, defined as
"the quality necessary to sustain a household and a community"
was a central form of excellence (p. 122).

Heroic societies demand hospitality for the stranger, place a high
value on human life, and accept death as the unavoidable end of
human life. The evidence MacIntyre gleans from extant literature
shows that the people who lived in heroic societies were quite unlike
the pre-social individuals of Hobbes, Locke, and Rousseau; they are
more like the natural citizens of Aristotle's *Politics*.[2] For the citizens
of heroic societies, membership in the community is not an option;
they do not enter civil society by choice.[3] For people of the heroic
age, to reject the norms of society is to deny one's identity as a member of the community with its attendant roles and duties.

The kind of human culture that we find in the heroic age is
the foundation for the tradition of the virtues. Its people remained
very aware that the moralities of their communities were particular
rather than universal, and they understood the role of community
relationships in human excellence. Although these cultures are in
one sense the foundation of the tradition of the virtues, from what
is said in chapter eleven, it may be better to think of them as pre-
cursors to it, because their moralities were tied to their particular
communities and they lacked any coherent theory of virtue.

Chapter ten introduces the notion of theory as narrative and
social structure as enacted narrative. "Epic and saga . . . portray
. . . a society which already embodies the form of epic or saga"
(p. 125). "Heroic social structure *is* enacted epic narrative" (p. 129).
MacIntyre develops this idea more fully later in the book, and narrative is very important to the overall argument.[4]

Chapter eleven: The virtues in Athens

Literature from fourth- and fifth-century Athens marks a transition from savagery to civility in which the very concept of human

excellence was transformed. This chapter owes much to the work of Arthur Adkins. According to Adkins, by the end of the fifth century, the heroic notion of human excellence was being challenged by a new conception of morality:

> In broad outline, there are still two groups of ethical terms: one, consisting of αγαθός, αρετή, κακός, κακία, καλόν, αἰσχρόν[5] and similar words, commends success, prosperity, victory in war, high birth, courage, and similar qualities, and decries their opposites. (These I shall term competitive values and excellences.) The other consists in words commending justice, temperance and similar qualities, and decrying their opposites—cooperative values and excellences.[6]

Adkins neatly summarizes the transition by comparing Agamemnon and Socrates. Agamemnon, the heroic commander of the Greeks in the Trojan War, was excellent because of his high birth, his wealth, and his success in battle, while his murder at the hands of his wife's lover ruins him, "when Agamemnon was murdered, he died ἀισχρως [more shameful], . . . and this was ἀισχρόν [shame]—than which nothing can be worse—for Agamemnon."[7] Socrates, on the other hand, was not high born, lived in poverty, and allowed himself to be unjustly prosecuted and executed out of his concern for justice.[8] Agamemnon was a hero according to the competitive virtues, while Socrates was a paragon of moral excellence according to the cooperative virtues.

In this transitional period, MacIntyre notes that Plato, Sophocles, and many authors, including philosophers, poets, and historians, deliberately reorganized and redefined the moral vocabulary to make it coherent and systematic (p. 135). Of the various competing coherent views of the virtues that resulted, MacIntyre directs us to four: the sophists', Plato's, Aristotle's, and the tragedians', each of which should be viewed as a somewhat different answer to a somewhat different question.

MacIntyre cautions his readers to avoid reading contemporary notions of virtue and vice into the Greek terms (p. 136), and he suggests that the competitiveness of our modern liberal individualist culture may frustrate our efforts to understand Greek ethics. He demonstrates this challenge by discussing the difficulty of understanding two Athenian moral concepts on their own terms. First, "*pleonexia*," the vice of "acquisitiveness," no longer appears to be a vice in the competitive culture of modern liberal individualism. Second, again owing to the inherent competitiveness of our culture, the "*agôn*," or "contest," tends to appear to us as an individualistic struggle for private goods or personal opinion, while for the Greeks, the *agôn* had a shared social dimension in the common quest for the victory of the city, or the common quest for excellence and truth through drama, philosophy, and shared deliberation in politics.

After drawing these contrasts between the worldviews of modern liberal individualism and classical Athenian civic life, MacIntyre returns to three of the four contrasting Athenian views of the virtues: the sophists, Plato, and the tragedians. The sophists, represented in Plato's *Republic* by Thrasymachus, and in the *Gorgias* by Gorgias, Polus, and Callicles, take a relativist position. For the sophists, the virtues are whatever they are taken to be in each city, and "justice" is, according to Thrasymachus, "what is to the interest of the stronger."[9] Plato's account of the virtues stands in stark contrast to the sophists'. For Plato, the virtues are real, they are unified, and they are crucial to the real success of a person as a citizen. Here MacIntyre first raises his concern about the unity of the virtues. Saving Aristotle for the next chapter, MacIntyre explores the moral scheme of Sophocles' tragedies. Where Plato argues for an objective and consistent moral order, Sophocles presents an objective but incoherent moral order, in which human efforts to resolve problems end with the acceptance of a divine verdict.

On page 144, MacIntyre presents the hypothesis that forms the backbone of the constructive argument: "to adopt a stance on the virtues will be to adopt a stance on the narrative character of human life." He explains this in the next paragraph:

> If human life is understood as a progress through harms and dangers, moral and physical . . . the virtues will find their place as those qualities the possession and exercise of which generally tend to success in this enterprise and the vices likewise as qualities which likewise tend to failure. (p. 144)

If the virtues are qualities that enable people to succeed in living a good life, adopting a stance on the virtues will require us to develop an account of the good life, and a way to evaluate our progress toward that goal.

We have to develop an account of the good life

Chapter twelve: Aristotle's account of the virtues

Chapter twelve introduces Aristotle as the primary author in the tradition of the virtues that MacIntyre intends to defend, but MacIntyre will defend the Aristotelian tradition without defending Aristotle on all points. So the chapter begins with some caveats about traditions: Aristotle did not take himself to be making a limited contribution to an ongoing tradition; he took himself to be replacing error with truth.[10] Aristotle talks about his predecessors, but lacks the sense of history that could allow him to speak of his place in a tradition.

According to Aristotle's *Nicomachean Ethics*, human agents act to pursue goods that they desire. So moral education is an education in recognizing, knowing, desiring, and choosing actions that make us better as human agents. Good choices develop habits of good choice,[11] while bad choices degenerate into habits of moral blindness and vice.[12] According to Aristotle, nature determines the specific good that human beings seek;[13] thus, defending Aristotle's account of virtue may appear to presuppose a defense of Aristotle's "metaphysical biology."[14]

Aristotle holds that the natural goal or *telos* of human life is *eudaimonia* or happiness, and MacIntyre presents an Aristotelian definition of virtue according to the pattern he had set out in chapter eleven:

> The virtues are precisely those qualities the possession of which will enable an individual to achieve *eudaimonia* and the lack of which will frustrate his movement toward that *telos*. (p. 148)

Training in the virtues involves the training of desire, taking control over one's emotional responses, and learning how to act and how to feel. Remarkably, for the modern reader who approaches ethics as a study of rules, the *Nicomachean Ethics* says very little about rules, and when Aristotle does talk about rules, they are the rules laid down by the city-state. This does not contradict natural teleology because for Aristotle, the city is not a human artifact invented to raise the individual out of the dangers of the state of nature, as in Hobbes, Locke, and Rousseau. For Aristotle, the city is a natural development of human community, because the human person is a political animal (politikon zôon).[15]

MacIntyre argues that Aristotelian ethics requires those who adhere to it "to develop two . . . kinds of evaluative practice" (p. 151). First, the community must come to recognize and celebrate the qualities of character that help them to meet their goals, and to shun attitudes that are counterproductive. Second, the community must determine which courses of action help them to reach their goals, and celebrate these while condemning activities that hinder the pursuit of the common good, including activities that hinder the common good of developing a moral culture that supports the pursuit of the common good. These two components of moral culture—virtues and laws—are interconnected. Lawmakers need the virtues to make just laws; the people need just laws to support their development of the virtues; and community leaders need virtue in order to apply the laws of the city in a just and equitable manner. We cannot understand prudential laws without the virtues, and communities cannot develop the virtues without the support of prudential laws.

To illustrate the problems of the equitable application of law, MacIntyre presents the complicated issues of the Mashpee Wampanoag land suit.[16] Mashpee, Massachusetts is a vacation community on Cape Cod near Boston with some very valuable real estate.[17] "In 1976, the tribe sought the return of 11,000 acres of [public and private] undeveloped land in Mashpee and named New Seabury[18] and 145 other private land-owners who held title to 20 or more acres."[19] President Carter sought a mediated solution to the conflict, but the suit went to trial in 1977. In January 1978, "District Court Judge Walter J. Skinner dismissed the Indian's case (sic) . . . after a jury ruled that the Wampanoags did not meet the legal definition of an Indian tribe."[20] The Supreme Court of the United States rejected the Mashpee Wampanoag Tribal Council's appeal in October 1978 and the Council has made no effort to revive the suit, even after the Bureau of Indian Affairs recognized the tribe in 2007. Individual Mashpee Wampanoags have filed subsequent lawsuits, but those have been dismissed. Victory for the Mashpee would have voided every sale of Mashpee Indian land since 1790 and given the Mashpee a world-class location to operate a resort and casino.[21]

The Trade and Non-Intercourse Act of 1790 made the sale of Indian lands illegal unless the sale was approved by Congress. The Mashpee argued that they did exist as a tribe in 1790, and that this law therefore protected them and their land. Consequently, they held that the nineteenth-century sale of their land—some of it compelled through tax sales—was illegal. The city and the developers argued that the Mashpee had ceased to be a tribe by 1790, that their land was not "Indian land" as specified in the law, and that their members had sold their property as ordinary US citizens under ordinary property law. This was a difficult case because the jury had to determine which law to apply, before the judge could determine what the law demanded. MacIntyre used the Mashpee Wampanoag land suit to underscore the role of the judge—in this case, ultimately the jury—and the importance of the judge's prudence.

For Aristotle, *phronêsis* or prudence is a central virtue, and it is an intellectual virtue. To be good, one must also be wise, and to be wise, one must also be good (p. 154). To put this in medieval terms, one cannot exercise prudence without justice, temperance, and courage, and one cannot exercise temperance, courage, or justice without prudence. Aquinas calls this the unity of the virtues.[22] The modern tradition to which Kant belongs denies that moral virtue consists in desiring what is good and best, it denies that moral education is an education in feeling (p. 149). On the contrary, Kant argues that "To act virtuously is . . . to act against inclination" (p. 149).[23]

For Aristotle, friendship is a virtue, and it is this virtue that holds communities together, whether it is citizens in a *polis* or family members in a household. This civic friendship "is that which embodies a shared recognition of and pursuit of a good" (p. 155). Civic friendship is not a negotiation among individuals, it is a relationship that draws people into a common pursuit. The importance of civic friendship sets Aristotle's notions of citizenship and the common good against those of modernity, which constructs a view of the individual as a naturally autonomous agent who enters society by choice, in order to protect his own interests. MacIntyre says that such citizens of the modern state are, from Aristotle's point of view, "citizens of nowhere,"[24] which, according to the characterization given two pages later (p. 158), makes them barbarians (see p. 263).

Aristotle defends the unity of the virtues, and holds that the virtues are not available to those who are not free, including "non-Greeks, barbarians, and slaves" (p. 159). Aristotle identifies happiness as the end of human life but distinguishes that happiness from mere enjoyment or pleasure, and for good reason.

MacIntyre completes his summary of Aristotle by moving from virtues and their relationship to rules, civic life, and success, to the issue of practical reasoning. Notice that this is *practical reasoning*, rather than moral reasoning; Aristotle acknowledges certain moral absolutes (including those against murder, adultery, and theft[25]), but Aristotle is chiefly concerned with achieving the *telos*, the goal, not with obeying any revealed moral code. So the first essential element in Aristotle's account of practical reasoning is "the wants and goals of the agent." The second is the major premise that an action of a given kind is needed to move the agent toward her or his goal. The third is the minor premise that a proposed action is of that kind. The fourth element is the conclusion, the action (pp. 161–2).

MacIntyre raises three sets of objections to adopting this Aristotelian account of virtue, ethics, and practical reasoning. The first is MacIntyre's notorious rejection of "Aristotle's metaphysical biology": "If we reject that biology, as we must, is there any way in which that teleology can be preserved" (p. 162)? This is a real problem for anyone who would present a secular account of Aristotelian ethics; for Aristotle held that the form determined the *telos*. If there is no form, how could there be an objective *telos*? The second set of objections deals with the connection between Aristotle's notion of the virtues and Aristotle's notion of the *polis*; if a peculiar set of virtues presupposes a particular *polis*, then it seems impossible to maintain those peculiar virtues without that particular *polis*. The third set deals with what MacIntyre took to be the mistake of Aristotle's position on the unity of the virtues; MacIntyre determined later that this was a mistake on his part.[26]

Chapter thirteen: Medieval aspects and occasions

The purpose of this chapter is to distinguish medieval Christian thought from the properly Aristotelian tradition of the virtues. On this account, the Aristotelian tradition of the virtues is absent from the mainstream of European thought in the middle ages.

Medieval European Christian culture maintained many pre-Christian influences, including those of its still recent heroic past, which shaped medieval law and social practices. Inasmuch as it was Christian, medieval ethics was moral *theology*, it was concerned with revealed moral law and sin and *moral* reasoning, rather than with human goals, human excellence, and *practical* reasoning. Stoicism, with its emphasis on the will, had a great impact on medieval thought.

When Aristotelian thought was adopted, it was transformed in fairly specific ways, through the addition of Christian virtues and the modification of the notion of the *telos*.

Aristotle had distinguished between an activity that is united with its *telos* (going for a walk) and acts performed for the sake of an external *telos* (walking to the store). It is reasonable to seek an external *telos* by some other means (getting a ride to the store) but one can achieve the telos internal to an activity only by doing the activity (getting a ride from a friend when one is going for a walk only ends one's walk). Aristotle took the human *telos* to be an end internal to living the good life, Christianity, on the other hand, appears to present the *telos* as salvation, an outcome beyond this life, which one can achieve at the end of a vicious life, provided one repents before dying.[27]

This may be a fair portrayal of some medieval moral theology, but it is not an adequate portrayal of the Thomistic position. Thomism combines Aristotle's notion of the good life as an activity to be lived in this life with the Christian revelation that something better awaits. For Aquinas, the Christian lives the good life in this world as a sign and foretaste of the life that awaits all who are saved.

MacIntyre asserts that Augustine transformed the human *telos* in another way by asserting that Augustine's position that "the will can delight in evil" means that the will is able to choose evil as an end. This, too, is inadequate, as it would make Augustine a Manichean.[28]

MacIntyre finds two benefits to the medieval modifications of Aristotelian teleology: First, eudaimonia is opened to all people, regardless of the external circumstances of their lives, since the focus of virtue moves from earthly success to moral goodness. Second, the medieval view of virtue has an awareness of its history. This provides a "stance on the narrative character of human life" (p. 144) that leads to a new definition for virtue: "The virtues are then on this kind of medieval view those qualities which enable men to survive evils on their historical journey (p. 176)."

Thomas Aquinas is "a highly deviant medieval figure" and "an unexpectedly marginal character" in the history presented in chapter thirteen (p. 178). Thomas writes as a philosopher and a theologian, but what Thomas takes from Aristotle only reiterates a metaphysical cosmology that we must reject, and what Thomas takes from Christian theology is not available to contemporary secular philosophers. MacIntyre was not yet a Thomist when he wrote *AV*, and MacIntyre's thinking on Thomas, Thomas's contribution to Aristotelianism, and Thomas's value as a philosopher develops considerably through the decades following *AV*.

MacIntyre ends the chapter by criticizing Aquinas's account of the unity of the virtues. This is an important mistake, which MacIntyre explicitly recognized in the preface to *WJWR* and in the essay "Moral Dilemmas."[29] Given MacIntyre's clear support for Aristotle's argument for the unity of the virtues in the previous chapter (p. 154), it seems that this criticism of Aquinas is more properly a critique of neo-Thomism.[30]

Chapters ten through thirteen specify what MacIntyre is interested in when he proposes that we choose Aristotle over Nietzsche. If the rejection of the "Aristotelian account of action" led to the culture of emotivism (p. 82), the recovery of practical reasoning must begin with the recovery of Aristotle's account of human action.[31] Aristotle's account of human action links the virtues of human excellence to social life and practical reasoning. MacIntyre does not begin with Aristotle's *Physics*, but his *Nicomachean Ethics*. MacIntyre does not begin with Aristotle as presented through the lens of Medieval Thomism and its rejection, but with Aristotle considered in himself. MacIntyre does not seek to resurrect Aristotle's theory of virtue as an ahistorical relic of history, but to join Aristotle's tradition by developing Aristotle's insights concerning virtue and human action.

Defining virtue

Chapters fourteen and fifteen draw on the insights of Aristotle and the virtue tradition to set out a new theory of virtue. As with

Aristotle, it is a theory that begins with the interests of agents and the shared interests of members of communities. As such, it unites the virtues with practical reasoning and community life. Unlike Aristotle, it understands its place in history, and sees a role for the history of the community in the explication of virtue.

Chapter fourteen: The nature of the virtues

Against the backdrop of conflicting notions of virtue presented so far, MacIntyre seeks to identify a "single core conception of the virtues" (p. 181). Comparing and contrasting Homer, Aristotle, the New Testament, Benjamin Franklin, and Jane Austen, MacIntyre finds considerable differences among the things they take to be virtuous, and even in what they take virtue to be. Thus, the "unitary core conception of the virtues" is not to be found in the concrete practical claims of the contending parties, but in a study of what the contending parties are doing when they define the virtues.

In every case, the virtues name what are taken to be excellences in practical reasoning and human action. The virtues make us better agents because they enable us to achieve excellence in practices. The rest of this chapter explains what practices are and how the virtues enable us to meet and extend the standards of excellence in practices. Practices occupy only the first place in MacIntyre's three-part definition of virtue. The account of virtues in terms of (1) practices is incomplete until it is supplemented in chapter fifteen with additional definitions in terms of (2) the narrative order of a whole human life, and (3) moral traditions.

We do not need the virtues to perform simple tasks. We do not need to be virtuous to change tires, cook meals, or even to run for public office. We do need the virtues to excel in practices. We need the virtues to maintain automobiles, to become chefs, or to govern communities wisely. These latter practices, unlike the former acts, have an inherent moral component to them. What is a practice?

> By a "practice" I am going to mean any coherent and complex form of socially established cooperative human activity through which goods internal to that form of activity are realized in the course of trying to achieve those standards of excellence which are appropriate to, and partially constitutive of, that form of

activity, with the result that human powers to achieve excellence, and human conceptions of the ends and goods involved, are systematically extended. (p. 187)

MacIntyre gives examples of what is and what is not a practice, and some of these have been controversial. Practices are complex enough to develop over time, and they are coherent enough to make sense on their own. Tic-tac-toe is not complex, neither is throwing a football, and bricklaying is intelligible only within the broader practice of architecture. It does not make sense to say, "I am going to go lay some bricks," unless the speaker is building something.[32]

Practices have goods internal to them. One becomes a competent builder only by learning the practices of architecture. The only way to gain the skills of chess is by playing chess. These goods, competence as a builder and skill in the game of chess, cannot be purchased, they come only through committed engagement in the practice; thus, there is a moral dimension to developing them successfully.

There are other goods, goods external to practices, which can be gained in a variety of ways. Wealth can be earned or stolen, victory can be won honestly or dishonestly, and the appearances that bring fame may be real or fabricated. If an agent pursues apparent success in a practice for the sake of wealth or fame, there is good reason for that agent to cut corners to gain empty appearances of excellence. If, on the other hand, an agent pursues the goods internal to the practice, if the agent pursues true excellence in the practice, cutting corners becomes a plainly irrational choice, and the rational motivation to cheat disappears.

This difference between the pursuit of goods external to practices and the pursuit of the goods internal to a practice is the point of the parable of the chess-playing child. An intelligent and clever child who learns to play chess to win candy has every reason to cheat if doing so will help the child to win more candy. When that same child learns to play for the sake of excellence in the game of chess, cheating becomes counterproductive, whether it helps the child to win more candy or not. MacIntyre has identified this story as one of the most important passages in the book.

Practices may be conventional, but in many cases, their standards of excellence are real. Chess is conventional, but some players really are better than others, and the level of excellence developed over time through the literature of chess is a real development. American football is conventional, but its development is real, and if Walter Camp[33] or Knute Rockne[34] were to attend a contemporary college football game, they would probably be surprised at the size, strength, speed, skill, and achievements of today's players. These early football coaches would also be amazed by the architectural achievements of specialized football stadiums that accommodate more than 100,000 fans.

To succeed in a practice, to meet and extend its standards of excellence, new initiates need to accept "the authority of the best standards realized so far" (p. 190). This amounts to learning what the practice really is on its own terms, and developing an eye, an ear, and an acquired taste for its peculiar forms of excellence. This prepares the practitioner to pursue the goods internal to the practice independently. By obeying the rules of the practice and meeting its standards, the practitioners maintain the practice, and if they surpass those standards, they may improve them, raising the bar for the next generation.

Success in practices has a moral dimension, because we cannot succeed in them unless we are able to commit ourselves to excellence in the practice. MacIntyre thus gives his first definition of virtue in terms of preparing people to succeed in practices:

> A virtue is an acquired human quality the possession and exercise of which tends to enable us to achieve those goods which are internal to practices and the lack of which effectively prevents us from achieving any such goods. (p. 191)

It takes honesty and courage to continue to seek the goods internal to practices when it might be easier to settle for the appearances or cut corners to enjoy the external goods more quickly; the virtues help us to overcome those temptations.

Communities provide objective structures to practices by setting up institutions that set and enforce the rules and standards of practices. These institutions also celebrate and reward achievements in practices. Such institutions include professional associations, sports leagues, hospitals, churches, universities, and governments. Institutions are not to be confused with the practices they serve. Inasmuch as practices discover rather than create or choose their standards, those standards, like the goods internal to the practices, must always hold a certain priority over the decisions of those who control the institutions. Keeping institutions honest can be challenging, however, because institutions tend to prefer the pursuit of external goods. Maintaining the institutions' orientation to the internal goods and to the best standards so far depends entirely upon the virtues of the institutions' practitioners. "Without them," writes MacIntyre, "without justice, courage, and truthfulness, practices could not resist the corrupting power of institutions" (p. 194).

This relationship between goods, practices, virtues, communities, and institutions brings some of the key shortcomings of modern liberal individualist society into focus. If MacIntyre is correct, civic life would be best pursued through an Aristotelian kind of politics, in which establishing and maintaining social communities is seen as a practice, and government serves as the central institution of that practice. But it is a central tenet of liberal individualism that government is to be neutral regarding substantive conceptions of the good (p. 195),[35] and while there is no debate that "the modern state is indeed totally unfitted to act as moral educator of any community" (p. 195), this places the institutions of modern government in the peculiar position of serving the practice of maintaining social communities while willfully blinding itself to the goods internal to practices and turning its attention to external goods. This condition carries a considerable risk, for if a society were to be dominated by the pursuit of external goods, MacIntyre writes, "competitiveness would become the dominant and even exclusive function" of its social interactions; society could collapse into Hobbes's state of nature (p. 196).

MacIntyre concludes that all virtues find their initial definition in relation to practices. This claim is unlike that of Aristotle on the two points where Aristotle seemed most problematic to him, yet it supports the three elements of Aristotle's insight that MacIntyre finds most valuable.

Unlike Aristotle, (1) MacIntyre does not depend on "Aristotle's metaphysical biology" to explain teleology, and (2) he makes room for tragedy and moral dilemmas by rejecting the unity of the virtues. MacIntyre would eventually modify his position on Aristotle's metaphysics, and reverse his position on the unity of the virtues, but these developments do not change the larger argument of *AV*.

Like Aristotle, (1) MacIntyre's treatment of virtues and practices demands a rich account of human agency that investigates the limits of voluntary action and distinguishes moral and intellectual virtues. (2) MacIntyre, like Aristotle, demands that we distinguish happiness from pleasure, and embrace happiness, properly understood, as our goal, so that the relationship between practical and moral reasoning may be renewed. Finally, MacIntyre's account is like Aristotle's in that (3) "it links evaluation and explanation in a characteristically Aristotelian way" (p. 199); both Aristotle and MacIntyre hold that practical options and choices cannot be understood without the moral evaluation of agents who choose or fail to choose what is good and best.

The definition of virtue in relation to practices appears to offer the kind of objective basis for a definition of virtue that contemporary philosophy cannot offer, until MacIntyre allows that some practices may be evil (p. 199), and that virtuous acts that supported success in such evil practices would be evil acts (p. 200). For MacIntyre, the problem of evil practices shows that the definition of virtue as a quality of character that enables success in practices is inadequate, unless it is supplemented with additional points about the role of virtue in an agent's pursuit of the good over a lifetime, and the agent's responses to the realities of that agent's moral starting point.

I am not convinced that genuine practices can be evil, and I have argued elsewhere that they cannot be,[36] but the definition of virtues (1) in relation to practices certainly is incomplete. MacIntyre notes that it is incomplete because it lacks a notion of the overall *telos* of human life, and because it provides no basis for the virtue of integrity or constancy, which can be defined only in terms of the life of an agent (pp. 202–3). In chapter fifteen, MacIntyre completes his three-part definition of virtue by considering (2) its relationship to success in a whole human life, and (3) its relationship to a community's successful accommodation of those inherited relationships, responsibilities, and debts that constitute its tradition.

Chapter fifteen: The virtues, the unity of a human life, and the concept of a tradition

In the essay "Social Structures and Their Threats to Moral Agency" (1999),[37] MacIntyre discusses his discovery in the mid-1970s of a problem in contemporary social life that he calls "compartmentalization."[38] The compartmentalized self lacks a fully unified identity, and is defined instead by a variety of sometimes overlapping, sometimes conflicting social roles. This makes the compartmentalized person's life inconsistent and episodic. MacIntyre illustrates this with an anecdote about power company executives he interviewed for his contribution to *Values in the Electric Power Industry*[39]:

> Power company executives tended to a significant degree to answer what were substantially the same questions somewhat differently, depending on whether they took themselves to be responding qua power company executive or qua parent and head of household or qua concerned citizen. That is to say, their attitudes varied with their social roles and they seemed quite unaware of this.[40]

MacIntyre found that the compartmentalized power company executive was able to advance the interests of the company or the family or the community, but seemed unable to consider practical questions in terms of any overarching, integrated common good.

MacIntyre begins chapter fifteen by noting how compartmentalization precludes the achievement of Aristotelian virtue, and he wants to propose that we use the unity of a human life as the criterion for the next level of his definition of virtue, but this poses a difficulty. What is it that unifies a human life? Aristotle would say that the human person is a substance, a composite of matter and form; this substance is generated in its mother and exists as a distinct metaphysical entity until its death brings substantial change to its matter. MacIntyre cannot answer in the same way, at least not in 1981, and not to the audience of this book, given that many of the modern, postmodern, Marxist, and post-Marxist readers of *AV* reject not only Aristotle's metaphysics of substance, but any notion of metaphysical truth, including truth about personal identity.

What MacIntyre advances as a basis for enduring human identity is the unity of the story that is to be told about a given material being, from conception to death. He makes no metaphysical assertions (as he had not developed the commitments that would enable him to do so in 1981). He does not advance a concept of the objective person as substance, nor does he reduce the person to a physical entity. He proposes only the ordinary way that people name and explain themselves and their actions; he makes the case for "a concept of a self whose unity resides in the unity of a narrative which links birth to life to death as narrative beginning to middle to end."[41]

"Narrative," as MacIntyre used it in "Epistemological Crises, Dramatic Narrative, and the Philosophy of Science," and as he uses it in *AV*, encompasses stories, histories, fairy tales, scientific theories, religious doctrines, philosophical claims, and arguments of every kind. When MacIntyre had explained in that earlier essay how one could regain confidence in one's understanding of the world after the failure of one's former beliefs and theories, he wrote, "it is by the construction of a new narrative,"[42] that is, a new theory, a new account. The unity of the self is to be the unity of one's autobiography; this is not arbitrary, and it promises to liberate the issue of personal identity from any kind of metaphysical debate. MacIntyre writes: "the unity of an individual life" is "the unity of a narrative embodied in a single life" (p. 218).[43]

With the argument for a narrative concept of the self, MacIntyre's defense of human agency against the claims of the behaviorists takes a step forward. Not only is it necessary to understand human activity in terms of purposes and intentions, it is also the case that no fully adequate account of human action can be given until it includes the settings—the social settings and histories—in which those agents act. He concludes: "There is no such thing as 'behavior' to be identified prior to and independently of intentions, beliefs, and settings" (p. 208).

Human action is so tied to intentions, beliefs, and settings that the things we do and say are to be understood as the acting out of our understanding of the world. As MacIntyre puts it: "I am presenting both conversations in particular then and human actions in general as enacted narratives" (p. 211). Human action is intelligible precisely because through our actions, we manifest our views of the world; our actions enact our narratives.[44]

One essential element of any narrative is the relationship of the present to the future, and inasmuch as an agent sees some goal in the future that is to be pursued through present action, that goal serves as the *telos* for that person's acts. This teleology begins subjectively, in the subjective narrative, with the subjective question: "What is the good life for me?" But this question seeks an

It's an adventure

objective answer, and the quest for the truth about the good life for me, and for the truth about the good life for humankind, becomes an adventure through which I learn more about what I am looking for, and more about myself (p. 219).

The requirements for success in this narrative quest provide the criteria for the second level of MacIntyre's definition of virtue:

> The virtues therefore are to be understood as those dispositions which will not only sustain practices and enable us to achieve the goods internal to practices, but which will also sustain us in the relevant kind of quest for the good, by enabling us to overcome the harms, dangers, temptations, and distractions which we encounter, and which will furnish us with increasing self-knowledge and increasing knowledge of the good. (p. 219)

This second-level definition of virtue considerably narrows the range of qualities that might reasonably be considered virtuous. Given MacIntyre's claim that there might be evil practices, the first-level definition might be used, on its own terms, to specify the virtues of a successful torturer; that move is not available with the second-level definition. The shattered conscience that might seem like a virtue with respect to a wicked practice (or better: wicked pseudo-practice) would truly be revealed as a vice with respect to an agent's quest for the good life.

MacIntyre moves toward the third-level definition of virtue when he begins to consider the "moral starting point" for human agents. MacIntyre holds that the life of one's community, its historic debts toward others along with its responsibilities, and the debts owed to it, make up an ineliminable part of the setting for human agency. It is in this sense that "moral traditions" provide the criteria for the third-level definition of virtue.

MacIntyre's appeal to tradition is not a conservative call to return to historic moral norms.[45] It is a final and thorough rejection of individualism. As MacIntyre seeks to define virtue entirely in terms of human agency, he has to work out a complete picture of human agency and its excellence. The first-level definition is incomplete, because having the kind of character that enables one to seek excellence in practices is not enough to make one excellent as a human being. This incompleteness is evident in stories of master artisans who are fully committed to excellence in their arts but live otherwise corrupt lives. The second-level definition is likewise insufficient, because it stops with the individual. One could imagine a highly talented, highly educated, and widely accomplished aristocrat or gentleman who embodied all the traditional virtues while ignoring the fact that his forefathers built his family fortune through corrupt business practices or the exploitation of poor laborers. Such a man could appear to be virtuous according to the insufficient first- and second-level definitions, but he could hardly be considered excellent as a human being.

MacIntyre lists historic debts as constitutive elements of tradition: US debts to the descendents of slaves, the English debts to the Irish, the German debts to Jews. These debts are real; consider only the US example. African Americans suffered slavery and then second-class citizenship. Prior to the Civil War, it was illegal in some states to teach African Americans to read and write; after the Civil War, during Reconstruction, it became legal to educate them, but teachers were murdered for doing so. Segregation excluded African Americans from the best neighborhoods, the best schools, even from politically connected churches and civic organizations, and hence from national leadership until the 1960s. The individualist may assert that US law has leveled the playing field since then, and that lingering disparities in achievement are no longer important. But any US citizen who asserted such a thing would be denying a real dimension in our relationships with our fellow citizens that remains a real component of the setting of human agency in many parts of the United States.

As MacIntyre puts it: "I am born with a past; and to try to cut myself off from that past, in the individualist mode, is to deform my present relationships" (p. 221). To agree with MacIntyre is to accept that morality is social and concrete, and constituted largely by human relationships, and it is to deny that morality can be reduced to abstract universal norms or to natural rights or to the choices of the individual in civil society. Anyone who accepts this third level of MacIntyre's definition of virtue must recognize and reject the mushroom people of Hobbes's *De Cive*, sprung from the ground unrelated to others, along with his and his successor's versions of the state of nature, as the ideological fictions that they are.

Tradition provides one's moral starting point in this historical sense of what one owes and what one owns because of the history into which one has been born; but it also provides one's moral starting point in an epistemological sense. Here MacIntyre is not interested in pushing any conservative ideological traditionalism, he is only sharing a hard-won insight about the difficulty of transcending tradition.

One of MacIntyre's driving questions since the 1960s has been the problem of ideology. He has been asking how an individual might transcend what she or he has been taught so that she or he might see and understand the world more clearly; this includes seeing and understanding more clearly one's real debts and one's best opportunities to contribute constructively in one's social community. The modern liberal individualist approach has always been to reject tradition and to start over; but MacIntyre finds that this leads only to moral and ideological blindness.

Modern moral philosophy has demonstrated repeatedly, beginning with Descartes, that the decision to transcend tradition by abandoning it has the opposite effect. Descartes had asserted that he would reject everything he knew and start over; but after telling his readers that he had rejected everything he had learned, imagined, or sensed, he produces an argument for his own existence, the existence of God, and the reception of innate ideas from God, using logic, vocabulary, and theories drawn directly—and quite obviously—from his scholastic education. One might claim that Descartes was lying when he wrote that he had rejected everything he knew, but that would be a mistake.

Descartes began his *Discourse on Method* and also his *Meditations* with the claim that reason is universal; and this became a central presupposition of modern thought. In his work on rationality, particularly *WJWR*, *3RV*, and *DPR*, MacIntyre puts this presupposition under a different light. In their rejection of the many doubtful elements of the tradition that they had received, there was a large part of the peculiar substantive rationality of Western thought that remained unquestioned for Descartes and his modern successors. Since it remained unquestioned, it also remained invisible to them because it constituted the lens through which they viewed the world. The moderns took this peculiar form of substantive rationality drawn from Christian medieval, scholastic sources to be universal reason. Thus, in his effort to transcend tradition by rejecting it, Descartes bequeathed to all of modernity a false belief in the universality of this peculiar form of substantive rationality. Not only did he fail to free himself from his tradition, he blinded himself to his inheritance from and continued participation in that tradition.

Traditions do not transcend their limitations by rejecting the past and starting over, they do so "through criticism and invention" (p. 222), and such criticism demands understanding of and attention to what has gone before. A living tradition, for MacIntyre, is the property of a community engaged in practices that continues to seek new and better ways to pursue the goods internal to those practices.

MacIntyre distinguishes his appeal to tradition from those that reduce tradition to a static set of received norms. Edmund Burke, author of *Reflections on the Revolution in France* (1790) exemplifies the conservative appeal to tradition. Burke contrasted the French Revolution, with its *Declaration of the Rights of Man* (1789) and its theory of social contract[46] against the Glorious Revolution in Great Britain (1688), and its theory of rights.[47] Burke, a Whig, interpreted the Glorious Revolution as a defense of the inherited rights of Englishmen. Burke defends the liberal individualism of the Glorious Revolution[48] against the liberal individualism of the French Revolution. MacIntyre rejects both, and notes that contemporary conservatives "for the most part" continue this liberal critique of liberalism (p. 222). In *AV*, MacIntyre altogether rejects "natural rights" and other features of modern liberal individualist ethics and politics as fictions. His concern with tradition is directed entirely to the inherited conditions of life as they affect practical reasoning and human agency.

The third-level definition of virtue completes MacIntyre's social account of human teleology:

The virtues find their point and purpose not only in sustaining those relationships necessary if the variety of goods internal to practices are to be achieved and not only in sustaining the form of an individual life in which that individual may seek out his or her good as the good of his or her whole life, but also in sustaining those traditions which provide both practices and individual lives with their necessary historical context. (p. 223)

A virtue is a quality of character that enables one to excel as a human agent. So an adequate definition of virtue must encompass all the conditions of human action that are available to contemporary philosophy. Therefore, the definition of virtue in terms of practices and whole human lives is only complete when those practices and whole human lives are considered in relation to their social setting in the histories of the communities to which human agents belong.

The virtues of courage, honesty, and truthfulness support practices. Excellence in a whole human life demands something like Austen's virtue of constancy. MacIntyre's notion of excellence in the agent as a bearer of tradition requires a specific virtue: "the virtue of having an adequate sense of the traditions to which one belongs or which confront one" (p. 223). On MacIntyre's account, recognition and appreciation of one's own culturally developed moral and intellectual peculiarities, and awareness and appreciation of those of others, is to be accounted a high virtue. This awareness of one's peculiarities is a crucial virtue for diplomatic and political success in times of social conflict. MacIntyre illustrates this virtue of historical sensibility with the examples of Reginald Cardinal Pole (1500–1558), and James Graham, the Marquis de Montrose (1612–1650). Cardinal Pole was a prudent statesman and a leading figure in the political wrangling between the Catholic Church and Tudor England, who served as an advisor to Mary I (1515–1558). The Marquis de Montrose was the chief of a Scottish clan, an able general, and a gifted diplomat who supported Charles I (1600–1649) in the English Civil War.

MacIntyre ends the chapter by returning to the theme of tragedy and moral dilemma before transitioning to the final phase of the argument.

Applying the theory

Now that MacIntyre has defined virtue and laid out "the kind of understanding of social life which the tradition of the virtues requires" (p. 225), he returns to the history of the emotivist culture of modern liberal individualism. In this examination of that history, MacIntyre considers the social structures within individualist theory and emotivist culture that exclude the culture of the virtues. He contrasts the sociology of the virtue tradition that he has developed in the foregoing chapters against that of modern "liberal or bureaucratic individualism."

"Bureaucratic individualism," a term that echoes Trotsky's critique of Stalin's "bureaucratism," was first explained on page 35, then defined more succinctly on page 71, and is now reintroduced on page 225. Bureaucratic individualism is the bifurcated ideology that allows the contemporary inhabitants of the culture of emotivism to discuss morality in terms of rights and then make political plans in terms of utility. The final chapters of the book show how and why the culture of emotivism, rooted in bureaucratic individualism, opposes the culture and tradition of the virtues. These chapters also argue that the culture of the virtues is the only authentic approach to human and social development.

Chapter sixteen: From virtues to virtue and after virtue

Chapter sixteen first describes the dissolution of the culture of the virtues in terms of the three-part definition worked out in chapters fourteen and fifteen (pp. 226–8), and examines the problem of redefining virtue without teleology or divine command (pp. 228–36). Then the chapter considers three efforts to renew the culture of the virtues (pp. 236–43). The chapter title, "From Virtues to Virtue and After Virtue," refers to two changes in Western moral culture. First, there is a change from the traditional emphasis on a variety of virtues to an emphasis on the singular virtue of rule-following (p. 235). Second, there is the challenge of maintaining the culture of the virtues after virtue has ceased to play a role in civic life (p. 243).

In the first three pages of chapter sixteen, MacIntyre provides anecdotal evidence of a large shift in Western society, away from a culture that pursues excellence in practices and seeks to understand and advance its own moral development through art and literature. He finds the people of late modernity shifting toward a non-culture—a collection of competing individuals, who lack any shared conception of their goals as human beings.[49] MacIntyre notes the transformation of art and literature (pp. 226–7), and the marginalization of practices from arts and community life, especially in politics (p. 227). He credits this partially to the shift from cottage industry to factory production. But he finds that the developments that created the four[50] characters of emotivist culture are not reducible to economics;[51] they have a philosophical cause as well (p. 228).

Without the "background concepts" of teleology and the common good that make it intellectually coherent, the tradition of the virtues became an empty shell in the dominant culture of modernity. Yet, the language of virtue has remained a central part of the Western moral vocabulary, and this has led to several redefinitions of virtue over the past few centuries. The tradition of the virtues celebrated the excellent character of agents whose pursuit of their personal good was inextricably linked to their service to the common goods of their communities. Aquinas taught that "the natural law in us"[52] inclines us to defend and protect of human life, to preserve our species through the nurture and education of children, "to know the truth about God and to live in society."[53] These goods were naturally desirable, and the one who pursued them well was thereby virtuous both in terms of nature and in terms of divine law.

Late medieval moral theologians rejected natural teleology as a basis for morality, and replaced it with divine command ethics. This entailed identifying moral virtue with obedience to divine commands. Modern secular philosophers who maintained the late-medieval rejection of teleological ethics would have to find another way to explain virtue. Like the divine command theorists who preceded them, they saw a conflict between morality and desire. They saw a conflict between egoistic selfishness and altruistic service to others. So they began to define the virtues as dispositions that help individuals to manage the conflicts between natural egoism and moral altruism (pp. 228–9).

The tradition of the virtues begins from an Aristotelian account of human action, in which the human person has a set purpose, and the suitability of any given human action is to be assessed in terms of its support for the agent's progress toward that purpose. The virtues are likewise tied to the purpose of the human person, as habits of character that will enable the agent to recognize actions that support her or his pursuit of the good, and that will provide her or him with the moral freedom to act on that judgment. With the rejection of the concept of a natural end or *telos* for the human person, the virtues become indefinite, for they lose the criteria that had determined their meaning and content. In the same way that modern moral philosophy had to find either a new teleology or a new categorical status for the rules of morality (discussed in Chapter 6), modern moral philosophy also needed to find a new status for the virtues:

> *Either* the virtues—or some of them—could be understood as expressions of the natural passions of the individual *or* they—or some of them—could be understood as dispositions necessary to curb and limit the destructive effect of some of those same natural passions. (p. 228)

Where the tradition had defined the virtues as habits of transformed desire that enable people to seek the common good, modernity sees the virtues either as good natural desires or as dispositions to serve the public good against one's own desires.

In modern moral philosophy, all goods are private, and one person's pursuit of her or his private good might prevent others from seeking theirs. So the question of balancing concern for one's own pursuit of one's private good against concern for others and their pursuits of their goods becomes a central issue in moral philosophy. Moral sentiment becomes a struggle between egoism and altruism. MacIntyre dates this development to the seventeenth and eighteenth centuries (p. 229). The virtue of "altruism" received its name from the pen of Auguste Comte (1798–1857), in the 1850s.

Between the extremes of the egoistic pursuit of one's own good and the altruistic commitment to helping others in the pursuit of theirs, David Hume proposed a theory of enlightened self-interest (p. 229). MacIntyre identifies three features of Hume's account of virtue that recur in the work of Hume's contemporaries and their successors: First, since individualistic society did not share the values or the notion of the common good that had informed the tradition of the virtues, novel and sometimes remarkable definitions have to be assigned to the names of the traditional virtues. Second, the virtues are defined in terms of their service to moral rules, as sentiments or dispositions that enable individuals to obey moral rules. Third, there is "the shift from a conception of the virtues as plural to one of virtue as primarily singular" (p. 233).

The shift from plural "virtues" to singular "virtue" is significant. It is part of a larger contraction and transformation of moral vocabulary. The precise terminology that supported the culture of the virtues—the morality of character that enables the desirous pursuit of human excellence—breaks down when the culture abandons teleology. The precision of that language is no longer needed as the culture moves to embrace a Stoic morality of rules. Stoicism, in the generic sense that MacIntyre uses it here, as in chapter thirteen, is a morality in which "the virtues" are replaced by "a monism of virtue" (p. 169), this singular virtue is identified with rule-following. The virtuous person does not follow those rules as means toward any human end, but only as ends in themselves (see pp. 168–70).

When the modern republican movement (the movement to replace monarchs with elected heads of state) arose as "the project of restoring a community of virtue" (p. 236), it understood and pursued virtue in a Roman, Stoic sense. Like the earlier Stoics, modern republicans were faced with conflicts between public and private goods with no way of adjudicating between them (see p. 170), and like the earlier Stoics, modern republicans demanded the pursuit of the common good before the private good. MacIntyre writes:

> What is central to that tradition *is* the notion of a public good which is prior to and characterizable independently of the summing of individual desires and interests. Virtue in the individual is nothing more or less than allowing the public good to provide the standard for individual behavior. The virtues are those dispositions which uphold that overriding allegiance. (pp. 236–7)

MacIntyre notes that the republican approach to virtue retrieves part of the classical tradition without depending on Aristotelian natural philosophy and without tying itself to Christian theologies of obedience to Church or king (p. 237).

MacIntyre presents the republican movement, and specifically the Jacobin Clubs of the French Revolution, on their own terms, as moral enterprises dedicated to egalitarianism, liberty, patriotism, and family life. MacIntyre rejects the claims of J. L. Talmon, Isaiah Berlin, Daniel Bell, and others that "this republican commitment to public virtue [was] the genesis of totalitarianism" and argues instead that "It was . . . the ways in which the commitment to virtue was institutionalized politically . . . which produced some at least of the consequences which they abhor" (p. 238). MacIntyre notes that the central purpose of the French Revolution, including the Reign of Terror, was to bring a new morality to the people of France. Totalitarianism proceeds from the "desperate expedient" of imposing a new morality through governmental coercion when those in power "already glimpse," but refuse to admit, that success in such an endeavor is utterly impossible (p. 238).

The failure of the Jacobin movement teaches us that it is impossible for a government to "re-invent" both the language and the demands of morality and to impose its reinvented morality on a whole nation for the sake of social progress. Is it also impossible for a government to "re-establish the virtues," by returning to the tradition? To answer this question, MacIntyre contrasts the careers of Cobbett and Austen: "Cobbett . . . crusaded to change society as a whole; Austen tried to discover enclaves for the life of the virtues within it" (p. 238).

Cobbett (1763–1835) was a politically active author and publisher whose writings cost him 2 years in prison (1809–1811) and 2 years in exile (1817–1819), although he was eventually elected to Parliament (1832). He is best remembered for his *History of the Prostestant Reformation in England and Ireland* (published serially 1824–1826), and *Rural Rides* (1830). E. P. Thompson, who influenced MacIntyre's Marxist work, used Cobbett's *Rural Rides* extensively in his book, *The Making of the English Working Class* (1966). Cobbett looked back into history to identify ideal circumstances for the development of virtue (although his list of virtues is modern), and he criticized the unjust social practices of his day, particularly usury (the taking of interest on loans).[54] Cobbett campaigned for parliamentary reform, and was an outspoken opponent of the Poor Law of 1834, which put poor relief in the hands of a bureaucracy, made confinement in workhouses a condition for public support, and demanded that living conditions in the workhouses be worse than those that people could achieve through the lowest-paying work. Cobbett had a public following, but his public efforts to renew the virtues through political action bore little lasting fruit.

Austen (1775–1817) was the daughter of an Anglican minister. She traveled little and lived a relatively quiet life with her family. Her moral writings took the form of novels about people living in her own time, seeking the happiness of virtuous lives, even in the

midst of the social challenges of her time. Austen's characters make
no attempt to change the world; instead, her heroines live their private lives virtuously even when their world makes that difficult.

For MacIntyre in 1981, Austen is "the last great representative of
the classical tradition of the virtues" and her writings "teach us to
observe . . . that both in her own time and afterwards the life of the
virtues is necessarily afforded a very restricted social and cultural
space" (p. 243). Contemporary social and cultural life honors the
modern virtues of obedience to law, not the Aristotelian virtues of
disciplined, prudent, and just action. Where the culture of the virtues
taught that the purpose of law is to make the members of the community good, modern liberal individualist culture restricts the purposes
of law according to Mill's "Principle of Liberty" or harm principle:

> That principle is, that the sole end for which mankind are
> warranted, individually or collectively, in interfering with the
> liberty of action of any of their number, is self-protection. That
> the only purpose for which power can be rightfully exercised
> over any member of a civilised community, against his will, is to
> prevent harm to others. His own good, either physical or moral,
> is not a sufficient warrant.[55]

The purpose of modern law is only to protect individual pursuits of
individual goods. The role of the harm principle in contemporary
legal reasoning rules out anything like a return to an Aristotelian
politics of civic friendship and public virtue.

If MacIntyre's task, like that of Cobbott or Austen, is to renew
the tradition of the virtues, then he must determine how to proceed.
MacIntyre's criticism of Cobbett and his praise for Austen fore-
shadow his preference for Austen's private approach. The discussion
of justice that follows in chapter seventeen will show why Cobbett's
public political work cannot serve as a model for MacIntyre's effort
to renew and preserve the culture of the virtues.

Chapter seventeen: Justice as a virtue: Changing conceptions

In chapter seventeen, MacIntyre argues that modern states "lack
the necessary basis for a political community" because they lack

"practical agreement on a conception of justice" (p. 244). MacIntyre supports this claim by comparing and contrasting the two leading conceptions of justice in contemporary political life, which he labels "A" and "B." "A," represented in theoretical literature by Robert Nozick, seeks the preservation of property and finds justice in respect for the inalienable rights of individuals. "B," represented by John Rawls, seeks to meet the needs of all people equally, and considers the redistribution of wealth to be an acceptable means toward this end. These two leading conceptions of justice in contemporary culture are incommensurable, and that alone might suffice to demonstrate our lack of "practical agreement on a conception of justice."

There is, however, a deeper problem in our contemporary notions of justice that comes into focus when we compare popular understandings of A and B, to the theories of Nozick and Rawls. Ordinary people explain A and B in terms of the things that people deserve: Ordinary A says he deserves what he has earned; Ordinary B says the poor do not deserve to suffer. This is a survival from the tradition of the virtues, but the notion of what a person deserves is entirely absent from the individualistic teachings of both Nozick and Rawls. MacIntyre argues that Nozick and Rawls rule out desert in two ways.

First, Nozick and Rawls rule out desert by defining justice in terms of the individual, rather than within the context of a political community. According to the tradition of the virtues, what a person deserves can be understood only in the context of a community, but communities have no place in the theories of Nozick and Rawls, who attempt to define justice for individuals prior to their involvement in any community. MacIntyre compares the individuals of Rawls and Nozick to shipwrecked strangers on some uninhabited island, "What have to be worked out are rules which will safeguard each one of us maximally in such a situation" (p. 250). Where justice in the tradition of the virtues helps to regulate the relationships of community members, modern justice helps to define the individual's position against the community. This criticism echoes Marx's critique of liberalism.[56]

Second, Nozick and Rawls rule out questions concerning what people deserve by refusing to examine history to determine the demands of justice. Rawls only looks to what people need; so history is not an issue for him. Nozick asserts that history supports his view of property rights, for "all legitimate entitlements can be traced to legitimate acts of original acquisition" (p. 251). History, MacIntyre reminds us, records very few "legitimate acts of original acquisition," in North America, the British Isles, and Prussia, where modern private land ownership began with arbitrary seizures, invasions, or enclosures of what had previously been foreign wilderness and common lands. This is precisely what is at issue in the Mashpee Wampanoag land suit that MacIntyre had discussed earlier in the book (p. 153).

When ordinary people argue that they deserve what they have earned or that the poor do not deserve to suffer, their appeal to desert echoes the tradition of the virtues. That tradition was still visible in the lives of certain marginalized religious communities when MacIntyre wrote AV, but even these communities had little choice but to adopt the moral language of modern liberal individualism in order to participate in political life. Tragically, in order to contribute to the rational deliberations of the larger society, such communities have traded the coherent moral and political language of the tradition of the virtues for the incoherence of liberal individualism, and they have done this to enter a political arena where moral consensus is increasingly impossible.[57]

The task of a government that rules a society that lacks moral consensus cannot be like an Aristotelian government that rules a community that shares a substantive understanding of its common good. In his summary of Aristotle's account of political friendship in chapter twelve, MacIntyre noted that an Aristotelian society would condemn actions that "destroy the bonds of community" (p. 151) and hold that "Civil war is the worst of all evils" (p. 157). Now MacIntyre argues that "Modern politics is civil war carried on by other means" (p. 253). Modern government is not the moral leadership of a people; it is only "a peacemaking or truce-keeping body" (p. 253). Modern laws do not have moral authority, rather, "Laws, whether civil or political, are expedients of policy to adjust the pretensions of the parties and to secure the peace of society."[58]

MacIntyre concludes that it is not possible to renew the tradition of the virtues through the political structures of the modern state. That renewal will have to be carried out within communities that still maintain the tradition of the virtues, and those communities will have to withstand pressures to assimilate themselves to the language and practices of contemporary politics. When those communities do engage modern political institutions to pursue their ends—and they will have no choice but to do so from time to time—they must be prepared to engage those institutions without being co-opted by them. Those who seek to renew the tradition of the virtues must reject "Modern systematic politics, whether liberal, conservative, radical, or socialist" because modern politics has rejected the tradition of the virtues (p. 255).

Chapter eighteen: *After Virtue*: Nietzsche *or* Aristotle, Trotsky *and* Saint Benedict

Chapter eighteen completes *AV* by doing two things. First, MacIntyre gives a new argument for the superiority of his Aristotelian action-centered approach to the tradition of the virtues over Nietzsche's rejection of morality. Second, MacIntyre brings the entire argument of *AV* to bear upon those who would defend Marxism against his critique.

In chapter nine, MacIntyre had accepted Nietzsche's critique of modern moralities of rules and proposed that the critical argument of chapters one through eight left us with a very real and, for many people, uncomfortable ultimatum: either Nietzsche was correct and all morality is ultimately arbitrary, or the modern rejection of the Aristotelian tradition of the virtues was mistaken, and there is something real about the demands of the virtues.

Now that MacIntyre has laid out his own account of the virtues, it is up to those who back Nietzsche's position to rebut it, but MacIntyre claims that they cannot succeed because "Nietzschean man, the *Übermensch*, the man who transcends . . . is wanting in respect of both relationships and activities" (p. 257). The role of the community in establishing goods and practices exposes the immorality of Nietzsche's *Übermensch*. He does not transcend; he simply fails to flourish as a human being. The *Übermensch* is just another moral fiction, and Nietzsche turns out to be one more representative of modern liberal individualism—the very moral framework that Nietzsche so ardently opposes (p. 259).

MacIntyre expected three groups to criticize his conclusion that Aristotelian ethics can be redeveloped through an account of human action, thereby avoiding the shortcomings of Aristotelian natural philosophy. The first critics would be "defenders of liberal individualism." These liberal individualists were likely to question

his notion of rationality. MacIntyre would answer their questions
in 1988 when he published *WJWR*.[59]

The second group of critics would be traditional Aristotelians and
Thomists. These scholars were certain to take exception to MacIntyre's
rejection of "Aristotle's metaphysical biology," his rejection of the unity
of the virtues, and MacIntyre's entirely social account of teleology.
MacIntyre promises to treat this as a dispute internal to contemporary
Aristotelianism. As he explained in the prologue to the third edition
of *AV* (p. xi), his understanding of the relationships between nature,
virtue, and metaphysics developed considerably after he became a
Thomist. These developments led to the publication of *DPR* (1999),
and shaped several of the essays collected in *Tasks* (2006), notably
First Principles, Final Ends, and Contemporary Philosophical Issues
(the 1990 Aquinas Lecture) and "Philosophy Recalled to its Tasks: A
Thomistic Reading of *Fides et Ratio*."

Marxists would make up the third group of critics, and
MacIntyre devotes the rest of the chapter to answering the questions he expected his former comrades to raise.

MacIntyre makes two general points in anticipation of the
Marxist critique of *AV*. First, Marxism is a form of modern liberal
individualism. There is evidence for this in Marxist history and literature, even in the writings of Marx, who writes about "a society
of free individuals."[60] MacIntyre calls that individual "a socialized
Robinson Crusoe" (p. 261), like the "shipwrecked" modern individuals of the previous chapter (p. 250).

The second general point is that even at their best, Marxists in
power become Weberians. Marxists in power become uncritical
bureaucrats justifying their authority on the basis of managerial
effectiveness rather than on any substantive evaluation of the quality of their acts,[61] and this in spite of the fact that Marxism presents
itself as "a peculiarly illuminating" "guide to practice" (p. 262).

MacIntyre presents the final writings of Leon Trotsky, one of the
most committed protagonists of Marxist socialism in the twentieth
century, to witness against the Marxist tradition, and concludes that
Marxists should take Trotsky seriously, and conclude, as Trotsky
himself would have had to conclude, that Marxism has failed:[62]

> For I too not only take it that Marxism is exhausted as a *political*
> tradition . . . but I believe that this exhaustion is shared by every
> other political tradition within our culture. (p. 262)

This is no cheap liberal or conservative critique of Marxism, it is an internal critique delivered by a man who had given nearly two decades of his life to the cause of Marxist politics.

In chapter sixteen, MacIntyre had presented Cobbett and Austen as two people who had tried to renew the tradition of the virtues. Cobbett had tried to renew the virtues in the public realm through political action, but the argument of chapter seventeen showed that recovering the tradition of the virtues through modern politics is impossible, because the two are fundamentally opposed to each other. If MacIntyre had proposed Cobbet's sort of public reform to his readers, then he would rightly have been accused of nostalgia. Anyone who follows Cobbet's path truly is committed to a quixotic enterprise. At the end of chapter eighteen, MacIntyre rejects the path of cultural renewal through political reform and embraces Austen's private alternative instead.

Austen recognized her world for what it was, criticized it, and adapted herself to its constraints. Austen's approach to virtue was neither nostalgic nor quixotic; it was thoroughly realistic. What MacIntyre proposes at the end of the chapter is modeled on the families and communities in Austen's stories. MacIntyre proposes the formation of local communities whose members join in the pursuit of common goods through practices. He proposes that the internal relationships of those communities can drive their members to develop the virtues. To look for a new Saint Benedict is to seek an architect for this new model of social life that will enable communities that embody the tradition of the virtues to flourish in the midst of a social and political culture that rejects that tradition.

Chapter nineteen: Postscript to the second edition

Many journals sought out established and respected scholars to review *AV*, and the quantity and quality of those early reviews testify to *AV*'s importance as a philosophical work. Given the implications of *AV* for the whole schools of thought that these reviewers represented, it was not surprising that many of them took issue with MacIntyre's argument. MacIntyre responded to a small number of his early critics in the "Postscript to the Second Edition"

(1984). He organized their concerns under three categories: "The Relationship of Philosophy to History" (pp. 265–72), "The Virtues and the Issue of Relativism" (pp. 272–8), and "The Relationship of Moral Philosophy to Theology" (p. 278).

"The Relationship of Philosophy to History" responds to analytic and historicist critiques of the book, and particularly to critiques from specialists in Hume and Kant. MacIntyre worked for many years in the field of analytic philosophy, which approaches philosophy as a study of the internal logic of arguments. There is a clear history to the discovery of the logic that analytic philosophers use, but that history plays no great role in analytic philosophers' application of that logic. Thus, the work of analytic philosophy has an ahistoric character that leaves its twentieth-century logical technicians equally qualified to comment on Anselm's ontological argument for the existence of God and John Locke's *Essay Concerning Human Understanding*. Analytic philosophy bears the brunt of MacIntyre's critique throughout *AV* as MacIntyre returns again and again to the theme that philosophy demands that we read and understand philosophical texts substantively on their own terms.

William Frankena, a leading analytic philosopher, complains that MacIntyre does not distinguish history from philosophy. MacIntyre responded to Frankena by questioning the appropriateness of that distinction. Philosophy happens in history, so where is the putative distinction to be drawn between philosophy and history? The dispute between MacIntyre and Frankena has to do with the nature of philosophy. Where Frankena sees philosophy as a discovery of timeless truths about logic and logical relationships among terms and propositions, MacIntyre sees philosophy as a tradition, bound in history, conditioned by history, which seeks timeless truth about the world and formulates its best approximations of that truth in theoretical narratives that cannot but be open to revision and improvement.

Annette Baier and Onora O'Neill question the quality of MacIntyre's history. They doubt that MacIntyre understands Hume (Baier) and Kant (O'Neill) on their own terms. MacIntyre acknowledges their concerns and agrees that he would have to answer their questions in order to establish the central claim of *AV* on its own terms.

Abraham Edel accuses MacIntyre of remaining an analytic philosopher and not enough of a social historian. MacIntyre uses his response to Edel to map out his own vision of the way the history of philosophy should be written.

The second section, "The Virtues and the Issue of Relativism," addresses the concerns of Samuel Scheffler, Stanley Hauerwas, Paul Wadell, and Robert Wachbroit, who questioned the determinateness of the virtues MacIntyre might derive from his historicist theory. MacIntyre restates his account of the virtues and their relationship to practices. He argues that excellence in practices can demand very specific kinds of virtues. In the end, he admits that what his theory offers is to be taken as "*the best theory* so far," and that this is the best that any philosophical theory can offer (p. 278).

The third section identifies some of the shortcomings of *AV*'s treatment of "The Relationship between Moral Philosophy and Theology," and ends with the admission that "After Virtue . . . ought to be read as a work still in progress" (p. 278). MacIntyre concludes by thanking his critics for their contributions.

Notes

1   Hobbes, *De Cive* (1642), chapter 8; *Leviathan* (1651), chapter 13; Locke, *Second Treatise Government* (1688), chapter 2; Rousseau, *Discourse on the Origin and the Foundations of Inequality among Men* (1755), part 1.

2   See Aristotle, *Politics*, 1.1 [1253a].

3   See MacIntyre, "ToF:RNT," in *MacReader*, pp. 223–34, at p. 223.

4   See "CNS," *The Monist* (1977), reprinted in *Tasks*.

5   These terms mean: αγαθός, agathos—good; αρετή, arête—excellent; κακός, kakos—bad, mean, ugly, ill-born, ignoble; κακία, kakia—badness, moral badness, cowardice, wickedness; καλόν, kalon—moral beauty, virtue; αἰσχρόν, aischron—shameful, disgraceful, base, wicked, vice.

6   Arthur W. H. Adkins, "Aristotle and the Best Kind of Tragedy," *The Classical Quarterly*, New Series, 16, no. 1 (May 1966): 78–102, at 79.

7   Ibid., p. 86.

8   Ibid., p. 87.

9   Plato, *Republic*, I (338c), quoted in *AV*, p. 139.

10   Compare Aristotle on this point to the "Emmas" of "CNS," in *Tasks*, p. 6.

11 Aristotle, *Nicomachean Ethics*, 2.1.

12 Ibid., 3.5 [1114a3–23].

13 Ibid., 1.13.

14 See Aristotle, *Physics* 2; *De Anima* 2; and *On the Generation of Animals* 1; see also prologue to the third edition of *AV*, pp. x–xi.

15 Aristotle, *Politics* 1 [1253a2].

16 To investigate the details of the land suit, the Mashpee Wampanoag museum recommends Jack Campisi, *The Mashpee Indians: Tribe on Trial* (Syracuse, NY: Syracuse University Press, 1991). For additional background on the Mashpee Tribe, see Lisa Brooks, *The Common Pot: The Recovery of Native Space in the Northeast* (Minneapolis: University of Michigan Press, 2008), pp. 163–218.

17 According to the National Association of Realtors, median sales price for single-family homes in the United States in June 2010 was $182,900 and the average price was $230,000. (http://www.realtor.org/wps/wcm/connect/30532f00474c16e380a08e0e6e9f088e/REL1105EHS.xls?MOD=AJPERES&CACHEID=30532f00474c16e380a08e0e6e9f088e, retrieved July 7, 2011). According to AOL Real Estate, the Average price of existing "homes" (type not specified) sold in Mashpee, Massachusetts, in June 2010 was $320,855, while the "average estimated value" of the 9,385 properties in Mashpee was $355,824 (slightly lower than the "$366,721" average estimated value of homes in Massachusetts), and the median value was $450,000 (http://realestate.aol.com/Mashpee-MA-real-estate, retrieved July 7, 2011). From the AOL Real Estate data, we can estimate the total value of Mashpee real estate to be $3,339,408,240.00 in June 2010.

18 A private land developer: http://www.newseabury.com

19 http://www.capecodonline.com/apps/pbcs.dll/article?AID=/20081023/NEWS/810230312, retrieved July 7, 2011.

20 http://www.thecrimson.com/article/1979/10/2/supreme-court-refuses-to-hear-mashpee/, retrieved July 7, 2011.

21 The Indian gaming industry developed after the Supreme Court of the United States ruled in *Bryan v. Itasca County*, 426 U.S. 373 (1976) that state and local government could not regulate behavior on Indian reservations. This industry was placed under the authority of the National Indian Gaming Commission after the passage of the *Indian Gaming Regulatory Act of 1988*.

22 See Aquinas, *Summa Theologiae*, I–II, question 65, article 1.

23 See Kant, *Critique of Pure Reason*, A 802/B830 (animal vs free will); *Foundations of the Metaphysics of Morals*, pp. 399–401 (duty vs inclination), and pp. 432–4 (third formulation of the categorical imperative).

24 Ibid., p. 156; See Thomas Hobbes, *De Cive*, p. 8, and *Levianthan*,
    p. 14; Locke, *Second Treatise of Government*, p. 8; and Rousseau,
    Discourse on the Origin and Foundation of Inequality among Men,
    and *The Social Contract*.

25 See Aristotle, *Nicomachean Ethics*, 2.6 [1107a10–15].

26 See *WJWR*, p. x; *E&P*, p. ix; "Moral Dilemmas," in *E&P*, pp.
    85–100. MacIntyre does not list this among the developments of his
    reading of Aristotle in *AV*, 3rd edn, pp. x–xi.

27 "The story of the thief on the cross," which MacIntyre mentions on
    page 175 refers to "the good thief" of Lk. 23: 39–43. For MacIntyre
    in *AV*, the problem with viewing salvation as an end external to
    the virtuous life is that it threatens to separate practical from moral
    reasoning. In terms of the definitions that come in chapters 14 and
    15, it would make salvation an "external good," a good that could be
    achieved by other means. This is a complicated theological issue for
    Christians, since Christians believe that salvation cannot be *achieved*
    by any means, and that to believe that it could be achieved by human
    action is at the heart of the Pelagian heresy that Augustine rejected
    in the fifth century (see Augustine, *On Nature and Grace*, in *The
    Fathers of the Church: Saint Augustine—Four Anti-Pelagian Writings*
    (Washington, DC: Catholic University of America Press, 1992). It
    therefore should be noted that philosophical ethics must confine
    itself to a discussion of human action in pursuit of the good, while it
    remains to theology to discuss the dynamics of human relationships
    with God.

28 For Augustine's treatment of a question like this one, see *On the Free
    Choice of the Will*, book 1, chapter 1. When Augustine rejected the
    metaphysical dualism of Manichaeism, he developed a metaphysics
    rooted in Neo-Platonism, which sees God as the source of all being,
    and treats evil as a privation of being, rather than as a being in
    itself. Thomas Aquinas's *Disputed Questions on Evil* (*De Malo*)
    summarizes the main tenets of the privative notion of evil in its two
    opening articles: "Whether Evil Is Something" and "Whether Evil
    Exists in Good."

29 Alasdair MacIntyre, "Moral Dilemmas," *Philosophy and
    Phenomenological Research* 50 supplement (Fall 1990): 369–82;
    reprinted in *E&P*, pp. 85–100.

30 The main lines of MacIntyre's critique follow Peter Geach, *The
    Virtues* (Cambridge University Press, 1977), pp. xxxi, 164–5. Geach's
    argument responds to poor neo-scholastic interpretations of Thomas
    Aquinas, rather than to Thomas Aquinas himself. For MacIntyre's
    subsequent assessments of Neo-Thomism, see *God, Philosophy,
    Universities: A Selective History of the Catholic Philosophical*

Tradition (Lanham, MD: Rowman and Littlefield, 2009), pp. 151–63; and *3RV*, pp. 105–48.

31 See Knight, "A Revolutionary Arsitotelianism," in *Aristotelian Philosophy*, pp. 102–221.

32 Bricklaying can be construed to name the basic work of laying bricks in straight, even, courses, or it can name the complex art of the brick mason. Readers familiar with the work of talented brick masons often bristle at the notion that it is not a practice, but this is a mistake. Such brick masons participate in the practice of architecture, along with other skilled construction workers, engineers, and architects.

33 Walter Camp (1859–1925) is called "the Father of American Football."

34 Knute Rockne (1888–1931) coached the Fighting Irish of the University of Notre Dame from 1918 to 1930.

35 See John Rawls, *A Theory of Justice* (Cambridge, MA: Belknap Press of Harvard University Press, 1971).

36 Christopher Stephen Lutz, *TEAM*, pp. 98–104.

37 Alasdair MacIntyre, "Social Structures and Their Threats to Moral Agency," *Philosophy* 74 (1999): pp. 245–57; reprinted in *E&P*, chapter 11, pp. 186–204.

38 *E&P*, pp. 196–202.

39 Alasdair MacIntyre, "Utilitarianism and Cost Benefit Analysis," in Kenneth Sayre, ed., *Values in the Electric Power Industry* (Notre Dame, IN: University of Notre Dame Press, 1977), pp. 217–37.

40 *E&P*, p. 196.

41 *AV*, p. 205.

42 "CNS" (1977), in *Tasks*, p. 5.

43 *AV*, p. 218.

44 In his subsequent book *DPR*, MacIntyre caused some controversy by asserting that animals have beliefs (pp. 37–9), but that argument is to be seen as a continuation of this one; beliefs, even indeterminate ones, are essential to MacIntyre's account of teleological action.

45 MacIntyre makes this more explicit in his rejection of the ideological use of tradition at *AV*, pp. 221–22.

46 Jean-Jacques Rousseau (1712–1778), the author of *Discourse on the Origin and Foundation of Inequality among Men* (1755), and *The Social Contract* (1762), had a strong influence on the French Revolution. *The Declaration of the Rights of Man and Citizen* (*Déclaration des droits de l'Homme et du Citoyen*) was approved by the National Assembly of France on August 26, 1789, establishing the principles for the French Revolution that followed.

47 John Locke, the theorist/ideologue of the Whig political party, published *Two Treatises of Government* in 1688 to justify the acts

of Parliament that had deposed King James II, and called William
of Orange and Mary Stuart to reign as king and queen. The *First
Treatise* refutes Robert Filmer's argument for "the absolute divine
right of kings." The *Second Treatise* asserts that human society begins
with the defense of private property, argues that the purpose of
government is to defend private property, and concludes that citizens
retain the right to depose a government that threatens their property,
in much the same way that they retain the right to kill a highwayman.

48 See Locke, *Two Treatises of Government* (1688), especially the
    Second Treatise.

49 Peter McMylor points out MacIntyre's debt to Michael Polanyi
    on this point in "Moral Philosophy and Economic Sociology:
    What MacIntyre Learnt from Polanyi," *International Review of
    Sociology—Revue Internationale de Sociologie* 13, no. 2 (2004):
    393–407; see also Peter McMylor, *Alasdair MacIntyre: Critic of
    Modernity* (New York: Routledge, 1994).

50 Chapter 16 lists the three characters from chapter 3 (p. 30) and the
    fourth comes from the prologue to the 3rd edn (p. xv).

51 By declaring that there is more to the conditions that create the
    characters of emotivism than economics, MacIntyre implicitly
    criticizes Marxism. In "Socialism: Utopian and Scientific," Frederick
    Engels declared "that the economic structure of society always
    furnishes the real basis, starting from which we can alone work out
    the ultimate explanation of the whole superstructure of juridical
    and political institutions as well as of the religious, philosophical,
    and other ideas of a given historical period" (section II, http://www.
    marxists.org/archive/marx/works/1880/soc-utop/ch02.htm, retrieved
    May 5, 2011). If the explanation of the characters of the culture of
    emotivism is not reducible to economics, Engels and all those who
    agree with him are wrong.

52 Aquinas, *Summa Theologiae*, I–II, question 91, article 2. It is
    important to note that for Aquinas, the natural law is "in us"
    (*in nobis aliqua lex naturalis*), "as in something that is ruled and
    measured" (*sicut in regulato et mensurato*), and that it is "nothing
    else an imprint on us of the divine light" (*nihil aliud sit quam
    impressio divini luminis in nobis*).

53 Aquinas, *Summa Theologiae*, I–II, question 94, article 2.

54 Cobbett recounts the role that institutionalized debt and usury played
    in the Glorious Revolution of 1688 in "Letter XIV" of *A History of
    the Protestant Reformation in England and Ireland*.

55 John Stuart Mill, *On Liberty*, chapter 1, in Stefan Collini, ed., *On
    Liberty and Other Writings* (Cambridge: Cambridge University Press,
    1989), p. 13.

56 Compare to Marx, *On the Jewish Question, Deutsch-Französische Jahrbücher* (February 1844). Marx's essay was a critical response to Bruno Bauer, "The Jewish Question" (1843).

57 There are notable examples of Catholic writers embracing rights language in the latter half of the twentieth century. Jacques Maritain supported the use of rights language in Catholic social teaching and contributed to the UN Declaration on Human Rights, John Courtney Murray, S. J. spoke about the compatibility of US Constitutional thought and Catholic teaching in *We Hold These Truths* (Kansas City, MO: Sheed and Ward, 1960; republished and repaginated, Lanham, MD: Rowman and Littlefield Publishers, Inc, 2005). The Second Vatican Council's *Dignitatis Humanae*, "declares that the human person has a right to religious freedom" (p. 2).

58 Adam Ferguson, *Principles of Moral and Political Science ii*, p. 144, quoted in *AV*, pp. 253–4.

59 For a study of MacIntyre's account of rationality, see Lutz, *TEAM*, paperback edition with new preface.

60 Marx, *Capital*, chapter 1, quoted in *AV*, p. 261.

61 See MacIntyre's treatment of Weber above, in chapters 3, 6, 7, and 9.

62 MacIntyre discusses Trotsky's assessment of Soviet socialism in detail in the essay "Trotsky in Exile" Encounter (December 1963), reprinted in *Against the Self-Images of the Age*, pp. 52–9.

6
Commentary on the constructive argument

Moral philosophy or ethics is in every case a guide to conduct, but conduct can be understood in two very different ways, as behavior or as action. Human conduct may be regarded as human behavior, as external acts considered apart from their purposes. Alternatively, one may view human conduct as human action, as free acts of the will that include decisions that lead to external acts. Human acts are largely internal events, and they are unintelligible if they are considered apart from their purposes. Aristotelian ethics is a study of rational human action. Modern moral philosophy is a search for criteria to determine correct human behavior.

In the first half of *AV*, MacIntyre examined and rejected not only the theories of modern moral philosophy, but also the individualism on which those theories were built. Now in the second half of the book, MacIntyre examines the notion of excellence in rational human agency and considers the role that our choices and actions play in making ourselves effective as rational human agents. What emerges is the opposite of the isolated individual of Hobbes's[1] and Rousseau's[2] states of nature. For MacIntyre, the human agent is naturally social, enters the world as a member of a community, and owes debts and exercises rights as a member of that community. This community member becomes excellent as a human agent, and lives the good life for humankind by cultivating virtue and seeking the good within human relationships.[3]

[margin note, top: Liberal moral philosophy is about knowing & doing what we ought]

[margin note, left: re the rules were to thwart human desire]

[margin note: to do via universal demands vs doing]

The purpose of the constructive argument of *AV* is to present free and deliberate human action as the central concern of moral philosophy. Modern moral and political philosophy, the philosophy of Kant, Mill, Prichard, Moore, Hare, and Rawls would tell us how we, as free people, can know what we ought to do, in spite of whatever we might want. Their theories ignore human goals and focus on the universal demands of morality. MacIntyre rejected all of those modern theories in the first half of the book as moral fictions. What MacIntyre proposes in the second half of the book is that we make sense of the demands of morality only by viewing those demands in terms of the conditions that support the human pursuit of human goals.[4]

[margin note, right: what we want w/ AV moral demands flow from the human pursuit of certain goals / Why can't the liberal order itself be a societal goal?]

In the Aristotelian tradition, "the subject matter of moral philosophy is human action."[5] Aristotle distinguishes voluntary and involuntary actions in the *Nicomachean Ethics*,[6] Aquinas examines the same distinction in the *Summa Theologiae*,[7] as does Anscombe in her little book, *Intention*. Knight's *Aristotelian Philosophy* traces the study of action from Aristotle to MacIntyre and identifies Aristotelian philosophy not with its metaphysics, but with its theory of action.

Historically, however, Aristotelian philosophy was identified with its metaphysics and abandoned with its metaphysics. For Aristotle and Aquinas, virtue is excellence according to "nature,"[8] and by "nature," they meant metaphysical form.[9] So MacIntyre's non-metaphysical account of the virtues in *AV* stirred controversy among Aristotelians from the beginning. Some Aristotelians and Thomists found its "historicist defense" (p. 277) of the Aristotelian account of the virtues incoherent and relativistic.

Other philosophers also took issue with MacIntyre's conclusions. Some Marxists found MacIntyre's critique of Marxism and his lack of a specific political program pessimistic, even despairing.[10] Some believed that MacIntyre's interest in tradition and the tradition of the virtues was little more than nostalgia for some imaginary golden age.[11] These controversies first appeared in scholarly reviews of *AV* and they have lingered in the secondary literature ever since.

The commentary in this chapter will first address the strengths and weaknesses of MacIntyre's effort to discover the virtues through an account of human action. Then it will take up these three claims against *AV*: that its so-called Aristotelianism is incoherent and relativistic, that its retreat into private life is pessimistic, and that its interest in tradition is falsely nostalgic.

Action and practice as the subject matter of ethics

The moral fictions MacIntyre exposed in the critical argument had been created to justify rules—or to authorize managers to make rules. The purpose of those rules was to thwart human desire and direct human behavior either to perform right actions or to serve the goals of an institution or state. What exposed the arbitrariness of those moral fictions was their failure to explain the establishment and maintenance of those rules in terms of human action, human ends, and human purposes. In place of those moral fictions, the constructive argument offers an account of the conditions that support human agency. For MacIntyre, virtue is excellence in human agency.

MacIntyre's virtuous agent is a protagonist in history; like Jane Austen, the virtuous agent refuses to conform to debasing social customs; like Aquinas, the virtuous agent seeks to transcend the conventional and the traditional and to struggle for progress in the pursuit of truth. Where conventional modern moral philosophy thwarted human desire, MacIntyre holds that virtue enables agents to educate their desires so that they may pursue their goals more effectively. Where behaviorist social scientists sought a causal understanding of human behavior, MacIntyre seeks to understand the choices that inform human actions. MacIntyre's agent becomes virtuous by learning to recognize what is good and best to do and by developing moral habits that allow her or him to follow through on good judgments, even when doing so demands difficult choices and the rejection of dominant ways of thinking. This standing, striving, struggling agent is an active protagonist, not a passive victim, in history.

The development of practices in MacIntyre's work

AV is the most important text for understanding MacIntyre's agency–based account of virtue, but some other short works help to clarify MacIntyre's project. The first is "NMW."[12] The second is

"Freedom and Revolution" (1960). The "MacIntyre and Marxism" chapter already introduced these essays to show MacIntyre's general debts to and criticisms of Marxism; we are now ready to return to these articles to illuminate MacIntyre's notion of a practice.

MacIntyre summarized the problem facing him in 1958 in the opening sentence of "NMW": "A position which we are all tempted into is that of moral critic of Stalinism."[13] MacIntyre saw the moral criticism of Stalinism as a temptation, rather than as an imperative, because he lacked the conceptual resources to justify that condemnation. MacIntyre accepted Marx's materialism and Marx's critique of human rights, along with contemporary critiques of modern moral philosophy. Marx had denounced human rights as inventions that severed the ties that held communities together. Others could complain that Stalinism had trampled human rights, but the Marxist MacIntyre could not use those terms. Stalin and Stalinists had done terrible things, but to say that their policies violated rules, one must first explain why those rules should be, or even *could be,* moral absolutes. Where are they written? What authority do they have?

MacIntyre found it troubling that some Marxists were willing to invoke modern liberal moral principles to condemn Stalinism. Modern liberal individualism asserts individual moral autonomy by founding morality upon individual choice. The individual choice at the root of liberal ethics is precisely what robs it of any authority. MacIntyre writes: "His 'I ought' is the most tremulous of modern utterances. For it represents nothing but his own choice."[14] This individual choice appears to have no more authority than any other arbitrary preference; so MacIntyre rejects it in 1958, just as he had rejected it in 1951,[15] and as he would continue to reject it in the critical argument of *AV.*

In 1958, MacIntyre believed that Marxism promised the best course to discover an authoritative moral critique of Stalinism. Unlike the liberal, MacIntyre writes, "The Marxist sees himself as discovering [his values]."[16] Where liberalism takes as its starting point the autonomy of the individual before the demands of society, Marxism takes as its starting point the solidarity of the people before the challenges of the world. In 1958, MacIntyre believed that the Marxist approach to the discovery of values would enable him to develop "a theory which treats what emerges in history as providing us with a basis for our standards."[17] This new theory would look to practice to establish, "a Marxist morality."[18] MacIntyre's Marxist morality would take history seriously, affirm human action as the subject matter of ethics, and explain moral absolutes objectively: "As against the Stalinist it is an assertion of moral absolutes; as against the liberal critic of Stalinism it is an assertion of desire and of history."[19]

MacIntyre's 1960 essay "Freedom and Revolution" is a meditation on the notion of freedom. It does not focus on political freedom from coercive government, but on moral freedom to judge and act. "To say that men are free," writes MacIntyre, "is to say that they are able to make their desires, intentions and choices effective."[20] Freedom is to be understood as freedom to act effectively.

Freedom to act effectively is not a merely formal condition; it is a real human ability, and it builds upon other abilities and achievements. Freedom requires knowledge—wisdom—about the kinds of activities that can satisfy human desire, and this demands that human agents learn such things from others. MacIntyre writes:

> Moreover, to know what will really satisfy one, one has to rely on the decisions that other men have made throughout history. And the discovery of the kind of life that will satisfy is the discovery of the kind of life in which fundamental desires, intentions, and choices are made most effective, in which man is most agent and least victim.[21]

For the MacIntyre of 1960, freedom is not just lack of constraint. It is the positive ability, informed by substantive knowledge, to seek and to do what is good and best.

The isolated individual who is left to seek the good life alone is a person adrift. That isolated individual is every bit as unlikely to succeed in the Herculean task of finding the good life as the citizen of a tyrannical collectivist state, whose freedom of agency is smothered by the forced conformism of governmental power. Thus, MacIntyre rejects the tendency to discuss freedom only in the political terms of the tension between individualism and collectivism. Instead, he turns his focus to the conditions of, and impediments to, effective human agency.

Because the individual exists in his social relations and because the collective is a society of individuals, the problem of freedom is

[Handwritten marginalia: "Freedom = Freedom to act effectively on your desires, intentions & choices i.e. to undertake activities that through knowledge you have of relating w/ satisfy human desire"; "& it requires others"; "The isolated individual"]

not the problem of the individual against society but the problem of what sort of society we want and what sort of individuals we want to be. Then unfreedom consists in everything which stands in the way of this.[22]

For MacIntyre, external constraint is not the only thing that hinders free agency, lack of constraint may also impede human agency and reduce human freedom if it hinders moral formation.

Freedom, thus defined, needs to learn from history. What emerges in history that MacIntyre proposes as a basis for moral absolutes is the revolutionary practice that Marx had spoken of in the third thesis on Feuerbach,[23] but Marx himself never developed his account of practice into a moral philosophy; this task was reserved, it seems, for MacIntyre.[24] Two decades after the "NMW" and "Freedom and Revolution," MacIntyre published *AV*, and he tells us in its preface that this book embodies the conclusions to the project that he had announced in those essays (pp. ix–x, third edition, pp. xvii–xviii).

What MacIntyre calls the tradition of the virtues is the approach to morality that finds excellence in human agency, the highest achievement of human freedom and good judgment, to be tied to certain habits of desiring, choosing, and acting. According to this tradition, human nature determines what these habits are, and having them makes a person morally good. Developing these habits is an essential goal in the good life, and enables us to contribute more effectively to the common good. These habits build on the more limited freedom that is natural to us, and so we are to be praised for our choices to pursue the virtues and blamed when we act against them.

The tradition of the virtues was rejected in one way by fourteenth-century Nominalist moral theologians who insisted that there is nothing to morality except the arbitrary decree of God.[25] The tradition of the virtues was rejected in another way by Protestant and Jansenist theologians whose theological determinism denied that human action contributed in any way to the salvation of one's soul. The tradition of the virtues was rejected in a third way by modern philosophers who denied that there is any real goal for human action, who reduced the pursuit of personal happiness to egoism, and who taught us to find moral value in actions that are contrary to our desires. The tradition of the virtues was rejected in a fourth way by philosophers like Baron d'Holbach and social scientists, including Auguste Comte, whose material determinism rejected the notion of moral freedom, and who sought to discover the causes of human behavior in environmental, biological, and developmental influences.

These rejections of the tradition of the virtues—theological, philosophical, and social scientific—appear to undermine the entire notion of natural morality, natural justice, or natural virtue. Yet, even as they appear to overturn the tradition of the virtues, their own theological, philosophical, and social scientific projects fail on their own terms. If it was right to reject the tradition of the virtues, and it has also proven impossible to provide a rational explanation of moral rules without the virtues, then it seems that Nietzsche was correct: There is nothing to moral judgments but the imposition of one person's will upon another's. If this is so, then morality is ultimately irrational. The only real difference between the atheist moral philosophy of Nietzsche and Christian moral theology of the divine command theorists is the latter's theism. Nihilism and Fideism are two sides of the same irrational coin.

If Nominalist Christian moral theologians were right to reject the tradition of the virtues and if Nietzsche was right to recognize the centrality of the will in modern ethics, then moral philosophy is simply an empty pursuit, unless it is reduced to the historical task of providing its own postmortem. The only philosophical alternative to Nietzsche is to return to the tradition of the virtues, if that can be justified.

If a return to the tradition of the virtues can be warranted, we must be ready to show that Aristotle is correct in his belief that the pursuit of virtue is choice-worthy. If Aristotle is correct on this one point, it is because striving effectively for human goals demands that we develop our habits of judgment and action so that we gain and keep both the intellectual wisdom to recognize what is good and best and the qualities of character that can free us to act on those judgments.

MacIntyre does not build his case for Aristotle by turning back the clock. He does not ask his readers to try to understand the world as Aristotle imagined it. He does not demand in *AV* that we return to Aristotle's biology and metaphysics and define virtue in terms of the perfection of human nature.

MacIntyre builds his case for Aristotle by taking up the language of the present and moving forward. He presents a history of ethics that emphasizes the historicity of classical notions of virtue. In chapter fourteen, "The Nature of the Virtues," MacIntyre argues that "a unitary core concept of the virtues," drawn from reflection on historical notions of excellence, must proceed through three levels: first, the concrete experience of the demands of a practice; second, "the narrative order of a whole human life"; and third, "a moral tradition" (pp. 186–7). To examine the three-level definition of virtue more carefully, it is necessary to return to four passages already quoted in the summary.

The foundation for this approach is MacIntyre's notion of a practice:

> By a "practice" I am going to mean any coherent and complex form of socially established cooperative human activity through which goods internal to that form of activity are realized in the course of trying to achieve those standards of excellence which are appropriate to and partially definitive of, that form of activity, with the result that human powers to achieve excellence and human conceptions of the ends and good involved, are systematically extended. (p. 187)

A practice is a complex social activity that stands on its own. Practices enable us to get certain goods. Practices have goals and standards that have been identified through the progress of the practice.

Practices pursue internal goods. Just as "going for a walk" has a good internal to it that is only frustrated if one decides to quit, practices have internal goods that can be attained only by participating in the practice in a committed way. Practices can also help a person to attain external goods, but the pursuits of external goods do not always demand excellence in the practice. Just as the person who decides to walk to the store loses nothing by accepting a ride from a friend, those who use a practice only to gain wealth or notoriety lose nothing if they find a different way to reach their goal. Consider two examples:

Medicine is a practice that includes the whole body of arts and sciences dealing with the healing, health, and maintenance of the human body. The practice of medicine includes all the disciplines that support the delivery of its internal good, namely, health care. Those who work in health care who are committed to excellence may seek better treatments, less invasive surgeries, and more effective therapies for their patients. When they succeed, the practice as a whole improves.

Medicine has standards, and those standards change when new discoveries lead to new treatments, or changes in technology enable medical professionals to imagine new ways to approach their work. Consider the changes in surgery between 1862 and 2012. Today's surgeons maintain sterile fields around incisions, treat infections with antibiotics, repair traumatic injuries to limbs, perform open-heart surgery, and transplant organs to replace failed kidneys, hearts, and lungs. The best military surgeons of the US Civil War routinely amputated limbs in crude battlefield hospitals with unsterilized instruments and washed their hands only after surgery to remove the blood. These physicians of the 1860s could not have imagined the remarkable innovations that would fill the following century. But those innovations have since become standard practice. The intervening 150 years have seen great progress in medical procedures and that progress has changed the way that medical practitioners understand the ends and goals of their practice.

Motor vehicle manufacturing is also a practice. Its internal goods involve the production of safe, efficient, comfortable cars, trucks, and buses to transport people and goods. In little more than a century, this practice has progressed from the modification of wooden buggies, carriages, and wagons to the engineering of vehicles that can travel 200,000 miles with very little maintenance.

In the last 50 years alone, progress in automotive engineering has made automobiles remarkably safer. In 2009, the Insurance Institute for Highway Safety celebrated its role in this progress with a 40-mile-per-hour, frontal offset crash test between a 1959 Chevrolet Bel Air and a 2009 Chevrolet Malibu.[26] Video of the test showed the Malibu absorbing the energy of the collision in its engineered crumple zones as it plowed through the decorative fenders of the Bel Air and shattered the Bel Air's passenger compartment. The progress demonstrated in that short video came about because people who wanted to make crashes more survivable sought innovative ways to make cars safer and raised the standards of excellence in their practice with each incremental success.

Not every form of cooperative activity is a practice. "Bricklaying" MacIntyre controversially asserted, "is not a practice; architecture is" (p. 187). Bricklaying does not stand on its own. If we see someone laying bricks, and ask, "What are you doing?" "I am laying bricks" is not a sufficient answer. The art of bricklaying is indeed quite complex, but it belongs to the practice of architecture; it might be better to think of highly skilled brick masons as highly specialized architects. To put it in a slightly different way, bricklaying does not have its own internal goods; the purpose of bricklaying is to build structures, but there are always other ways to build the same structures; bricklaying promotes the goods internal to the practice of architecture.

Practices have four distinctive characteristics: (1) People pursue the practice because they want to, because it addresses some need or desire that they have by providing certain goods. (2) A practice has internal goods. There are things that can be gained only through participation in the practice, and it is the pursuit of these internal goods that leads to true excellence in the practice. People may also use the practice well or badly to pursue other goods, like wealth, power, or honor, which are external to the practice. (3) A practice has standards of excellence that develop along with the practice. (4) The success of a practice depends upon the moral character of its practitioners.

MacIntyre illustrates the relationship between success and moral character with the example of the chess-playing child (p. 188). As long as the child is interested only in candy, the child has every reason to cheat in the game of chess. Cheating is likely to help the child to get more candy, so the child's pursuit of the external good of candy endangers the adult's efforts to teach the game of chess to the child. But if the child ever decides that he really does want to learn to play chess well, cheating becomes counterproductive, whether it yields more candy or not. When the child realizes that he can learn more by losing well than by cheating, he begins to pursue the internal goods of the game of chess. Seeking the skills one gains by playing chess well replaces the pursuit of candy as the child's main motivation in playing the game. It may take considerable moral strength to overcome the temptation to cheat in some instances, so the child will need to develop that strength in order to achieve the ends that the child has set.

Practices require institutions to support them. "Chess, physics and medicine are practices; chess clubs, laboratories, universities and hospitals are institutions" (p. 194). The institutions supporting the practice of medicine include government regulatory agencies, professional medical associations, hospitals, religious organizations, and for-profit agencies. There is always a potential for tension between the standards of a given practice and the demands of the institutions that sustain it. Concerns about costs or profitability might impinge upon the practice of medicine or automobile manufacturing.[27] The political ideology of a regulatory body may put it at odds with the policies of a professional organization. In such cases, it is up to the practitioners to maintain the practice against these threats, to continue to pursue the goods internal to the practice, and to "resist the corrupting power of institutions," and for this, they will need the virtues (p. 194).

MacIntyre introduced the notion of a practice in order to offer a definition of virtue in three stages. The first stage of MacIntyre's three-part definition of virtue focuses on the role of the virtues in enabling agents to pursue excellence in practices:

> A virtue is an acquired human quality the possession of which tends to enable us to achieve those goods which are internal to practices and the lack of which effectively prevents us from achieving any such goods. (p. 191)

The success of a practice depends on the moral character of its practitioners. This first definition reconnects desire and morality by showing how the virtues are related to our pursuits of our goals. But this definition is insufficient.

A more complete definition of the virtues needs to show how they are related to our personal goals. What if the chess-playing child is hungry one day? Will his resolution to play for the internal goods overcome his desire for extra candy? How will his experience with this temptation affect his choices as an adult to respect the demands of human relationships when the risks and rewards for infidelity might be much greater? The qualities of character that we want to study and to inculcate are the habits that prepare us to persevere in the face of adversity. This brings us to MacIntyre's second definition of virtue:

> The virtues . . . are to be understood as those dispositions which will not only sustain practices and enable us to achieve the goods internal to practices, but which will also sustain us in the relevant kind of quest for the good, by enabling us to overcome the harms, dangers, temptations, and distractions which we encounter, and which will furnish us with increasing self-knowledge and increasing knowledge of the good. (p. 219)

The habits of judgment and action that we seek to develop are habits that will enable us to stay in the fight and continue our quest, even when things become difficult and we are tempted to find some easy way out. But this definition, too, is insufficient, because it does not address my broader goal as a human person. Why not abandon the quest?

We maintain our quests because of relationships and responsibilities that define our place in the social fabric through the communities and traditions that form us. This brings MacIntyre to the third phase of his definition of virtue:

> The virtues find their point and purpose not only in sustaining those relationships necessary if the variety of goods internal to practices are to be achieved and not only in sustaining the form of an individual life in which that individual may seek out his or her good as the good of his or her whole life, but also in sustaining those traditions which provide both practices and individual lives with their necessary historical context. (p. 123)

Tradition in this context is not to be taken as any arbitrary set of beliefs, but as the setting, in terms of human relationships and social debts, that partially defines the agent. By tying virtue to the achievement of human goals, the advancement of practices, the development of individuals, and the contribution of the individual to the life of the community, MacIntyre has offered his readers a way to reconnect ethics and desire without atavism, without turning back the clock to the metaphysics of Aristotle.

Nearly everything of any value that people do is either a practice or a part of a practice. Communication is a practice. Journalism is a practice. Government is a practice. Farming is a practice. Health care is a practice. Manufacturing is a practice. Marriage is a practice. Living in society is a practice. If we need the virtues to do well in practices, then morality and moral action cannot belong to an isolated part of human life. Human life is a profoundly moral enterprise, in which the judgments we make and the actions we take can have lasting effects on our own lives and the lives of others.

Two problems: The unity of virtue and evil practices

The constructive argument has two inconsistencies—MacIntyre has called one of them an error—that remain out of phase with the rest of MacIntyre's project. The first is MacIntyre's rejection of the unity of virtue (pp. 179–80, 199–200). The second is MacIntyre's allowance that there might be evil practices (pp. 199–200). The two are so closely related that MacIntyre's recantation of the first error in the preface to *WJWR*[28] implicitly corrects both of them. Both the errors and MacIntyre's response to them bear investigation.

The goal of the constructive argument is to derive the virtues from the conditions that support excellence in human agency, so that we might discover criteria that could justify the moral condemnation of Stalinism, or any other form of injustice. How are the virtues to be defined?

One may define the virtues either formally or substantively. Defining them substantively involves taking a stand on the content of the virtues, a move that MacIntyre wants to avoid. He has good reason to avoid imposing the content of the virtues: Determining the content of the virtues might appear arbitrary, so that MacIntyre's virtues would have to join the catalog of moral fictions dismissed in the first half of the book.[29]

MacIntyre chose instead to define the virtues formally or procedurally: We will find out what the virtues are when we find out what enables people to pursue excellence in practices, to pursue the good of their whole lives, and to make good on the responsibilities that come to them through their communities. Discovering the virtues through this procedural definition presupposes the unity of the virtues that MacIntyre explicitly adopts in chapter twelve (p. 154). But it is incompatible with the equally explicit rejection of the Thomistic unity of the virtues in chapter thirteen (p. 179). What is the unity of the virtues, and how do the rejection of the unity of the virtues and the notion of evil practices undermine MacIntyre's procedural definition?

The unity of the virtues is a doctrine developed in the scholastic tradition concerning the connections between the four cardinal virtues: Prudence, Justice, Fortitude, and Temperance. It has to do with the difference between knowing what is good and acting to achieve that good. According to the doctrine of the unity of the virtues, prudence without the moral virtues would be incapable of action, while the moral virtues without prudence would lose their substantive content.

Aristotle defines prudence or practical wisdom as "a true and reasoned state of capacity to act with regard to the things that are good or bad for man" and "a reasoned and true state of capacity to act with regard to human goods."[30] Aristotle's prudence is not only the ability to recognize what is good, it is also the capacity to act according to that judgment. But in order to act when doing so demands that one stand up against danger or set aside pleasures, one needs the virtues of justice, fortitude, and temperance. Without those virtues, the agent might fall to weakness, having known what was best to do, but having failed to do it. The agent might be repentant, yet remain no better prepared to overcome similar challenges in the future.[31]

Aristotle defines the moral virtues in terms of our ability to act on the kind of judgment that a wise person would make:

> We may thus conclude that virtue or excellence is a characteristic involving choice, and that it consists in observing the mean relative to us, a mean which is defined by a rational principle, such as a man of practical wisdom would use to determine it.[32]

The person who has practical wisdom is able to judge what is appropriate to a given person, and the person who is virtuous is able to make the same kinds of determinations for herself or himself.

For Aristotle, any substantive explanation of courage or temperance depends on the kinds of judgments that come from the intellectual virtue of practical wisdom. Aristotle explains this in the *Nicomachean Ethics* by distinguishing five false forms of courage displayed by soldiers who appear to be brave.[33] All of Aristotle's falsely courageous soldiers do brave things, but in each case, something is missing. The first, the conscript, is motivated by fear, rather than standing against fear. The second, the mercenary, feels no fear because he knows the limits of the danger he faces. The third—a raging soldier bent on revenge—acts irrationally, and thus not virtuously. The fourth, the sanguine person, fails to acknowledge the danger he faces because he is used to winning, and the fifth, the ignorant person, simply does not understand the danger that awaits him. All of them do brave things, but none of them chooses to stand his ground in battle for the sake of honor knowing that his life is at risk;[34] thus, in none of these cases do those brave things flow from the virtue of courage. Brave deeds without knowledge, foresight, free choice, and settled character directed toward the good are not virtuous deeds in the Aristotelian sense of the term.

We should not confuse the classical virtue of courage with looser notions of courage like the one Kant mentions in the first section of *The Foundations of the Metaphysics of Morals.* Kant lists several qualities analogous to the classical virtues—"intelligence, wit, judgment, . . . courage, resoluteness, and perseverance"—but Kant does not call these things excellences or virtues; he describes them as "qualities of temperament" and asserts:

> they can become extremely bad and harmful if the will, which is to make use of these gifts of nature and which in its special constitution is called character, is not good.[35]

What Kant writes in this passage supports the unity of virtue. Aquinas, would be compelled to agree with Kant that prudence, courage, and temperance are incomplete without justice, the virtue of the will. But Kant gives name of courage to a quality of temperament that falls far short of the Aristotelian or Thomistic notion of a virtue.

For Aquinas, the unity of virtue is not an arbitrary dogma; it is a conclusion drawn from observations about the kind of excellence in human agency that makes a person a good candidate for the leadership and management of a community. Excellence in human agency demands at least three distinct kinds of excellence: (1) foresight and good judgment about fitting means to ends, (2) a settled and habituated commitment to give to others what is due to them, and (3) mastery over our passions so that we can follow our best judgment and give to others their due, even when it demands sacrifice on our part. Aquinas presents this unity in terms of the Aristotelian psychology of the powers of the soul, but the unity of the virtues remains quite plausible even if we find it necessary to separate it from that psychology.

The unity of the virtues may, in fact, be more plausible when it is separated from Aristotelian psychology than when it remains embedded in the powers of the soul. Peter Geach, for example, defends the interconnection of the virtues in his 1977 book *The Virtues*, but rejects what he takes to be Aquinas's all-or-nothing interpretation of the unity of the virtues.[36] Geach argues that Thomas was wrong to hold the thesis of the unity of virtue,[37] but defends the thesis that there is "No courage, then, without the other moral virtues: in particular, no courage without prudence."[38] This is the book that MacIntyre cites when he rejects the unity of the virtues in *AV* (p. 179), arguing that the courageous Nazi must have true courage, since there would be no need to retrain the Nazi in courage as part of his moral reeducation (p. 180).

The problem with *AV*'s rejection of Aquinas's unity of the virtues along with Geach's interconnection of the virtues is that it makes it impossible to specify what kinds of actions could be described as "virtuous" in any objective manner. Standing one's ground, for whatever reason, whether just or unjust, whether prudent or foolish, could be considered virtuous, in the absence of the unity of virtue, so long as the agent considered it to be something that merited standing one's ground. Cowardice, courage, and rash foolishness would have to be distinguished either subjectively or arbitrarily, and the other virtues would become similarly amorphous, confirming Kant's judgment that such "qualities of temperament . . . can become extremely bad and harmful" without good will.

If we are to recover the virtues by examining the requirements of excellence in human agency, then it seems that we will need to speak of the virtues as something more substantive than Kant's "qualities of temperament." If we are to approach what Aquinas presents as the conventional thirteenth-century definition of an acquired moral virtue, "a good quality of the mind by which we live righteously, of which no one can make bad use,"[39] then it seems that the interconnection of the virtues must be maintained. Maintaining the unity of the virtues is not arbitrary, it is compatible with a formal approach to the conditions that support excellence in human agency, for it amounts to recognizing the interrelatedness of these qualities of excellent agents: these qualities of character include a demonstrated, habituated commitment to justice, a demonstrated ability to judge well, and mastery over temptations to pleasure and the avoidance of pain that might hinder one from acting on one's judgments.

The second mistake in *AV* that threatens the effort to recover the virtues through a study of agency is MacIntyre's allowance that there might be evil practices:

> I want to allow that there *may* be practices—in the sense in which I understand the concept—which simply *are* evil. I am far from convinced that there are, and I do not in fact believe that either torture or sadomasochistic sexuality answer to the description of a practice which my account of the virtues employs. But I do not want to rest my case on this lack of conviction. (p. 200)

MacIntyre does not contend that there are evil practices; he only allows that there may be such practices. MacIntyre presents this as evidence of the insufficiency of a definition of virtue in terms of practices alone, and then he moves on to the second and third parts of the definition of virtue, in terms of the narrative unity of a whole human life and the connection of individual agents to traditions. The possibility of evil practices remains a problem, however, because it suggests that it may be possible to develop excellence in human agency, at least initially, through evil action, and through participation in fundamentally evil enterprises.

There are at least two good reasons to reject the notion of an evil practice. The first has to do with the notion of evil, and the second has to do with the relationship between practices and goods.

First, it is possible to conceive of an evil practice only if the notion of evil employed is a voluntarist or arbitrary one. Aristotle distinguished good and evil in terms of natural desire:

> There being three objects of choice and three of avoidance, the noble, the advantageous, the pleasant, and their contraries, the base, the injurious, the painful, about all of these the good man tends to go right and the bad man to go wrong.[40]

For Aristotle, good and evil are practical, and moral formation requires the development of practical judgment, so that one can distinguish the noble, the advantageous, and the pleasant from the base, the injurious, and the painful, and understand when to choose what is noble or useful, even when it is painful, over base or injurious pleasure.

From this perspective, it appears that an evil practice would pursue ends that are either injurious or base, and it is difficult to imagine how an injurious practice or a base practice could fulfill the requirements of MacIntyre's definition of a practice:

> By a "practice" I am going to mean any coherent and complex form of socially established cooperative human activity through which goods internal to that form of activity are realized in the course of trying to achieve those standards of excellence which are appropriate to, and partially constitutive of, that form of activity, with the result that human powers to achieve excellence, and human conceptions of the ends and goods involved, are systematically extended. (p. 187)

Practices are forms of activity that draw people together into shared enterprises that help to develop the character of the agents involved, as those same agents contribute to the development of the practice. It is difficult to imagine base or injurious practices that could contribute to social life in these ways.

There are evil activities that may seem like practices, but these evil pseudo-practices cannot have internal goods,[41] and engaging in them is more likely to harm than to develop one's character and one's abilities as an independent practical reasoner.[42] If any practice that fits the criteria of MacIntyre's definition is to be counted evil, then the notion of evil employed must be an arbitrary one, and if this were the case, we would have to look to the will of some lawgiver, and not to the conditions of human agency to determine the content for the virtues and the foundation for ethics.

MacIntyre's allowance, in AV, that some genuine practices might be evil seems to be connected to his rejection on the unity of the virtues. His subsequent acceptance of the unity of the virtues[43] and his related rejection of true moral dilemmas[44] seem to take away with them any grounds to maintain the allowance for evil practices. If it is possible to discover the conditions for excellence in human agency through practices, then that excellence has to be integral, and those practices will have to be good. MacIntyre's subsequent development of his account of the virtues, particularly in his *DPR*, corrects *AV* implicitly on both of these points.

Aristotle without metaphysics?

In chapter twelve of *AV*, MacIntyre rejects "Aristotle's metaphysical biology" even though he admits on the same page that "Aristotle's ethics, expounded as he expounds it, presupposes his metaphysical biology" (p. 148). There can be no question that Aristotle's account of virtue presupposed his metaphysical account of the soul as the form of the body. Aristotle defines the human good as "activity of soul in accordance with virtue, and if there are more than one virtue, in accordance with the best and most complete."[45] Aristotle distinguishes the virtues in the *Nicomachean Ethics* according to the powers of the soul that he had distinguished in *De Anima*,[46] and he concludes that the highest human virtues are those that serve the rational principle of the soul.[47] Given that Aristotle presupposed the metaphysics of nature in his account of virtue, it seems strange to many of MacIntyre's readers that he claims we can recover anything like Aristotle's account of virtue without recovering his account of nature.

MacIntyre argues that we can discover the Aristotelian virtues through practices, through the unifying narratives of whole human lives, and through traditions. MacIntyre says that this is possible because Aristotle's approach to the virtues has two components: a theory of practice and a theory of metaphysics, or as Knight has described it, "the ethical image" and "its theoretical projector."[48] Rather than tying the explanation of human excellence to a fixed metaphysical conception of human nature, as Aristotle had done, MacIntyre was satisfied in *AV* to define virtue in terms of the ability of human agents to pursue the kinds of goods that we take to be worthy of pursuit, so that

> the good life for man is the life spent in seeking the good life for man, and the virtues necessary for the seeking are those which will enable us to understand what more and what else the good life for man is. (p. 219)

This leads to a question: if the notion of virtue, expounded as MacIntyre expounds it, does not presuppose Aristotle's metaphysics, then is it really Aristotle's notion of virtue? What is the issue here? We may come to understand the problems involved by considering the roles of metaphysics and practice in the thought of Aristotle, Aquinas, and MacIntyre.

Metaphysics and practice in Aristotelian philosophy

The core theory of the Aristotelian research program in natural philosophy is teleology, the notion that natural substances are attracted to determinate ends. For Aristotle, teleology explains why grass seeds grow into grass plants, why acorns grow into oaks, and why tadpoles mature into frogs. The natures of the grass, the oak, and the frog are present from the beginnings of their lives; these natures or forms make these substances what they are, and direct their development through maturity. Similarly, teleology explains why "All men naturally desire knowledge,"[49] and why human excellence is identified with intellectual and moral virtue. As the natures of plants and brute animals direct their development toward maturity, so does human nature direct us not only to develop physically, but also to pursue knowledge and practical wisdom. To speak of Aristotelian teleology is to speak of the natural substance, composed of matter and form. Aristotle's form is present within the substance, so Aristotle's substance is not a participation of some transcendent form, but a real and independent instantiation of that form in the material world.[50] For Aristotle, teleology and metaphysics go hand in hand, for it takes metaphysics to account for what he takes to be our experience of teleology in nature and in human action.

Aristotle approaches teleology in another way, however, in his ethics, when he considers how a person develops moral virtue. For although Aristotle uses metaphysics to explain the causal mechanism behind teleology, he does not attempt to use it to provide a moral epistemology. Knowledge of justice and virtuous action does not flow from one's form or from knowledge of metaphysics, but from the activity of moral formation.

The origin of virtue in the activity of moral formation is the central theme of *Nicomachean Ethics*, book 2. Aristotle begins by declaring that the moral virtues do not arise by nature but through training:

> Neither by nature, then, nor contrary to nature do the virtues arise in us; rather we are adapted by nature to receive them, and are made perfect by habit.[51]

Knowledge of virtue arises through training, and acting virtuously is not reducible to adherence to a transcendent code of universal moral norms, rather it amounts to acting and choosing as the *sophron*, the wise person, would act and choose:

> Virtue, then, is a state of character concerned with choice, lying in a mean, i.e. the mean relative to us, this being determined by a rational principle, and by that principle by which the man of practical wisdom would determine it.[52]

Aristotle defines virtue in relation to the *sophron* because goodness is not only difficult to achieve, it is difficult to describe. Consequently, Aristotle's efforts to describe virtue and virtuous action always have a certain approximation to them, and even though Aristotle does specify a few universal moral norms,[53] the text leaves most of the questions about what is right or wrong to those who are in a position to advise us about appropriate actions in particular circumstances:

> Hence it is no easy task to be good. For in everything it is no easy task to find the middle . . . anyone can get angry—that is easy—or give or spend money; but to do this to the right person, to the right extent, at the right time, with the right motive, and in the right way, *that* is not for everyone, nor is it easy; wherefore goodness is both rare and laudable and noble.[54]

The content of Aristotle's ethics lacks anything like Plato's ascent to the world of the forms.[55] Aristotle's human agents learn what is virtuous from other human agents, whose understanding may be more or less adequate, and whose virtue may be more or less complete, so that the understood content of virtuous agency remains open to both development and corruption within the life of any given community.

Aristotle may explain teleology through metaphysics, but the agent's understanding of the demands of that teleology develops through reflection on human action. Aristotle never pretends to use metaphysics to offer us an adequate guide to morals; he never transforms it into a moral epistemology. The research program of Aquinas differs from Aristotle's in some important respects; Aquinas agrees with Aristotle on these two counts: metaphysics explains the causes of teleology, but metaphysics does not provide a moral epistemology.

The core teaching in Aquinas's research program is not a philosophical theory at all; it is the Christian doctrine of creation.[56] Aquinas takes up Aristotelian categories and Aristotelian physical theories, but finds them inadequate until they are combined with the Christian Neo-Platonic worldview that had developed through the Augustinian tradition. This changes the character of Aquinas's Aristotelianism considerably. For Aquinas, teleology in the human person is intrinsic; we have a natural desire for God, but the natural law in us is a participation of the Eternal Law in the Divine Intellect, and thus an extrinsic principle of action.[57] For Aquinas, the intellectual and moral virtues are to be understood in terms of the perfection of the Aristotelian powers of the soul,[58] but the moral virtues are also to be understood in terms of greater participation in the exemplar Ideas of the virtues in the mind of God.[59] Thus, Aristotle's virtues, the habituated excellences of Aristotle's *Nicomachean Ethics,* are reduced to true but imperfect images of the virtues infused by the Holy Spirit along with the theological virtues of faith, hope, and charity in Aquinas's *Summa Theologiae.*[60]

The metaphysical doctrine of creation explains the sources of teleology and describes the activity of God in creation; it even addresses the sources of knowledge of real moral norms, but it does not provide a moral epistemology, for knowledge of Thomas's metaphysical theory does not yield a thoroughgoing knowledge of good and evil action, nor does it provide the basis for a procedure to guide moral judgment.

We may gain a clearer picture of the limits that Aquinas places on natural moral knowledge if we compare two statements about the natural law in the *Summa Theologiae.* The first is I–II, question 100, article 1, "Whether the moral precepts of the Old Law

belong to the Law of Nature." The question is whether or not
the hundreds of moral commandments promulgated in the Old
Testament could be derived from natural reason. The three objections deny that the moral precepts of the divine law could be
derived from natural reason since (1) "the law of nature is not
learnt but instilled by natural instinct," (2) it seems that the divine
law should add to the law of nature, and (3) the divine law commands things that are "above nature." Thomas, however, affirms
the rational basis of the moral precepts of the Old Testament
divine law.

After distinguishing between matters that can be known by
most people, matters that can be understood only by the wise, and
matters that God alone understands, Thomas concludes:

> It is therefore evident that since the moral precepts are about
> matters which concern good morals; and since good morals
> are those which are in accord with reason; and since also every
> judgment of human reason must needs be derived in some way
> from natural reason; it follows, of necessity, that all the moral
> precepts belong to the law of nature; but not all in the same
> way. For there are certain things which the natural reason of
> every man, of its own accord and at once, judges to be done
> or not to be done; eg., *Honor thy father and thy mother,* and,
> *Thou shalt not kill, Thou shalt not steal;* and these belong to the
> law of nature absolutely.—And there are certain things which,
> after a more careful consideration, wise men deem obligatory.
> Such belong to the law of nature, yet so that they need to be
> inculcated, the wiser teaching the less wise: *e.g., Rise up before
> the hoary head, and honor the person of the aged man,* and the
> like.—And there are some things, to judge of which, human
> reason needs Divine instruction, whereby we are taught about
> the things of God: *e.g., thou shalt not make to thyself a graven
> thing, nor the likeness of anything; Thou shalt not take the name
> of the Lord thy God in vain.*[61]

Thomas's response allows that human reason may recognize what
is right and wrong in many cases, yet by asserting the absolute
limits of human reason, and the relative limits of the wise and the
unwise, Thomas implies that rational knowledge cannot yield any
fully adequate moral epistemology.

Given the claim that there are commands "which the natural reason of every man, of its own accord and at once, judges to be done or not to be done" like "thou shalt not steal," it might seem that Thomas is laying some foundation for at least a partial moral epistemology, but his earlier statements about universal knowledge of the natural law undermine that claim:

> But as to certain matters of detail, which are conclusions, as it were, from those general principles [of the natural law] it is the same for all in the majority of cases . . . and yet in some few cases it may fail, both as to rectitude . . . and as to knowledge, since in some the reason is perverted by passion, or evil habit, or an evil disposition of nature; thus formerly, theft, although it is expressly contrary to the natural law, was not considered wrong among the Germans, as Julius Caesar relates.[62]

Comparing the German and Gallic cultures in the sixth book of the *Gallic Wars*, Caesar writes:

> Acts of brigandage committed outside the borders of each several state involve no disgrace; in fact, they affirm that such are committed in order to practice the young men and to diminish sloth.[63]

If Aquinas accepts that it was possible for the whole German culture of the first-century BC to make such a broad exception to the law against theft, it follows that however broadly possible natural knowledge of the demands of the law may seem in principle, in practice, he finds such knowledge no easier to grasp than Aristotle did. Aquinas's human agents, like Aristotle's, learn the specifics of what is virtuous from other human agents, whose understanding may be more or less adequate, whose virtue may be more or less complete, and whose worldviews are shaped by the specific traditions that they inherit. Thus Thomas, like Aristotle, allows that the *humanly understood* content of virtuous agency remains open to both development and corruption within the life of any given community, even though he maintains that the truth of the virtues is to be measured by their divine exemplars.[64]

The conclusion that Thomas provides a metaphysical explanation of human teleology without a moral epistemology is confirmed by this treatment of subjectivity in human action in *Summa Theologiae*, I–II, question 19. In this question, "Of the Goodness and Malice of the Interior Act of the Will," Aquinas argues that it is the "understood good," the *"bonus intellectus"*—the choice-worthiness of the action, in its concrete circumstances, as understood by the agent—that stands before the will as an object of choice.[65] For this reason, Thomas holds that the erring conscience binds, that when one must act, one must act according to one's subjective grasp of the good or evil of the action.[66] Yet, Thomas holds that the erring conscience does not always excuse, since one may be morally responsible for one's misapprehension of the good or evil of the act in question.[67]

For Aquinas, the true measure of human action is not the natural law in us (our apprehension of which can be distorted), but the Eternal Law in the Divine Intellect. Yet, our natural knowledge of the Eternal Law is partial at best.[68] So it seems that our apprehension of the natural law in us depends in large measure on the moral character of the communities that form us, that is, it depends on practice, self-understanding and life-goals, traditions, and institutions.

MacIntyre advances what he takes to be an Aristotelian research program in *AV*, and the core of that program is human action or human agency. Human agents act for ends and purposes; we do so in order to achieve; we struggle in order to overcome. Describing the rationality of human action in "NMW" (1958), MacIntyre wrote, "we make both individual deeds and social practices intelligible by showing how they connect with characteristically human desires, needs, and the like."[69] Human agency, thus understood, stands in stark contrast to human behavior, as theorized in the social sciences, which is to be described "in a vocabulary which omits all reference to intentions, purposes, and reasons for action" (p. 83). MacIntyre's account of human action also stands against so much of modern ethics, which separates desire from morality, so that "The 'ought' of morality is utterly divorced from the 'is' of desire."[70] Two central goals of the project announced in "NMW," and continued through *AV*, were to show the inadequacy of behaviorist descriptions of human activity, and to show that the demands of morality were tied to the goals of human action. When MacIntyre praised Leon Trotsky in "Breaking the Chains of Reason" (1960), he praised him precisely in terms of his support for action and agency; he praised Trotsky for "providing throughout his life a defense of human activity, the powers of conscious and rational human effort."[71]

MacIntyre's concern for human activity and for the conditions that support conscious and rational human effort has remained a central theme in his ethical and political work throughout his career.[72] The eighth chapter of DPR (1999), for example, asks "How do we become independent practical reasoners?"[73] and MacIntyre answers by examining moral development. Similarly, the essay "Social Structures and Their Threats to Moral Agency" (written in 1999 and republished in E&P in 2006) considers the ways that social norms can fracture practical reasoning and undermine the relationships and commitments that support justice in human agency.[74] For MacIntyre, the virtues are just those qualities of character that support human agency and make us better and more effective practical reasoners and human agents, and they are to be discovered and identified by examining the conditions in which human agents act.

All three of these Aristotelian research programs—Aristotle's, Aquinas's, and MacIntyre's—are teleological, but they account for that teleology in different ways. Aristotle is concerned with human agents as self-contained, teleologically ordered substances, as people whose ultimate happiness is a life of intellectual and moral virtue in keeping with their nature. Aquinas is concerned with human agents as created substances whose excellences are to be understood Neo-Platonically as participations in a divine exemplar, as creatures whose virtues perfect the powers of their souls. MacIntyre is concerned with human agents as "dependent rational animals" who develop a capacity for rational deliberation and sharpen their ability for teleologically directed human agency through a "partial . . . transformation . . . of our first animal nature."[75]

When he wrote AV, MacIntyre was not willing to propose a metaphysical explanation for teleology. Instead, MacIntyre concerned himself only with evidence about human action drawn from experience and offered us only the "provisional conclusion" that "the good life for man is the life spent in seeking for the good life for man" (p. 219). Where Aristotle seeks an explanation of teleology in the metaphysics of substances composed of matter and form, and Aquinas draws Aristotle's metaphysical theory into his own understanding of human beings as creatures made in the image and likeness of God, MacIntyre's *AV* simply prescinds from the metaphysical question altogether. *AV* studies the phenomena of teleology in intentional actions and social practices, whole human lives, traditions, and institutions. In short, unlike his predecessors who experienced teleology in the interactions of human agents in society, and offered metaphysical explanations for it, the teleology of MacIntyre's *AV* is socially discovered, but remains metaphysically unexplained.

MacIntyre had good reason to refuse to explain his Aristotelian account of virtue using Aristotle's metaphysics. And since he "was not yet a Thomist" (third edition, p. x), he had even less reason to consider Aquinas's synthesis of Aristotle's metaphysics of substance and the Christian Neo-Platonist metaphysics of the exemplar Ideas in the Divine Intellect. MacIntyre was writing as a twentieth-century philosopher schooled in modern science, and he was well aware of the shortcomings of Aristotle's natural philosophy, and of the theological nature of Thomas's doctrine of creation.

The teleology of the substances at the heart of Aristotle's research program comes from forms, which are active, immaterial, and immutable. In *Physics* 2.8, Aristotle explains that evolution is impossible because the form gives the final cause that guides the development of each animal. In *On the Generation of Animals* 1.22, Aristotle explains how the nature or form of the male parent imparts its activity to the matter provided by the female parent by means of the semen. It may be possible to draw some analogies between these Aristotelian teachings and current science, but the differences are more important than the similarities.

Modern science has discovered that the formal principle imparted by the semen is material; and it delivers only one half of the chromosomes for the offspring; the mother provides the rest, so that both parents make a formal contribution to their combined offspring. Genes are material, and therefore mutable; and their mutation can bring about evolutionary changes. Scientists who have learned to control genetic changes in plant and animal chromosomes have established a new industry of genetic engineering.

Aristotle was a man of his time, and his time was 350 BC. While it is possible to respect the wisdom that Aristotle showed

[handwritten marginalia: conceive being as a compound of matter & form]

on many issues in the *Nicomachean Ethics* and the *Politics*, it is impossible to rehabilitate the hylomorphism of Aristotle's *Physics* on its own terms, especially after we see that theory worked out in practice in *On the Generation of Animals*. Aristotle's metaphysical biology is false, and we can say that it is false on scientific grounds because its central thesis, that form or nature is immutable and immaterial, is falsified by the evidence of evolution and by the experience of successful, deliberate, heritable modifications of plant genomes.

Aquinas is not engaged in a scientific research program; and it would stretch the meaning of the term to call his work a philosophical research program. Aquinas is a theologian. As Anton Pegis wrote, "St. Thomas 'was not a theologian *and a philosopher*, he was a theologian *even in philosophy*.'"[76] So, what can we say about Aquinas's work as a theological research program? Philosophically, we cannot say very much. When philosophers explicate the work of Aquinas, we work historically, laying out Thomas's sources and Thomas's arguments, so that our students and readers can understand Aquinas on his own terms. When Thomists turn to the practice of philosophy, however, we must proceed with caution, following Aquinas's own counsel,[77] for the practice of philosophy demands the rational justification of every premise and every conclusion, and many of Thomas's philosophical claims cannot be adequately defended within contemporary secular philosophy, because they presuppose faith in God as a rational Creator. Where Aristotle was a man of his time, Aquinas was a man both of his time and of his faith.

Writing as a secular philosopher in the late twentieth century, MacIntyre was not prepared to explain teleology either in terms of a falsified natural philosophy or a peculiar theological doctrine of creation that he did not accept. The teleology of *AV* is "social" rather than metaphysical, and this led some of MacIntyre's critics to question whether it is possible for someone who accepts MacIntyre's account of virtue to avoid relativism. This relativist question, raised in one way by Thomists who view metaphysics as the key to Thomistic moral epistemology, and in another by relativists who want to undermine MacIntyre's attempt to transcend the personal preferences of the culture of emotivism, has followed MacIntyre for more than 30 years.

Relativism?

Moral relativism is the position that objective truth in moral matters is an empty category because truth claims about virtue, appropriateness, right, and justice always depend on some limited view of the world. From the relativist perspective, anyone who commits herself or himself to the religious, moral, and political claims of a particular tradition only reveals a provincial preference for the familiar or unquestioning complacence with the status quo. When philosophers attempt to overcome the challenge of relativism, they usually try to do so by arguing from some new viewpoint that, from their point of view, transcends perspective and tradition. MacIntyre completely rejects this approach. What is the alternative?

One of MacIntyre's best short responses to the relativist challenge is his 1984 Presidential Address to the Eastern Division Meeting of the American Philosophical Association, "Relativism, Power, and Philosophy" ("RP&Ph").[78] In this essay, MacIntyre presents relativism as the point of view of a person who experiences a clash between two contrary worldviews that speak different languages. He gives two examples of this kind of clash: the Zuni people of sixteenth-century New Mexico and the Irish people of seventeenth-century *Doire*, whose town was renamed Londonderry by the English in 1613.

At the initial stage of this kind of clash of cultures, everyone on each side speaks her or his own language, judges according to the standards of her or his own language community, and imagines the world in terms of the canonical texts of her or his own language tradition. As time goes on, the communities learn to translate their languages. But the trivial "phrasebook" translations that develop in the early stages of a clash of cultures will have limits; they may translate nouns and verbs, but they will not be able to translate the conflicting elements of the contrary worldviews expressed in the languages of the contending parties that justify the kinds of judgments that organize the lives of each community.[79] As long as each language remains strange to the other, relativism fails to become a problem.

Relativism becomes a problem only in the case of a person who really comprehends two or more conflicting traditions:

For our imagined person who has the abilities to understand both, but who must choose to inhabit only one, the nature of the choice is bound, if he or she is adequately reflective, to transform his or her understanding of truth and of rational justification.[80]

Relativism becomes a problem for this person because she or he can justify her or his judgments according to either worldview; the problem now is to justify the choice of one worldview over the other. As long as "our imagined person" is unable to justify that choice, she or he will remain locked in relativism.

There seem to be two ways to respond to relativism. Either a person or community may choose to impose their opinions on people they cannot convince[81] or they may seek "impersonal standards of judgment, neutral between competing claims."[82] To seek neutral standards, one would begin by learning a third, neutral language that could speak objectively and neutrally about the contending communities.[83] This neutral language would comprehend every culture and collect every culture's literature,[84] and in the process, it would only exacerbate the problem of relativism for its speakers:

> The culture that is able to make such a language available is so only because it is a culture offering for the relevant kinds of controversial subject matter, all too many heterogeneous and incompatible schemes of rational justification. And every attempt to advance sufficient reasons for choosing any one such scheme over its rivals must always presuppose the prior adoption of that scheme itself or of some other.[85]

This artificially neutral culture faces the problem of relativism no more effectively than the imaginary person who spoke two languages. Each inhabitant of this artificially neutral culture is committed either to one of the partisan standpoints that it comprehends or to the neutral standpoint that comprehends them all. MacIntyre concludes: "Relativism after all turns out to be so far immune to refutation, even by us," even by the inhabitants of the modern English-speaking academic culture.[86]

MacIntyre holds that we will not overcome relativism by learning to judge rival claims from an objective neutral standpoint, yet he claims that the kinds of questions that tend to yield relativism can be answered rationally. How? Relativism begins when an isolated individual finds it necessary to choose a way to judge, to choose a worldview with all the standards that flow from that worldview, while the criteria for that choice can only come from within some given worldview. Rational engagement with the questions that lead others to relativism begins when a person joins a community that investigates those questions according to its own tradition, language, and standards.

Philosophical work done within the context of a tradition aims to understand the world, and to the extent that its theories fail to comprehend the world, those theories raise questions for the practitioners of that tradition. We cannot overcome relativism by treating competing conceptual schemes as self-enclosed language games and comparing them formally from a neutral perspective. MacIntyre holds that we can overcome the temptation to relativism only by interrogating alien conceptual schemes by the standards of our own, and allowing them to raise questions for us.

> Rationality, understood within some particular tradition with its own specific conceptual scheme and problematic, as it always has been and will be, nonetheless requires *qua* rationality a recognition that the rational inadequacies of that tradition from its own point of view . . . may at any time prove to be such that perhaps only the resources provided by some other quite alien tradition . . . will enable us to identify and to understand the limitations of our own tradition; and this provision may require that we transfer our allegiance to that hitherto alien tradition.[87]

The criterion of truth is not some metaphysical principle, but the world itself. It is by testing our theories against the world that we may discover which of them are more truthful, which are more inadequate, and which only seemed truthful from an inadequate point of view.

In short, MacIntyre treats sincere relativism as a kind of "Buridan's ass" problem. Buridan's ass starves to death because it cannot choose between two equally attractive alternatives. MacIntyre's relativist fails to make progress because she or he cannot decide which tradition or conceptual scheme to adopt. In either case, the only solution is to test one of the alternatives.

The approach MacIntyre advises in "RP&Ph" is the approach MacIntyre drew from the philosophy of science[88] and used throughout *AV*. The constructive argument of *AV* does not appeal to a metaphysical account of human nature or a theological account of the natural law. It only appeals to the kinds of questions that people are able to ask about their own experience, and metaphysicians and theologians should recognize this as one of the book's greatest strengths. For if the truth about the world is metaphysical and theological, then we should expect the questions that MacIntyre asks about modern moral theories, human agency, and virtue to yield the kinds of answers he defends.

Nostalgia?

Some readers of *AV* complained that MacIntyre was nostalgic for a fictional past. And his critics renewed this complaint after MacIntyre embraced the Thomistic tradition in the argument of *WJWR*.[89] One of the the strongest condemnations of *AV*'s supposed nostalgia came in Martha Nussbaum's review of *WJWR*, in which she accuses MacIntyre of longing "nostalgically for a unanimity that human life has never really had."[90] MacIntyre attributes this criticism to "careless misreading" in the prologue to the third edition of *AV* (third edition, p xi), but the claim remains.

There are three reasons why the nostalgia complaint seems plausible. First, MacIntyre argues in *AV* that the culture of modern liberal individualism lacks the kind of shared conceptual scheme or tradition that would allow us, as a culture, to settle social questions about morality and justice. Second, MacIntyre speaks of the Aristotelian tradition of the virtues as an alternative to modern moral philosophy and modern management. Third, MacIntyre argues that virtues cannot be fully defined without appeal to tradition. For MacIntyre, these three senses of tradition are distinct elements of an approach to philosophy that respects "the situatedness of all enquiry" (third edition, p. xii). For MacIntyre's critics to transform these elements into nostalgia, it seems necessary to misread them in fairly specific ways.

First, when MacIntyre argues that modern culture lacks a shared conceptual scheme, the critic who sees this as evidence of nostalgia must infer that MacIntyre imagines a time when "our culture" or "our tradition" or "the tradition" did have a shared conceptual scheme. It seems plausible that if he is complaining that we no longer have something, there must have been a time when "we," or some predecessor of ours, did. Yet, there is nothing in the text that supports this inference.

In the history of virtue that covers chapters ten through thirteen, MacIntyre emphasizes the disagreements and debates that characterized each period he presents. Each heroic community had a shared conceptual scheme of sorts, but the agreements of each were essentially local (pp. 126–7). Classical Athens saw conflicts between sophists, Platonists, Aristotelians, and tragedians (p. 135). Medieval Europe was still largely pagan, and many of its communities still celebrated the heroic virtues (p. 172), and Aquinas was "an unexpectedly marginal figure" (p. 178). Even the shared conceptual scheme that prevailed among the elite that led the kingdoms and local churches of medieval Christendom had collapsed by the time that Henry VIII executed Thomas More (1535) (p. 173). While MacIntyre does argue that public debates about moral and political issues are difficult in the contemporary world because we lack a shared conceptual scheme, it does not follow that any society as diverse as that of the modern world ever has had such a thing. Even the comparatively homogeneous communities of classical Athens and medieval Europe saw considerable disputes over these matters. What does follow is that moving forward as a society will demand that we question our own conceptual schemes, and there is nothing nostalgic about that.

Second, to construct the nostalgia critique, it is necessary to conflate what MacIntyre calls the Aristotelian tradition of the virtues, with "Aristotelian virtues" or "traditional virtues," or to identify the tradition of the virtues with traditional morality. This, too, is unsupported by the text. For MacIntyre in *AV*, the Aristotelian tradition of the virtues is nothing more than the Aristotelian research program of the virtues, which finds the habituation of desire and judgment essential to a life of effective rational agency. MacIntyre says little in *AV* about the kinds of actions that a virtuous person would pursue or avoid, and leaves those questions to his readers. So here, too, there is nothing particularly nostalgic.

Third, when MacIntyre speaks of "tradition" as part of the social setting for human action (p. 220), the critic of his supposed nostalgia takes this as the embrace of an uncritical and conservative traditionalism. This, too, would be a mistake. In the examples MacIntyre cites in this passage, the relationships between African Americans and the United States, between Ireland and England, and between Germany and the Jews, MacIntyre insists that past injustices, all of them sanctioned by cultural traditions, form an ineliminable component of the relationships between the heirs of the oppressed and the heirs of their oppressors. The virtues defined through the constructive argument would demand the criticism of the oppressive practices that shaped these inheritances and the unjust cultural traditions that had sanctioned them. Coming to terms with the evils of one's parents and ancestors is neither comforting nor nostalgic, it is difficult and forward looking, transformative work.

Pessimism?

AV does not propose any political program to advance the tradition of the virtues. Instead, it councils its readers to abandon "systematic politics" (p. 255) and to promote the life of the virtues within the context of small communities, as we live through "the new dark ages which are already upon us" (p. 263). Some commentators have rejected the conclusion of *AV* as a gloomy and pessimistic, passive expression of defeat. But that interpretation misses the point.[91] In a world in which a corrupted moral language is used politically to manipulate society to accept the arbitrary choices of those who have the power to command the mass media, setting aside systematic politics—the systematic manipulation of parties and their coalition partners—is a necessary first step to freedom and action. Waiting for a new Saint Benedict is not passive; it requires active resistance to the dominant culture. Waiting for a new Saint Benedict is not pessimistic, for hope is the essence of anticipation.

Notes

1 Hobbes, *De Cive*, chapter 8; *Leviathan*, chapter 13.
2 Rousseau, *Discourse on the Origin of Inequality*, part I, summarized in part II, paragraph 2.
3 See MacIntyre, "Truthfulness and Lies: What Can We Learn from Kant?" in *E&P*, pp. 122–42, at 139.

4 See MacIntyre, "What Morality is Not," *Philosophy* (1957), reprinted in *Against the Self-Images of the Age*, pp. 96–108.

5 Ralph McInerny, *Ethica Thomistica* (Catholic University of America Press, 1982), p. 1; McInerny attributes this position to Thomas Aquinas.

6 Aristotle, *Nicomachean Ethics*, book 3.

7 Aquinas, *Summa Theologiae*, I–II, question 6.

8 See Aristotle, *Nicomachean Ethics*, book 2, chapter 1.

9 See Aristotle, *Physics*, book 2, chapters 1 and 7, and *De Anima*, book 2, chapter 1.

10 See Marx Wartofsky, "Virtue Lost or Understanding MacIntyre," *Inquiry: An Interdisciplinary Journal of Philosophy* 27, no. 1 (1984): 235–50.

11 Martha Nussbaum, "Recoiling from Reason," review of Alasdair MacIntyre, *WJWR*, *New York Review of Books* 36, no. 19 (December 7, 1989): 36–41.

12 MacIntyre, "NMW" 1 and 2, in *MacReader*, ed. Kelvin Knight, pp. 31–49; also in *AMEM*, pp. 45–68.

13 Ibid., 1: §1.

14 Ibid., 2: §4.

15 Alasdair MacIntyre, *The Significance of Moral Judgments: Being a Thesis Presented for the Degree of M.A. in the University of Manchester under Ordinance II(a) in April 1951.* The original is in Manchester. For a summary of the text, see Thomas D. D'Andrea, *Tradition, Rationality, and Virtue*, pp. 3–18.

16 "NMW" 2: §4.

17 Ibid., 1: §2 (4).

18 Ibid., 2: §3.

19 Ibid., 2: §4.

20 "Freedom and Revolution," p. 124.

21 Ibid., p. 125.

22 Ibid., p. 129.

23 See Marx, *Theses on Feuerbach*.

24 See MacIntyre, "ToF:RNT."

25 See Heiko Augustinus Oberman, "Some Notes on the Theology of Nominalism: With Attention to Its Relation to the Renaissance," *The Harvard Theological Review* 53, no. 1 (January 1960): 47–76; Idem, *The Harvest of Medieval Theology: Gabriel Biel and Late Medieval Nominalism* (Cambridge, MA: Harvard University Press, 1963); Bonnie Kent, *Virtues of the Will: The Transformation of Ethics in the Late Thirteenth Century* (Washington, DC: The Catholic University of America Press, 1995); and Thomas M. Osborne, Jr, "Ockham as a Divine-Command Theorist," *Religious Studies* 41 (2005): 1–22.

26 http://www.youtube.com/watch?v=joMK1WZjP7g (accessed October 14, 2009).

27 The infamous case of the Ford Pinto, sent into production with a known design flaw to avoid the expense of protecting its fragile fuel tank from four bolts protruding from its differential housing, provides a stark example of a practice compromised by an institution's pursuit of goods external to the practice. See David Dowie, "Pinto Madness," *Mother Jones* (September/October 1977) http://motherjones.com/politics/1977/09/pinto-madness.

28 *WJWR*, p. x.

29 For an example of the contrary, substantive approach, see Edmund L. Pincoffs, *Quandaries and Virtues: Against Reductivism in Ethics* (Lawrence, KS: University Press of Kansas, 1986).

30 Aristotle, *Nicomachean Ethics*, 6.5 [1140b5 and 1140b20], trans. Ross.

31 For Aristotle's treatment of weakness or incontinence, see *Nicomachean Ethics*, 7.

32 Ibid., 2.6 [1106b36–1107a2], trans Ross.

33 Aristotle, *Nicomachean Ethics*, 3.7–3.8.

34 See Aristotle, *Nicomachean Ethics*, 3.7 [1115b10–15].

35 Kant, *Foundations of the Metaphysics of Morals*, trans. Lewis White Beck, 393.

36 P. T. Geach, *The Virtues* (Cambridge University Press, 1977), chapter 8.

37 Ibid., p. 165. Given Aquinas's statement in *Summa Theologiae*, I–II, question 61, article 5 that the virtues admit of degrees, it seems unlikely that Thomas held the kind of all-or-nothing position on the unity of the virtues that Geach imputes to him. Geach's apparent oversight may follow from a Neo-Thomist reading of Aquinas that ignores Thomas's Neo-Platonism and filters Thomas through the all-or-nothing implications of "the Principle of Excluded Middle." For a representative treatment of this principle, see John P. Noonan, S. J., *General Metaphysics* (Chicago: Loyola University Press, 1956), pp. 55–6.

38 Geach, *The Virtues*, p. 160.

39 Aquinas, *Summa Theologiae*, I–II, question 55, article 4, objection 1, modified according to the recommendation at the end of the corpus of the same article.

40 Aristotle, *Nicomachean Ethics*, 2.3 [1104b30–3], trans. Ross.

41 See Lutz, *TEAM*, pp. 98–102.

42 See *DPR*, chapter 8.

43 See *WJWR*, p. x.

44 See *E&P*, pp. viii–ix, and chapter 5; compare to Geach, *The Virtues*, p. 155.

45 Aristotle, *Nicomachean Ethics*, 1.7 [1098a.18], trans. Ross.

46 See Aristotle, *De Anima*, 2.2–4.

47 Aristotle, *Nicomachean Ethics*, 1.13.

48 Knight, *Aristotelian Philosophy*, p. 1.

49 Aristotle, *Metaphysics* 1.1 [980a22], trans. Hugh Tredennick.

50 For a much more thorough summary of the main elements of
    Aristotelian natural philosophy and its connection to Aristotelian
    ethics, see Kelvin Knight, *Aristotelian Philosophy*, chapter 1.

51 Aristotle, *Nicomachean Ethics*, 2.1 [1103a23–5], trans. Ross.

52 Ibid., 2.6 [1106b36–1107a2], trans. Ross.

53 Ibid. [1107a9–26].

54 Ibid., 2.9 [1109a24–9], trans. Ross.

55 See Plato, *Republic*, book 7 (514a–518d), and *Phaedrus* (246a–250e).

56 See Josef Pieper, "The Negative Element in the Philosophy of
    St. Thomas Aquinas," in *The Silence of Saint Thomas*, trans.
    John Murray, SJ, and Daniel O'Connor (New York: Pantheon, 1957).

57 See Aquinas, *Summa Theologiae*, I–II, question 90, prologue and
    question 91, article 2.

58 Ibid., question 58, article 2, and question 61, article 2.

59 Ibid., question 61, article 5.

60 See ibid., question 65, article 2, The moral virtues are imperfect
    without charity; I–II, question 61, article 5, levels of virtue; and II–II,
    question 47, article 13, distinctions between false and true prudence.

61 Ibid., question 100, article 1.

62 Ibid., question 94, article 4.

63 "Latrocinia nullam habent infamiam, quae extra fines cuisque
    civitatis fiunt, atque ea iuventutis exercendae ac desidieae minuendae
    causa fieri praedicant." Julius Caesar, *Gallic Wars*, chapter 6, trans.
    H. J. Edwards, Loeb Classical Library 72 (Harvard University Press,
    1997), p. 349.

64 Aquinas, *Summa Theologiae*, I–II, question 61, article 5.

65 Ibid., question 19, article 3.

66 Ibid., question 19, article 5.

67 Ibid., question 19, article 6.

68 Ibid., question 19, article 4, reply objection 3.

69 MacIntyre, "NMW," part 2; §III, in Knight, ed., *MacReader*, p. 41; in
    AMEM, p. 58.

70 MacIntyre, "NMW," part 2; §III, in Knight, ed., *MacReader*, p. 41; in
    AMEM, p. 58.

71 MacIntyre, "Breaking the Chains of Reason," reprinted in Paul
    Blackledge and Neil Davidson, eds, *AMEM*, p. 166.

72 For an excellent overview of MacIntyre's life long attention to the
    problems of human action see Knight, *Aristotelian Philosophy*,
    chapter 4.

73 MacIntyre, *DPR*.

74 MacIntyre, *E&P*, Selected Essays, Volume 2 (Cambridge: Cambridge University Press, 2006).

75 *DPR*, p. 49.

76 Anton C. Pegis, "After Seven Hundred Years: St. Thomas Aquinas in 1974," *Église et Théologie* 5 (1974): 144, quoted in Denis J. M. Bradley, *Aquinas on the Twofold Human Good: Reason and Revelation in Aquinas's Moral Science* (Washington, DC: Catholic University of America Press, 1997), p. 12.

77 Aquinas, *Summa Theologiae*, I, question 1, article 8.

78 Alasdair MacIntyre, "RP&Ph," Presidential Address delivered before the 81st Annual Eastern Division Meeting of the American Philosophical Association in New York City, New York, December 29, 1984, *Proceedings and Addresses of the American Philosophical Association* (1984), pp. 5–22, reprinted in *Relativism: Interpretation and Confrontation* (Notre Dame, IN: University of Notre Dame Press, 1989), pp. 182–204.

79 "RP&Ph," p. 187.

80 Ibid., p. 189.

81 Ibid., p. 191.

82 Ibid.

83 Ibid., p. 193.

84 Ibid., p. 196.

85 Ibid., p. 198.

86 Ibid., p. 198.

87 Ibid., p. 201.

88 See "CNS."

89 MacIntyre, *WJWR*, pp. 402–3.

90 Martha Nussbaum, "Recoiling from Reason," Review of *WJWR* by MacIntyre, *The New York Review of Books* 36, no. 19 (December 7, 1989): 36–41.

91 MacIntyre gives his own interpretation of the concluding paragraph of *AV* in the prologue to the 3rd edn, p. xvi.

7

Alasdair MacIntyre's constructive work since *AV*

Alasdair MacIntyre's 1977 article, "CNS," marked "a major turning point" in his philosophical development.[1] It was in that essay that MacIntyre first articulated the approach to philosophy that would govern his mature work. *AV* was only the first of MacIntyre's major works to bring that approach to the study of philosophy. Two more books, *WJWR* (1988) and *3RV* (1990), continued to develop MacIntyre's theory of rationality. Three additional books, *DPR* (1999), *Edith Stein* (2006), and *God, Philosophy, Universities* (2009), apply MacIntyre's method to ethics and politics, to philosophical biography, and to the history of philosophy in the Catholic intellectual tradition. This brief survey of MacIntyre's work since *AV* will consider the two books on MacIntyre's theory of rationality, and the application of that theory to moral philosophy and philosophical history.

MacIntyre ends the 1984 postscript to the second edition of *AV* by acknowledging the need for a successor volume to provide a theory of rationality to support *AV*'s conclusions (pp. 277–8). That successor volume, *WJWR*, was published in 1988. The theory of rationality that it proposes is tradition-constituted and tradition-constitutive rationality.

In simplest terms, a rationality is a way of judging. A rationality has formal elements—logic, mathematics, and certain broad categories—that are not tradition dependent, even if one tradition may be more advanced in logic or mathematics than another. A rationality also has substantive elements, ways of judging what counts as a good reason or appropriate evidence that are tied to a particular tradition, culture, or conceptual scheme. The title question "Which rationality?" suggests a response to the challenge of relativism: There is only one truth, but differences in rationalities may make conflicting claims that appear to be true from the standpoints of conflicting conceptual schemes.[2]

The most visible examples of differences in substantive rationality involve the kinds of traditional practices that modernity looks upon as superstitious nonsense. Medieval trial by ordeal seems completely absurd to the modern mind, to which it exemplifies the irrationality of the dark ages. Yet, to those who practiced it, trial by ordeal appeared to provide reasonable evidence of guilt or innocence. Whenever we find ourselves asking, "How could they think that?" we have discovered a border between our own conceptual scheme, our own substantive rationality, and another.

When children and young adults learn how to judge truth and falsity, we learn from others within some sort of language community or social tradition. What we learn are the substantive elements of that community's or tradition's rationality; we learn to judge from within their worldview, their conceptual scheme. In this way, an individual's rationality is "tradition-constituted." Left to themselves, many, if not most people, never have reason to question the conceptual scheme through which they organize and interpret their experiences. They live their lives within a kind of Kuhnian paradigm, in which ordinary life is like normal science. Initiation into the community's conceptual scheme "prepares the student for membership"[3] and they simply assume that their "community knows what the world is like."[4]

Conceptual innovation becomes possible only when a significant challenge[5] makes elements of the community's conceptual scheme untenable for one or more of its members. If these few community members struggle through their epistemological crises until they are resolved, they will have transformed their own substantive rationality in the process, and to the extent that they are able to share this transformation with others, their rationality may become tradition-constitutive. The tradition-constitutive rationality of this group is not Kuhnian; it recognizes the shortcomings in its conceptual scheme and recognizes the superior rational resources of other conceptual schemes in the way that Imre Lakatos describes the progress, failure, and replacement of research programs.

MacIntyre presents his theory of tradition-constituted and tradition-constitutive rationality in *WJWR* by four traditions in the history of philosophy. Three of these, the "Aristotelian tradition," the "Augustinian tradition," and "the Scottish blend of Calvinist Augustinianism and renaissance Aristotelianism," understood themselves as traditions, while the fourth, "liberalism," is the tradition of the rejection of tradition:

> Liberalism, beginning as a repudiation of tradition in the name of abstract, universal principles of reason, turned itself into a politically embodied power, whose inability to bring its debates on the nature and context of those universal principles to a conclusion has had the unintended effect of transforming liberalism into a tradition.[6]

The first three traditions illustrate the role of tradition in the methodology of rational enquiry. The failure of liberalism through its transformation into a tradition shows that tradition plays an ineradicable role in every human enquiry.

The lessons of the detailed history of *WJWR* are digested into the ten Gifford Lectures in *3RV*. In this book, MacIntyre treats three approaches to the study of ethics that have coexisted since the time when Adam Gifford endowed the Gifford Lectureship on his death in 1887. The first, "encyclopaedia," understands itself as a tradition-independent mode of enquiry that collects facts; MacIntyre takes its name from the ninth edition of the *Encyclopaedia Britannica* (1875–1889).[7] The second, "genealogy," recognizes the role of tradition in history, and works to liberate itself from all traditional presuppositions; MacIntyre takes its name from Friedrich Nietzsche's on the *Genealogy of Morals* (1887).[8] The third mode of enquiry, tradition, is represented by the work of Catholic scholars who responded to Pope Leo XIII's call to renew Christian philosophy along the lines of Aristotle and Aquinas in the encyclical letter, *Aeterni Patris* (1879).

Nineteenth-century Thomism *represents* tradition in *3RV*, but the methodology of tradition cannot be identified with or reduced to Thomism or Aristotelianism or any other particular tradition. It is precisely by showing that encyclopedia and genealogy cannot

but function as traditions, that MacIntyre demonstrates the incoherence of their a-traditional and antitraditional presuppositions.
The point MacIntyre is driving at in *3RV* is the same point he had
made in chapter 18 of *WJWR*, "The Rationality of Traditions":
philosophy makes its way through history according to the methodology of tradition. Thomism is a tradition that knows it is a
tradition, while encyclopedia and genealogy, like the liberalism of
WJWR, fail to give adequate attention to the implications of traditions that they do not fully acknowledge and cannot escape.

MacIntyre returns from the broader consideration of philosophical methodology to the specific concerns of moral philosophy in his 1999 Carus Lectures, *DPR*. This book is reminiscent
of the riddle of the sphinx in *Oedipus Rex*. The sphinx asked
what walks on four legs in the morning, on two legs at midday,
and on three legs in the evening. Oedipus solved the riddle when
he answered, "man." The human person crawls as an infant, and
walks as an adult, before hobbling with a cane in old age. The
answer to the riddle shows that the independence of healthy adult-
hood is only one phase in a life marked by dependence in child-
hood and old age. *DPR* calls its readers to approach ethics not
merely as a study of criteria for the moral decisions of healthy
adults, but as a study of the education and care of people who
live in human communities that treats "the facts of vulnerability
and affliction and the related facts of dependence as central to the
human condition."[9]

MacIntyre's most recent book, *God, Philosophy, Universities*,[10]
deploys the methodology of "CNS" to tell a cautionary tale about
the sometimes troubled history of the Catholic philosophical tradition. The narrative of this book tells how this tradition was reduced
at first to intellectual irrelevance and then to silence between 1600
and 1850 by the imposition of a kind of scholastic philosophical
orthodoxy.[11] When Catholic scholars did begin the work of renew-
ing Christian philosophy in the 1880s, it took decades to rede-
velop a fully adequate and appropriately critical understanding of
Aquinas and his contributions to the Catholic philosophical tradition.[12] Meanwhile, Catholic philosophers began to do valuable
work in analytic philosophy, existentialism, phenomenology, and
other non-Thomistic fields.[13] Catholic philosophy, freed from scholastic orthodoxy,[14] has been able to take up the methodology of
tradition and to make progress once again.

Through all of MacIntyre's mature work, he maintains three themes. First, he insists upon the earthly, human character of philosophical enquiry, and thus the inescapably traditional nature of human rationality. Second, he maintains the possibility of truth, and the place of truth as the goal of enquiry, even as he recognizes the always partial and imperfect character of philosophical narrative and theory. Third, since the 1950s, MacIntyre has treated moral philosophy as a study of practical reasoning, and of the conditions and habits that enable human agents to recognize and choose what is good and best, that aims at the liberation of the human agent through discipline and virtue.

In addition to these books, two other important collections of MacIntyre's writings complete the bookshelf of MacIntyre's recent primary works. Knight published *The MacIntyre Reader* in 1998. The essays and book sections contained in this book reflect and confirm the fine synthesis of MacIntyre's philosophy that Knight offers in the book's introduction. Knight's anthology provides a clear map from "NMW" through *AV*, to MacIntyre's mature work. Paul Blackledge and Neil Davidson present an equally useful collection of MacIntyre's earlier, Marxist work in *Alasdair MacIntyre's Engagement with Marxism: Selected Writings 1953–1974* (2008). This collection shows how MacIntyre's concern with the problem of human agency develops within Marxism. It provides a piece of the puzzle that had been largely unavailable to most people before its publication, and it reveals more clearly the continuity of MacIntyre's philosophy throughout his various conversions.

Secondary literature on MacIntyre

MacIntyre's mature work has given rise to a growing body of secondary literature. Much of the early secondary work was critical, initially in the form of book reviews, later in journal articles, and finally in two collections of essays. *After MacIntyre: Critical Perspectives on the Work of Alasdair MacIntyre* (1994)[15] presented 14 critical essays along with MacIntyre's response. *Kierkegaard After MacIntyre: Freedom, Narrative, and Virtue*[16] took issue with MacIntyre's interpretation of Kierkegaard. These critiques testify their author's assessment of the influence of MacIntyre's philosophy. Other recent secondary literature justifies MacIntyre's influence.

Peter McMylor, a sociologist from the University of Manchester, was the first to publish a book-length study of MacIntyre's mature work. McMylor shares MacIntyre's background in the social sciences, and his book, *Alasdair MacIntyre: Critic of Modernity* (1994),[17] includes two chapters, "An Excursus on the Possibility of an Aristotelian Marxism" and "MacIntyre's Evaluative History and Polanyi's Historical Sociology," that shed new light on the background to MacIntyre's work.

My own book, *TEAM* (2004), explores MacIntyre's theory of rationality. Surveying the claims of some of MacIntyre's critics, the book defends MacIntyre's assessment of the situatedness of human enquiry and his claim that no theory is ever more than "the best theory so far" in any given field of study. This demanded a response to the claims of contemporary Thomists that MacIntyre's position was incompatible with the metaphysics of Aquinas, to which MacIntyre had implicitly allied himself in *WJWR*. It also demanded a response to critics who dismissed MacIntyre's turn to Thomism as the embrace of a religious ideology.

Knight's *Aristotelian Philosophy: Ethics and Politics from Aristotle to MacIntyre* (2007) provides an excellent treatment of Aristotle's ethics and politics as a theory of action. This approach to Aristotle vindicates the Aristotelianism of *AV* and *DPR*, which investigate the development of human agency without defending "Aristotle's metaphysical biology." This frees Aristotle's ethics and politics from his physics and metaphysics and leaves the connection between virtue and nature an open question.

There are four other monographs on MacIntyre. Bruce Ballard's brief *Understanding MacIntyre* (2000) is a basic interpretative guide to MacIntyre's mature work, based on a solid understanding of MacIntyre's earlier Marxist work. In Italy, Sante Maletta published *Biografia della ragione: Saggio sulla filosofia politica di MacIntyre* (2007), and Marco D'Avenia has translated MacIntyre's principle works into Italian.[18] In France, Emile Perreau-Saussine won the Prix Philippe Habert for *Alasdair MacIntyre: Une Biographie Intellectuelle* (2005), before his tragically early death in February 2010. Perreau-Saussine's essay, "The Moral Critique of Stalinism," which appears in *V&P* (2011), gives the clearest account I have seen of this central problem in *AV*. In Great Britain, Thomas D'Andrea summarized many of MacIntyre's books and articles in *Tradition, Rationality, and Virtue: The Thought of Alasdair MacIntyre* (2006).

In addition to these monographs, several recent anthologies have appeared, interpreting MacIntyre's philosophy and applying it to problems in ethics, politics, and management. Mark Murphy's collection of interpretative essays, *Alasdair MacIntyre* (2003), gives a comprehensive and highly illuminating introduction to the elements of MacIntyrean enquiry. Paul Blackledge and Knight's *Virtue and Politics* (2011) is a collection of papers from the 2007 London conference that questions the contemporary Left's dismissal of MacIntyre's later work. Papers from the London conference also appeared in *Revolutionary Aristotelianism*, a special edition of the journal *Analyse & Kritik* (2008) edited by Knight and Blackledge, and in *MacIntyre, Empirics, and Organisation*, a special edition of the journal *Philosophy of Management* (2008) edited by Ron Beadle and Geoff Moore.

In London, the Centre for Contemporary Aristotelian Studies in Ethics and Politics (CASEP), founded by Knight, has established an internet site for research on MacIntyre's "Revolutionary Aristotelianism."[19] This site includes an extensive bibliography of MacIntyre's books and published papers, along with a growing list of "Engagements with MacIntyre's Aristotelianism."

The fruit of this growing body of secondary literature is a new kind of engagement with MacIntyre. It is no longer acceptable to present a critique of MacIntyre's philosophy on the basis of a faulty reading of a single book or essay. At the same time, it is no longer necessary to spend hours in libraries seeking out copies of *Marxism: An Interpretation*, the 1958 and 1959 issues of *The New Reasoner*,[20] the 1977 volume of *The Monist*,[21] or the festschrift for Marx Wartofsky,[22] to develop a more adequate understanding of MacIntyre's development. In the postscript to the second edition of *AV*, MacIntyre concluded that the book remained "a work still in progress" (p. 278). And so it still remains, but *AV* is no longer a single work; it has become the foundation for a tradition.

Notes

1 *Tasks*, p. vii.
2 See Lutz, *TEAM*, p. 68.

3   Kuhn, *The Structure of Scientific Revolutions*, p. 11.
4   Ibid., p. 5; Kuhn is talking about "the scientific community."
5   See Lutz, *TEAM*, pp. 85–7.
6   *WJWR*, p. 349.
7   *3RV*, p. 18.
8   Ibid., pp. 24–5.
9   *DPR*, p. 4.
10 MacIntyre, *God, Philosophy, Universities*.
11 Ibid., pp. 114, 132–3.
12 Ibid., pp. 153–7.
13 Ibid., pp. 157–63.
14 See John Paul II, *Encyclical Letter* Fides et Ratio (September 12,
    1998), Vatican translation (Boston: Pauline Books and Media, 1998),
    p. 49.
15 John Horton and Susan Mendus, eds, *After MacIntyre: Critical
    Perspectives on the Work of Alasdair MacIntyre* (Notre Dame, IN:
    University of Notre Dame Press, 1994).
16 *Kierkegaard After MacIntyre: Freedom, Narrative, and Virtue*, ed.
    Anthony Rudd and John Davenport (Chicago: Open Court, 2001).
17 Peter McMylor, *Alasdair MacIntyre: Critic of Modernity* (London:
    Routledge, 1994).
18 *Tre versioni rivali di ricerca morale* (Massimo: Milano, 1993);
    Animali razionali e dipendenti (Vita e Pensiero: Milano, 2001); *Dopo
    la virtù*, seconda edizione italiana (Armando: Rome, 2007); *Edith
    Stein. Un prologo filosofico* (Edusc: Rome, 2009); *Selected Works* (in
    progress, 2012).
19 http://www.londonmet.ac.uk/depts/lgir/research-centres/casep/
    research-resources/macintyre-publications/macintyre-publications_
    home.cfm
20 "NMW" 1 and 2 were first published in two issues of *The New
    Reasoner*.
21 "ECR" was first published in *The Monist* (1977).
22 "ToF:RNT" was first published in *Artifacts, Representations, and
    Social Practice: Essays for Marx Wartofsky*.

BIBLIOGRAPHY

Abelard, Peter. *Ethics: Or Know Thyself*. Trans. R. McCallum. In
  Philosophy in the Middle Ages. Ed. Arthur Hyman and James J. Walsh.
  Indianapolis: Hackett, 1973, pp. 188–202.

Adkins, Arthur W. H. "Aristotle and the Best Kind of Tragedy." *The
  Classical Quarterly*, New Series, 16, no. 1 (May 1966): 78–102.

Anscombe, Gertrude Elizabeth Margaret. "Modern Moral Philosophy."
  Philosophy 33 (1958): 1–19.

—. *Intention* (1957; reprinted by Harvard University Press, 2000).

Aristotle. *De Generatione Animalium (On the Generation of Animals)*.
  Book I. Trans. William Ogle. In *The Basic Works of Aristotle*. Ed.
  Richard McKeon. New York: Random House, 1941.

—. *Metaphysics*. Trans. W. D. Ross. In *The Basic Works of Aristotle*.
  Ed. Richard McKeon. New York: Random House, 1941.

—. *Metaphysics*. Trans. Hugh Tredennick. Cambridge, MA: Harvard
  University Press, 1989.

—. *Nicomachean Ethics*. Trans. David Ross. New York: Oxford
  University Press, 1990.

—. *Nicomachean Ethics*. Trans. Martin Ostwald. Englewood Cliffs, NJ:
  Prentice Hall, 1962.

—. *On the Generation of Animals*. Trans. A. L. Peck. Cambridge, MA:
  Harvard University Press, 1963.

—. *Physics*. Trans. R. P. Hardie and R. K. Gaye. In *The Basic Works of
  Aristotle*. Ed. Richard McKeon. New York: Random House, 1941,
  pp. 213–394.

—. *Politics*. Trans. Benjamin Jowett. In *The Basic Works of Aristotle* Ed.
  Richard McKeon. New York: Random House, 1941, pp. 1113–316.

Aron, Raymond. "Max Weber." In *Main Currents in Sociological
  Thought*. Trans. R. Howard and H. Weaver. Garden City, NY: Anchor
  Books, 1968.

Augustine, St. *Confessions*. Trans. John K. Ryan. New York: Doubleday,
  1960.

—. *Eighty-Three Different Questions*. Trans. David L. Mosher.
  Washington, DC: Catholic University of America Press, 1982.

Ballard, Bruce W. *Understanding MacIntyre*. Lanham, MD: University Press of America, 2000.

Beabout, Gregory. "The Silent Lily and Bird as Exemplars of Active Receptivity." In *International Kierkegaard Commentary: Without Authority*. Ed. Robert L. Perkins. Macon, GA: Mercer University Press, 2007, pp. 127–46.

Beadle, Ron and Geoff Moore, eds. *MacIntyre, Empirics, and Organization*, special issue, *Philosophy of Management* 7, no. 1 (2008).

Blackledge, Paul. "Morality and Revolution: Ethical Debates in the British New Left," *Critique* 35, no. 2 (August 2007): 211–28.

Blackledge, Paul and Neil Davidson, eds. *Alasdair MacIntyre's Engagement with Marxism*. Leiden: Brill, 2005; republished in paperback, Chicago: Haymarket Books, 2009.

Brooks, Lisa. *The Common Pot: The Recovery of Native Space in the Northeast*. Minneapolis: University of Michigan Press, 2008.

Burke, Edmund. *Reflections on the Revolution in France And on the Proceedings of Certain Societies in London Relative to That Event*. New York: Rinehart, 1959.

Caesar. *The Gallic War*. Trans. H. J. Edwards. Cambridge, MA: Harvard University Press, 1917.

Campisi, Jack. *The Mashpee Indians: Tribe on Trial*. Syracuse, NY: Syracuse University Press, 1991.

Camus, Albert. *L'Homme Révolté [The Rebel]*. Paris: Gallimard, 1951.

—. *The Rebel: An Essay on Man in Revolt*. Trans. Anthony Bower. New York: Vintage Books, 1956.

Carr, Edward H. *The Russian Revolution from Lenin to Stalin 1917–1929*, 2nd edn. New York: Palgrave Macmillan, 2004.

—. *The Bolshevik Revolution 1917–1923*. 3 vols. New York: W. W. Norton & Co., 1985.

Chappell, Vere Claiborne, ed. *Hume: A Collection of Critical Essays*. New York: Doubleday, 1966.

Cobbett, William, MP. *A History of the Protestant Reformation in England and Ireland*. New York: D & J Sadlier, 1849.

—. *Rural Rides* (1830). Ed. with introduction by Ian Dyke. London: Penguin, 2001.

D'Andrea, Thomas D. *Tradition, Rationality, and Virtue: The Thought of Alasdair MacIntyre*. Surrey: Ashgate, 2006.

Descartes, René. *Discourse on Method*. In *The Philosophical Writings of Descartes*, Volume I. Trans. John Cottingham, Robert Stoothoff, and Dugald Murdoch. New York: Cambridge University Press, 1992, pp. 109–51.

—. "Meditations on First Philosophy." In *The Philosophical Writings of Descartes*, Volume II. Trans. John Cottingham, Robert

Stoothoff, and Dugald Murdoch. New York: Cambridge University Press, 1992.

Diderot, Denis. *Le Neveu de Rameau ou La Satire seconde*. In *Rameau's Nephew and First Satire*. Trans. Margaret Mauldon. New York: Oxford University Press USA, 2009.

Dignitatis Humanae. In *The Documents of Vatican II*. Ed. Walter M. Abbott, S. J. Trans. Reverend Monsignor Joseph Gallagher. New York: America Press, 1966.

Encyclopædia Britannica. 9th edn. Edinburgh: Adam and Charles Black, 1875–89.

Engels, Friedrich. *Socialism: Utopian and Scientific*. *Revue Socialiste* (March, April, and May, 1880). Trans. Edward Aveling in 1892 (authorized by Engels). Transcription/Markup, Zodiac/Brian Baggins. Online version: Marx/Engels Internet Archive (marxists.org) 1993, 1999, 2003, http://www.marxists.org/archive/marx/works/1880/soc-utop/index.htm.

Flew, Antony and Alasdair MacIntyre, eds. *New Essays in Philosophical Theology*. New York: Macmillan, 1955.

Franks, Joan M., OP. "Aristotle or Nietzsche?" *Listening* 26, no. 2 (1991): 156–63.

Geach, Peter T. *The Virtues*. Cambridge: Cambridge University Press, 1977.

—. "The Religion of Thomas Hobbes." *Religious Studies* 17, no. 4 (December 1981): 549–58.

George, Robert P. "Moral Particularism, Thomism, and Traditions." *Review of Metaphysics* 42 (March 1989): 593–605.

Gewirth, Alan. *Reason and Morality*. Chicago: University of Chicago Press, 1978.

Hanson, Harry. "An Open Letter to Edward Thompson." *The New Reasoner* 2 (Autumn 1957): 79–91.

Hauerwas, Stanley, and Paul Wadell. Review of *After Virtue,* by Alasdair MacIntyre. *The Thomist* 46, no. 2 (April 1982): 313–23.

Hibbs, Thomas S. "MacIntyre's Postmodern Thomism: Reflections on *Three Rival Versions of Moral Enquiry.*" *The Thomist* 57 (1993): 277–97.

Hobbes, Thomas. *De Cive (The Citizen): Philosophical Rudiments Concerning Government and Society* (1651), rendered into HTML by Jon Roland of the Constitution Society, http://www.constitution.org/th/decive.htm; chapter 8, "Of the Rights of Lords over their Servant," http://www.constitution.org/th/decive08.htm, accessed June 11, 2009.

—. *Leviathan or the Matter, Forme, and Power of a Commonwealth Ecclesiasticall and Civil* (1651). Ed. C. B. MacPherson. New York: Penguin, 1988.

Horton, John, and Susan Mendus, eds. *After MacIntyre: Critical Perspectives on the Work of Alasdair MacIntyre*. Notre Dame, IN: University of Notre Dame Press, 1994.

Hudson, William Donald, ed. *The Is-Ought Question*. London: Macmillan, 1969.

Hume, David. *An Enquiry Concerning Human Understanding* [originally published 1751], 2nd edn. Ed. L. A. Selby-Bigge. Oxford: Oxford University Press, 1978.

—. *A Treatise of Human Nature*. [Originally published, London: for John Noon, at the White-Hart, near Mercer's-Chapel, in Cheapside, 1739.] Ed. Eric Steinberg. Indanapolis: Hackett Publishing Company, 1977.

James, Henry. *The Portrait of a Lady*. New York: Oxford University Press USA, 2009.

Jesseph, Douglas M. "Hobbes's Atheism." *Midwest Studies in Philosophy* 26 (2002): 140–66.

John Paul II, Pope. Encyclical Letter *Fides et Ratio* (September 12, 1998). Vatican translation. Boston: Pauline Books and Media, 1998.

Kant, Immanuel. *Critique of Pure Reason* [First Critique]. Trans. Norman Kemp Smith. Unabridged edn. New York: St. Martin's Press, 1929.

—. *Critique of Practical Reason* [Second Critique]. Trans. Lewis White Beck. Indianapolis, IN: Bobbs-Merrill Educational Publishing, 1956.

—. *Critique of Judgment* [Third Critique]. Trans. James Creed Meredith. Oxford: Clarendon Press, 1952.

—. *Foundations of the Metaphysics of Morals,* 2nd edn. Trans. Lewis White Beck. New York: Macmillan, 1990.

—. "What is Enlightenment?" In *Foundations of the Metaphysics of Morals,* 2nd edn. Trans. Lewis White Beck. New York: Macmillan, 1990, pp. 83–90.

Khrushchev, Nikita. "Speech to the 20th Congress of the Communist Party of the Soviet Union" [The Secret Speech]. February 24–25, 1956, http://www.marxists.org/archive/khrushchev/1956/02/24.htm.

Kierkegaard, Søren. *Either/Or Part I* [*Enten/Eller*, English]. Trans. Howard V. Hong and Edna H. Hong. Princeton: Princeton University Press, 1988.

—. *Either/Or Part II* [*Enten/Eller*, English]. Trans. Howard V. Hong and Edna H. Hong. Princeton: Princeton University Press, 1987.

Knight, Kelvin, ed. *The MacIntyre Reader*. Notre Dame, IN: University of Notre Dame Press, 1998.

—. *Aristotelian Philosophy: Ethics and Politics from Aristotle to MacIntyre*. Cambridge, UK: Polity, 2007.

Knight, Kelvin and Paul Blackledge, eds. *Revolutionary Aristotelianism: Ethics, Resistance, and Utopia*. Stuttgart: Lucius & Lucius, 2008, special edition of *Analyse & Kritik* 30, no. 1 (June 2008).

Kuhn, Thomas. *The Structure of Scientific Revolutions*, 2nd edn. Chicago: University of Chicago Press, 1962; 2nd edn, 1970.

Lakatos, Imre. "Falsification and the Methodology of Scientific Research Programmes." In *The Methodology of Scientific Research Programs*, Philosophical Papers, Volume I. Ed. John Worral and Gregory Currie. Cambridge: Cambridge University Press, 1978.

—. "Science and Pseudoscience." In *The Methodology of Scientific Research Programmes*, Philosophical Papers, Volume I. Ed. John Worral and Gregory Currie. Cambridge: Cambridge University Press, 1978, pp. 1–7.

Locke, John. *Two Treatises of Government* (1698). Ed. Peter Laslett. Cambridge: Cambridge University Press, 1992.

—. *An Essay Concerning Human Understanding*. New York: Oxford University Press USA, 2008.

Lutz, Christopher Stephen. *Tradition in the Ethics of Alasdair MacIntyre: Relativism, Thomism, and Philosophy*. Lanham, MD: Lexington Books, 2004.

—. "Alasdair MacIntyre's Tradition Constituted Rationality: An Alternative to Relativism and Fideism." *American Catholic Philosophical Quarterly* 85, no. 3 (Summer 2011): 391–413.

MacIntyre, Alasdair. *Marxism: An Interpretation*. London: SCM Press, 1953.

—. "Visions." In *New Essays in Philosophical Theology*. Ed. Antony Flew and Alasdair MacIntyre. New York: Macmillan, 1955.

—. "The Logical Status of Religious Belief." In *Metaphysical Beliefs: Three Essays*. Ed. Stephen Toulman, Ronald W. Hepburn, and Alasdair C. MacIntyre. London: SCM Press, 1957, pp. 159–201.

—. "Determinism." *Mind* 66 (1957): 28–41.

—. "Notes from the Moral Wilderness I." *The New Reasoner* 7 (Winter 1958–59): 90–100. Reprinted in *The MacIntyre Reader*, pp. 31–40 and in *Alasdair MacIntyre's Engagement with Marxism*, pp. 45–57.

—. "Notes from the Moral Wilderness II." *The New Reasoner* 8 (Spring 1959): 89–98. Reprinted in *The MacIntyre Reader*, pp. 41–9 and in *Alasdair MacIntyre's Engagement with Marxism*, pp. 57–68

—. *Difficulties in Christian Belief*. London: SCM Press, 1959.

—. "Freedom and Revolution." *Labour Review* 5, no. 1 (February–March 1960): 19–24. Reprinted in *Alasdair MacIntyre's Engagement with Marxism*, pp. 123–34.

—. Alasdair MacIntyre, "A Review of Neal Wood, *Communism and British Intellectuals*." *The Listener* 7 (January 1960): 21–3. Reprinted in *AMEM*, 115–22.

—. A Short History of Ethics: A History of Moral Philosophy from the Homeric Age to Twentieth Century. New York: Macmillan, 1966. Reprinted. New York: Touchstone, 1996.

—. "Kierkegaard, Søren Aabye." In *Encyclopedia of Philosophy*. Ed. Paul Edwards. New York: Macmillan, 1967, Volume 4, pp. 336–40.

—. "The Debate about God: Victorian Relevance and Contemporary Irrelevance." In *The Religious Significance of Atheism* (Bampton Lectures in America delivered at Columbia University, 1966). Ed. Alasdair MacIntyre and Paul Ricoeur. New York: Columbia University Press, 1969, pp. 1–55.

—. *Marxism and Christianity*. New York: Schocken Books, 1968.

—. "Preface to the 1970 Edition." *Metaphysical Beliefs: Three Essays*. New York: Schocken Books, 1970.

—. *Against the Self-Images of the Age: Essays on Ideology and Philosophy*. London: Duckworth; New York: Schocken Books, 1971.

—. "Can Medicine Dispense with a Theological Perspective on Human Nature?" In *Knowledge, Value, and Belief*. The Foundations of Ethics and Its Relationship to Science, Volume II. Hastings-on-Hudson, NY: The Hastings Center, 1977, pp. 25–43.

—. "A Rejoinder to a Rejoinder" [to "Can Medicine Dispense . . ."]. In *Knowledge, Value, and Belief*. The Foundations of Ethics and Its Relationship to Science, Volume II. Hastings-on-Hudson, NY: The Hastings Center, 1977, pp. 75–8.

—. "Epistemological Crises, Dramatic Narrative, and the Philosophy of Science." *The Monist* 60, no. 4 (October 1977): 453–72.

—. "Intelligibility, Goods, and Rules [abstract]." *The Journal of Philosophy* 79, no. 11 (November 1982): 664.

—. *After Virtue: A Study in Moral Theory*, 2nd edn. Notre Dame, IN: University of Notre Dame Press, 1984.

—. *Whose Justice? Which Rationality?* Notre Dame, IN: University of Notre Dame Press, 1988.

—. "The Privatization of Good: An Inaugural Lecture." *Review of Politics* 52 (1990): 344–61.

—. "Relativism, Power, and Philosophy." In *Relativism: Interpretation and Confrontation*. Ed. with introduction by Michael Krausz. Notre Dame, IN: University of Notre Dame Press, 1989, pp. 182–204.

—. *Three Rival Versions of Moral Enquiry: Encyclopaedia, Genealogy, and Tradition* (Gifford Lectures). Notre Dame, IN: University of Notre Dame Press, 1990.

—. First Principles, Final Ends, and Contemporary Philosophical Issues. The Aquinas Lecture, 1990. Milwaukee: Marquette University Press, 1990.

—. "Moral Dilemmas." *Philosophy and Phenomenological Research* 50 (1990): 367–82.

—. "An Interview for *Cogito*." *Cogito* 5, no. 2 (1991): 67–73. Reprinted in *The MacIntyre Reader*. Notre Dame, IN: University of Notre Dame Press, 1998, pp. 267–75.

—. "Incommensurability, Truth and the Conversation between Confucians and Aristotelians about the Virtues." In *Culture and Modernity: East-West Philosophic Perspectives*. Ed. Eliot Deutsch. Honolulu: University of Hawaii Press, 1991, pp. 104–92.

—. "Plain Persons and Moral Philosophy: Rules, Virtues, and Goods." 1991 Aquinas Lecture at the University of Dallas. *American Catholic Philosophical Quarterly* 66, no. 1 (Winter 1992): 3–19.

—. "My Station and Its Virtues." In Symposium in Memory of Edmund L. Pincoffs. *Journal of Philosophical Research* 19 (1994): 1–8.

—. "How Can We Learn What *Veritatis Splendor* Has to Teach?" *The Thomist* 58 (1994): 171–95.

—. "Moral Relativism, Truth and Justification." In *Moral Truth and Moral Tradition: Essays in Honor of Peter Geach and Elizabeth Anscombe*. Ed. Luke Gormally. Dublin: Four Courts Press, 1994, pp. 6–24.

—. "The *Theses on Feuerbach*: A Road Not Taken." In *Artifacts, Representations, and Social Practice: Essays for Marx Wartofsky*. Ed. Carol C. Gould and Robert S. Cohen. Dordrecht: Kluwer Academic Publishing, 1994. Reprinted in *The MacIntyre Reader*. Ed. Kelvin Knight. Notre Dame, IN: University of Notre Dame Press, 1998, pp. 223–34.

—. "Nietzsche or Aristotle?: Alasdair MacIntyre." Interview by Giovanna Borradori in *The American Philosopher: Conversations with Quine, Davidson, Putnam, Nozick, Danto, Rorty, Cavell, MacIntyre, and Kuhn*. Trans. Rosanna Crocitto. Chicago: University of Chicago Press, 1994, pp. 137–52.

—. Tape recording of Alasdair MacIntyre's appearance in David Solomon's class, "15 Years after *After Virtue*" (1995), at the University of Notre Dame.

—. "Truthfulness, Lies, and Moral Philosophers." In *The Tanner Lectures on Human Values*, Volume 16. Ed. Greth B. Peterson. Salt Lake City: University of Utah Press, 1995.

—. "*Kinesis* Interview with Professor Alasdair MacIntyre." Interview by Thomas D. Pearson. *Kinesis* 20, no. 2 (Spring 1994): 34–47.

—. *Dependent Rational Animals*. Chicago: Open Court, 1999.

—. *The Tasks of Philosophy*. Selected Essays, Volume 1. Cambridge: Cambridge University Press, 2006.

—. *Ethics and Politics*. Selected Essays, Volume 2. Cambridge: Cambridge University Press, 2006.

—. *Edith Stein: A Philosophical Prologue, 1913–1922*. Lanham, MD: Rowman and Littlefield Publishers, 2007.

Maletta, Sante. Biografia della ragione: Saggio sulla filosofia politica di MacIntyre. Soveria Mannelli (CZ), Italy: Rubbettino, 2007.

Marx, Karl. *On the Jewish Question* [by Bruno Bauer, 1843], *Deutsch-Französische Jahrbücher* (February 1844); http://www.marxists.org/

archive/marx/works/1844/jewish-question/index.htm; retrieved April 7, 2011.

McInerny, Ralph. *Ethica Thomistica: The Moral Philosophy of Thomas Aquinas.* Rev. edn. Washington, DC: The Catholic University of America Press, 1997.

McMylor, Peter. *Alasdair MacIntyre: Critic of Modernity.* London: Routledge, 1994.

Mill, John Stuart. *Utilitarianism.* In *Utilitarianism, On Liberty, Considerations on Representative Government.* Ed. H. B. Acton. Everyman's Library. London: J. M. Dent & Sons, Ltd, 1991.

Moore, George Edward. *Principia Ethica* [first published 1903]. 2nd edn. Cambridge: Cambridge University Press, 1993.

Murphy, Mark C. ed. *Alasdair MacIntyre.* Contemporary Philosophy in Focus. Cambridge: Cambridge University Press, 2003.

Murray, John Courtney, SJ. *We Hold These Truths.* Evanston, IL: Sheed and Ward, 1960. Reprinted and repaginated, Lanham MD: Rowman and Littlefield Publishers, 2005.

Nietzsche, Friedrich. *Beyond Good and Evil.* Trans. Walter Kaufmann. New York: Random House, 1966.

—.*On the Genealogy of Morals* [First German edition published, 1887] *and Ecce Homo.* Trans. Walter Kaufmann. New York: Random House, 1969.

Noonan, John P., SJ. *General Metaphysics.* Chicago: Loyola University Press, 1956.

Nussbaum, Martha Craven. "Recoiling from Reason." Review of *Whose Justice? Which Rationality?* by Alasdair MacIntyre. *New York Review of Books* 36, no. 19 (December 7, 1989): 36–41.

Oberman, Heiko Augustinus. *The Dawn of the Reformation.* Edinburgh: T & T Clark, Ltd, 1986.

—. "Some Notes on the Theology of Nominalism: With Attention to Its Relation to the Renaissance," *The Harvard Theological Review* 53, no. 1 (January 1960): 47–76.

Palmer, Donald. *Does the Center Hold?* 5th edn. New York: McGraw-Hill, 2010.

Perkins, Robert L., ed. *International Kierkegaard Commentary: Either/Or Part II.* Macon, GA: Mercer University Press, 1995.

Perreau-Saussine, Emile. *Alasdair MacIntyre: Une Biographie Intellectuelle.* Presses Universitaires France, 2005.

—. "The Moral Critique of Stalinism," in Paul Blackledge and Kelvin Knight, eds. *Virtue and Politics: Alasdair Macintyre's Revolutionary Aristotelianism.* Notre Dame, IN: University of Notre Dame Press, 2011), pp.134–51.

Pieper, Josef. "The Negative Element in the Philosophy of St. Thomas Aquinas." In *The Silence of St. Thomas.* Trans. John Murray, S. J. and Daniel O'Connor. New York: Pantheon, 1957.

Pinckaers, Servais, OP. *The Sources of Christian Ethics*. Trans. from the 3rd edn by Mary Thomas Noble, OP (Washington, DC: The Catholic University of America Press, 1995).

Popper, Karl. "Science: Conjectures and Refutations." In *Conjectures and Refutations: The Growth of Scientific Knowledge*. New York: Harper and Row, 1963.

Rawls, John. *A Theory of Justice*. Cambridge, MA: Belknap Press of Harvard University Press, 1971.

Reames, Kent. "Metaphysics, History, and Moral Philosophy: The Centrality of the 1990 Aquinas Lecture to MacIntyre's Argument for Thomism." *The Thomist* 62 (1998): 419–43.

Rousseau, Jean-Jacques. *Discourse on the Origin and Foundation of Inequality among Men* (1755). (Amsterdam: Marc Michel Rey, 1755); in The First and Second Discourses and Essay on the Origin of Languages, trans. Victor Gourevitch (New York: Harper and Row, 1990), pp. 116–230.

—. *The Social Contract* (1762) , in Rousseau, Jean-Jacques, *Basic Political Writings*. Trans. Donald A. Cress. Indianapolis: Hackett Pub. Co, 1987; pp. 139–227.

Rudd, Anthony and John Davenport, eds. *Kierkegaard After MacIntyre: Freedom, Narrative, and Virtue*. Chicago: Open Court, 2001.

Sartre, Jean-Paul. *L'Existentialisme est un Humanisme*. Paris: Les éditions Nagel, 1946.

—. *Existentialism is a Humanism*. Trans. Carol Macomber. New Haven: Yale University Press, 2007, pp. 30–3.

Scheffler, Samuel. Review of *After Virtue: A Study in Moral Theory*, 1st edn. In *The Philosophical Review* 92, no. 3 (July 1983): 443–7.

Taylor, Charles. "Marx and Humanism." *The New Reasoner* 2 (Autumn 1957): 92–8.

Thomas Aquinas, St. *Commentary on Aristotle's Nicomachean Ethics*. Trans. C. I. Litzinger, OP. © 1964 by Henry Regnery, revised. Notre Dame, IN: Dumb Ox Books, 1993.

—. *Summa Contra Gentiles*, book III. In *Basic Writings of Saint Thomas Aquinas*, Volume II. Ed. Anton C. Pegis. Indianapolis, IN: Hackett, 1997.

—. *Summa Theologiae*. Trans. Fathers of the English Dominican Province. New York: Benziger Bros., 1948.

Thompson, Edward P. "Socialist Humanism: An Epistle to the Philistines," *The New Reasoner* 1 (Summer 1957): 105–43.

—. *The Making of the English Working Class*. New York: Pantheon, 1964.

Toulman, Stephen, Ronald W. Hepburn, and Alasdair MacIntyre. *Metaphysical Beliefs: Three Essays*. London: SCM Press, 1957.

Trotsky, Leon. *The Permanent Revolution* (1930), Revised Edition, Seatle, WA: Red Letter Press, 2010.

—. *The Revolution Betrayed*. Trans. Max Eastman. Garden City, NY: Doubleday, Doran, & Co., 1937. Reprinted, Mineola, NY: Dover Publications, Inc., 2004.

Wachbroit, Robert. "A Genealogy of Virtues." Review of *After Virtue*, 1st edn. *The Yale Law Journal* 92 (1983): 564–76.

—. "Relativism and Virtue." *The Yale Law Journal* 94 (1985): 1559–65.

Wartofsky, Marx. "Virtue Lost or Understanding MacIntyre." *Inquiry* 27 (1984): 235–50.

Wittgenstein, Ludwig. *Philosophical Investigations*. The English Text of the Third Edition. Trans. Gertrude Elizabeth Margaret Anscombe. New York: Macmillan, 1958.

INDEX